W9-AKE-120

101
Kitchen Projects
for the Woodworker

Percy W. Blandford

EAU CLAIRE DISTRICT LIBRARY

TAB BOOKS Inc.
Blue Ridge Summit, PA 17214

73352

FIRST EDITION
FIRST PRINTING

Copyright © 1987 by TAB BOOKS Inc.
Printed in the United States of America

Reproduction or publication of the content in any manner, without express
permission of the publisher, is prohibited. No liability is assumed with respect to
the use of the information herein.

Library of Congress Cataloging in Publication Data

Blandford, Percy W.
101 kitchen projects for the woodworker / by Percy W. Blandford.
      p. cm.
   Includes index.
   ISBN 0-8306-7884-0   ISBN 0-8306-2884-3 (pbk.)
   1. Kitchen utensils. 2. Furniture making. I. Title. II. Title:
One hundred one kitchen projects for the woodworker. III. Title:
One hundred and one kitchen projects for the woodworker.
            TT197.5.K57B58   1987
            674'.8—dc19   87-19406
                     CIP

Questions regarding the content of this book
should be addressed to:

Reader Inquiry Branch
Editorial Department
TAB BOOKS Inc.
P.O. Box 40
Blue Ridge Summit, PA 17214

Contents

Introduction

Cooking and food preparation needs in a kitchen can provide ample opportunity to exercise your woodworking skills. The cook will welcome equipment and furniture planned to suit specific needs or to fit into certain places. Your kitchen might not be as big as you might wish, but by carefully fitting what you make into available space or by constructing dual-purpose items, you can make your kitchen more versatile.

Wood is particularly appropriate for kitchen items. It has traditionally been used with food, and for most kitchen purposes today, it is at least as good as plastic or metal. Most woods are safe to use with food. They are gentler on pots and pans and are easily cleaned. In large and professional kitchens, cooks and chefs still prefer wooden equipment to plastic gadgets.

Wooden kitchen equipment has the further advantage that a do-it-yourselfer can make the most of it. To the keen woodworking craftsman, this can be a very attractive opportunity. Kitchen projects can range from simple to more complex furniture. You can make articles for the kitchen with just a few hand tools, or you can use all the power tools you have in a well-equipped shop. If you are a beginner, there are many things you can produce satisfactorily with simple joints, but if you want to show your more advanced skills, you can make the same item with better joints and a high-quality finish. Many woodworking needs in a kitchen are utilitarian. Fitness for purpose is the first consideration, with good appearance arising from it.

The projects in this book have worthwhile purposes, as well as sound construction. They are designed for woodworkers with varying skills, with alternative constructions suggested for some projects. There are a few projects particularly meant for woodturners, but in most cases, alternative constructions are suggested for those without a lathe. If you are a beginner, you can tackle a few simple projects first. Then you can go on to construct the more advanced projects in stages, thus achieving the satisfaction of mastering a job that you had not thought possible.

Many projects can be made to sizes and shapes different from those shown. Each is described in particular sizes with materials lists to suit. Sections are shown to finished widths and thicknesses, but lengths are mostly full to allow for cutting. As far as possible, the number of sections required are kept to a minimum, and some sizes can be cut from others. If you prepare your own wood, start with the larger sections so other pieces can come from offcuts. If you buy the wood cut to size, let the supplier see the materials list, so he can select pieces to suit. Do not add all the lengths of one section and ask for one long piece. That might be impractical or cost more than several short pieces.

All sizes quoted are in inches unless marked otherwise. In some cases near sizes might be acceptable, but be careful of making parts thin and weak or so thick as to look clumsy. Straight-grained hardwood can be in thinner sections than knotty softwood.

There are probably more ideas here for things to make in wood for a kitchen than in any other book. I hope you get a lot of pleasure and satisfaction out of making these projects and that those concerned with cooking enjoy and appreciate your constructional efforts.

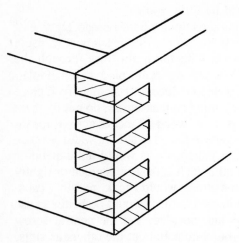

Preparation

Traditionally wood has been the material used in kitchens, and it still is regarded as best for most purposes where food is prepared. You can use plastic and stainless steel, but the foundation of kitchen furniture and equipment is wood. Suppliers of complete fitted kitchens proudly present their better products as solid wood rather than man-made versions of wood.

Anyone who hopes to make kitchen items from wood should know something of the choice of materials. The varieties of trees in the world runs into thousands. Not all are converted to lumber, but the number that are can still be bewildering. Follow the advice of your supplier if you like, but if you know the characteristics of the wood you want, you can select the most suitable from the available stock.

Woods are broadly divided into hardwoods and softwoods. Although the names indicate the characteristics of most woods, some hardwoods are softer than some softwoods. The names apply to the types of trees. *Softwoods* are pines, spruces, firs, and similar coniferous woods with needle leaves. *Hardwoods* come from the broad-leafed trees, most of which shed their leaves during the winter in temperate climates.

Softwoods have uses in a kitchen, but they tend to cut and splinter if used as a work surface. There is a fashion for natural softwood furniture, and it can be quite attractive, but it must be protected with a good varnish or other finish.

Hardwoods vary considerably. Some, such as oak, have very open grain. Although they are good structurally and look good as furniture, they are not the woods for close contact with food. Other woods, such as sycamore and beech, have grain so close that pores cannot be seen without magnification. They are better for working surfaces where you chop or cut food.

You should also consider color. Although it might not affect the food, it affects its appearance and desirability. Because a near-white color seems more hygienic, light, close-grained hardwoods make attractive items for food preparation. A dark color wood with similar characteristics would be just as good in every way, except appearance.

Some woods have an odor that is persistent. Others are naturally oily or contain resin. You might use them in the kitchen as furniture, but avoid using them for purposes of food preparation. Some softwoods contain a large amount of resin. Most of these can be identified by contrasting grain colors of alternating dark and light brown lines. The softwoods with little or no resin usually have a milder appearance with little to distinguish the grain lines. Undesirable hardwoods are not so easily identified, and you might need to rely on what your supplier tells you.

SHRINKING AND WARPING

As a tree grows, it increases in diameter with annual rings, which produce the grain markings. If you count the rings in a cut across a tree, you can determine its age in years. A considerable amount of sap goes up and down the tree, and most of this has to be dried out before the wood can be used for carpentry. Drying of sap is done during the process called *seasoning*, which reduces the moisture in the wood to an acceptable level of about 10 percent. The seasoned wood takes up or gives out moisture according to the humidity of the surrounding air. Humidity causes it to swell or contract, therefore altering its size and shape. You must allow for humidity, but you can limit the effects by your choice of wood and the way you use it.

If you keep the wood in conditions similar to where it will be used for some time before you make an article, there is unlikely to be any significant changes after it is put into use. This particularly applies if you work in an unheated shop and the thing you make will be used in a centrally heated kitchen.

If a board shrinks or expands, it does this mostly in the direction of the grain lines on its ends, so the part of the log it is cut from affects its behavior. A board cut radially has grain lines through its thickness (Fig. 1-1A). If cut across square to that, the lines form curves on the end (Fig. 1-1B). If the first piece (A) loses moisture, it gets thinner but remains flat; there is no important change in its width (Fig. 1-1C). If the other piece (B) loses moisture, it becomes curved or warps (Fig. 1-1D). You can visualize what will happen to a piece of wood that shrinks if you consider the grain lines on the end trying to straighten. This action is reversed if the wood absorbs moisture. In practice, shrinkage is more often a problem than swelling. If you let the wood become accustomed to the atmosphere in which the finished item will be used, there should be little trouble.

To make something where a broad expanse of wood has nothing to restrict or support it, use a piece of wood with the grain lines through the thickness. You can expect this piece to remain flat.

If you want to reduce the risk of a broad piece warping by putting battens across, do not fix them rigidly. A piece of wood 12 inches across, for instance, might be expected to alter in width as much as ¼ inch. A batten across would not expand or contract at all in its length. If it is glued or tightly screwed, something would break, possibly causing cracks in the board. It would be better to use slot screws and no glue. Put the central screw through a round hole and cut the others as slots, increasing the lengths towards the sides (Fig. 1-1E) so the screws can slide if the broad panel moves.

You can limit changes in moisture content by sealing the wood in a water-resistant way. Various paints, varnishes, and polishes can provide surface protection. Dry wood is less likely to absorb moisture if coated in this way, but the majority of these surface treatments are not fully waterproof. Some synthetic finishes are waterproof, but many of these tend to be brittle and hard, and some are unsuitable for contact with food.

Another way to prevent water absorption is to saturate the wood with something that does not mix with water. Linseed oil is sometimes used, and there are preservatives that have the same effect. Although these treatments are suitable for exterior woodwork, they obviously are unsuitable for kitchen use. Vegetable oil, of the type used for cooking, can be a successful treatment. Wood soaked in it for a few hours can be allowed to dry, then wiped to show a slight sheen. After that, the user can wipe the wood with more oil occasionally to keep its shape and appearance. For some

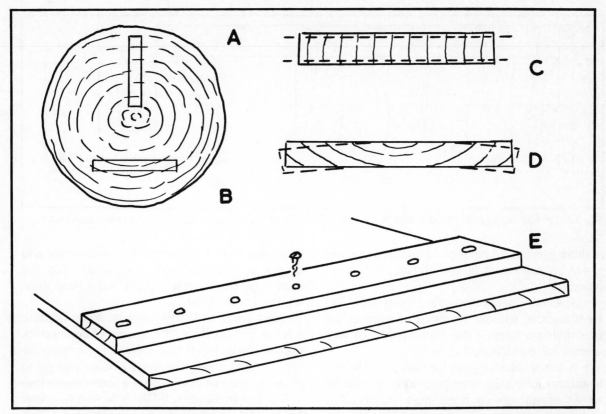

Fig. 1-1. Wood shrinks in the direction of the grain lines (A - D) and might need a batten with slotted screw holes (E) to flatten it.

articles, the wood must be left bare, so it can be washed when necessary, but for most things, such as cutting boards, the treatment with vegetable oil is best.

JOINTS

When you make articles for use in the kitchen, you must join pieces of wood. This is not a book on woodworking techniques, but some guidance on the choice of joints is offered. In addition to your own skill and equipment, you need to consider the use of what you are making. There is no need for elaborate or advanced joints if you are making a rough article for temporary use, but if the article is to have a permanent place in your kitchen, you will want to make the most suitable joints you can.

To a certain extent, you need to consider your tools and equipment. Power tools are valuable aids to accurate work, but most traditionally acceptable joints date from the days before power tools. If you have the skill, you can make joints with hand tools.

Nailing might be all that is needed. Sometimes it is advisable to drill a clearance or slightly undersized hole in the top piece to reduce the risk of splitting. For a long joint, you can increase strength by driving in alternate directions, dovetail fashion (Fig. 1-2A), with some closer nails near the end if it is an open box (Fig. 1-2B).

Nails on the surface are unattractive. If you use fine, small-headed nails or pins, set them below the surface with a punch. Cover them with stopping colored to match the wood (Fig. 1-2C) for an inconspicuous finish.

Modern *glues* are very strong, but no glue holds well on end grain, and most glues require surfaces to meet closely. If you must glue uneven edges, mix sawdust with the glue. The glue bonds

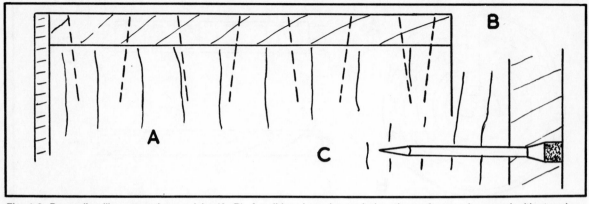

Fig. 1-2. Dovetail nailing strengthens a joint (A, B). A nail head can be set below the surface and covered with stopping.

to these particles where gaps have to be filled and gives reasonable strength, but it is better to fit joints closely.

Screws are better than nails as they draw surfaces together without the shock of hammering. For many purposes, a glued joint tightened with screws has considerable strength.

A screw holds by gripping the lower piece of wood and pulling the other piece to it by pressure from the head, so there is nothing to be gained by making the screw a force fit in the upper piece. You should drill a hole the size of the screw neck in the upper piece and a smaller hole for the screw thread to bite into the lower piece (Fig. 1-3A).

Make the hole for the screw thread larger and deeper in hardwood than in softwood. You can drive some small screws in softwood without drilling the lower wood.

Beware of excessive countersinking. Because a screw head pulls in, the amount of countersink usually can be less than the size of the screw head (Fig. 1-3B). Where the wood is thick enough to allow it, you can counterbore a screw head (Fig. 1-3C). For small sizes, fill the hole with stopping, but in most cases, gluing in a wood plug is better. Make it too long and plane it level after the glue has set.

For many assemblies, *dowels* are satisfactory.

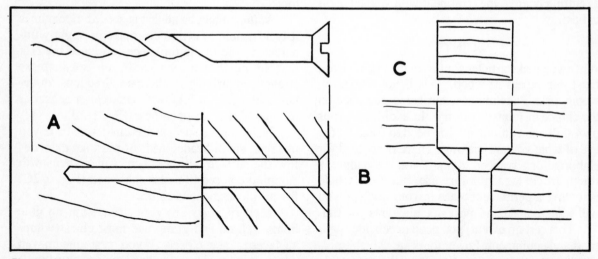

Fig. 1-3. Holes should be drilled for screws (A). Countersinking allows for the head pulling in (B). A counterbored head can be covered with a plug (C).

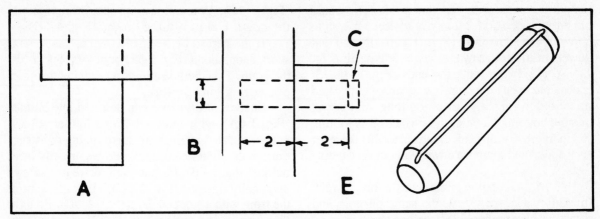

Fig. 1-4. Proportion a dowel to suit the wood (A-C). A groove and beveled end (D, E) makes driving simpler.

Normally, use at least two dowels in each joint, with the dowel diameter about half the thickness of the thinnest wood being joined (Fig. 1-4A). Much of the strength of doweled joints is in the glue area provided, so the further they penetrate, the better the glue bond. There are other factors, however, and if the wood is thick enough to allow it, the dowel should penetrate to a distance equal to twice its diameter (Fig. 1-4B).

A dowel enters a hole like a piston and at-

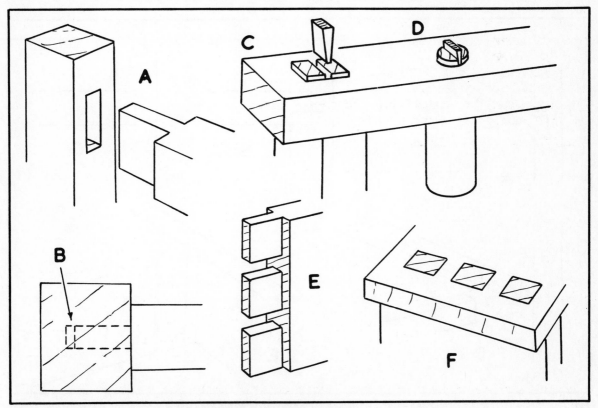

Fig. 1-5. Mortises and tenons are the traditional constructional joints.

tempts to compress air and glue inside. This could burst or crack wood. Make a hole deep enough to allow some clearance (Fig. 1-4C). If you cut dowels from a rod, saw grooves to release air (Fig. 1-4D). It helps to taper the ends (Fig. 1-4E). It is possible to buy cut dowels with grooves pressed in. Avoid having any dowel too long. If a dowel hits the bottom of a hole, the surfaces it is joining cannot meet. It is difficult to satisfactorily take apart such a joint and shorten a dowel without very messy results.

Mortise-and-tenon joints came before dowels. In many ways, they serve the same purpose and sometimes are preferable. Usually a tenon is about one-third the thickness of the wood (Fig. 1-5A). If the tenon does not go through, allow some clearance in the mortise (Fig. 1-5B) for the same reasons as when using dowels. If the tenon goes through, strengthen it with a wedge driven into a saw cut, but position it so it spreads the tenon end in the direction of the grain in the mortised piece (Fig. 1-5C). You can use the same technique on the dowel end of a turned piece (Fig. 1-5D).

If the part to be tenoned is wide, use several short tenons along (Fig. 1-5E) or across (Fig. 1-5F) the grain. This method avoids weakening the other part with a long mortise.

Shelves or divisions can be fitted into *dadoes* (Fig. 1-6A), which are not strong in themselves, but are usually retained by surrounding construction. You might need to use screws or nails from outside (Fig. 1-6B). For the shelf, drive thin screws diagonally upward (Fig. 1-6C). Hide the joint at the front with a stopped dado (Fig. 1-6D). Fit light divisions, as in a cutlery box, into V grooves (Fig. 1-6E).

If you want something better than a lapped joint at a corner, you have several choices. *Notching* one piece allows nails or screws to be driven both ways (Fig. 1-7A). *Finger* or *comb* joints (Fig. 1-7B) provide good glue area if properly cut. They are best made with a jig on a table saw. An un-

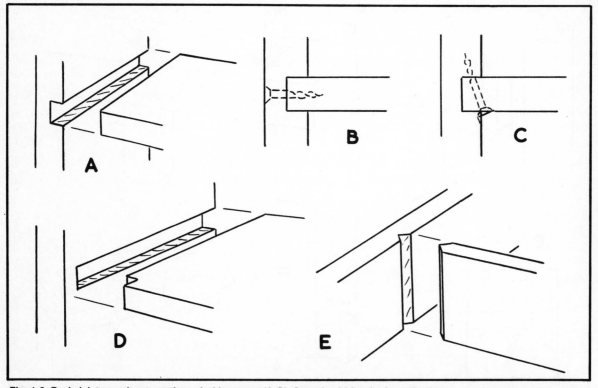

Fig. 1-6. Dado joints can be strengthened with screws (A-C). Stopping hides the front (D). A V section is better for thin wood.

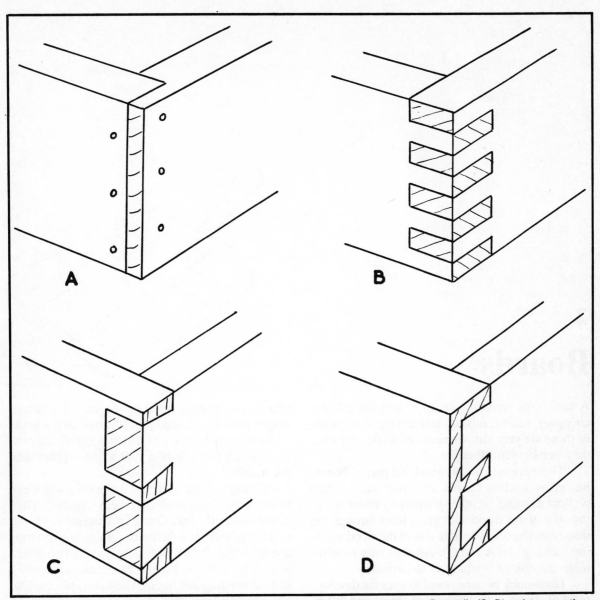

Fig. 1-7. Notching allows nailing both ways (A). Finger or tongue joints (B) are strong. Dovetails (C, D) resist separating.

even hand-cut joint looks bad and is weak.

Traditionally, the best corner joint is a *dovetail* (Fig. 1-7C). A tail width about 1½ times the thickness of the wood and pins between about ½ the thickness in width are the marks of a good cabinetmaking dovetail joint. For a drawer front, use a stopped dovetail joint (Fig. 1-7D). There are guides for mechanically cutting both types, but you will get a lot of satisfaction out of cutting them by hand if you use care.

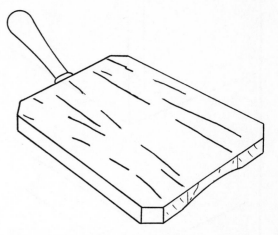

2

Boards

A cook uses various sorts of boards for cutting, chopping, rolling, mixing, and serving food. Some of these are very simple pieces of wood, but even they need careful thought.

There are uses for plywood and particleboard, but many kitchen boards are solid wood, often without framing or other support to resist warping. If you use wood with grain lines through the thickness, there will be little risk of the wood warping (see Fig. 1-1A and C). Another way to minimize the risk of warping is to laminate.

Laminating became possible with the development of strong, fully waterproof glues. The differing grains of the strips used (Fig. 2-1A) counteract each other's tendency to warp, which will not be much in any case, because of their narrow widths. The result gives the fashionable "butcher block" appearance.

Building up from strips lets you use up random widths, possibly offcuts from other jobs. Having different widths also might be regarded as a decorative feature.

Laminating requires care in matching thick-nesses and planing meeting edges. Use pieces longer than the finished job. It is best to plane the edges slightly hollow, then clamp across the center to pinch the ends of a joint a little tighter than the middle.

Gluing several pieces to make up a width can be difficult if you deal with them together. They might not settle flat. One might twist in relation to its neighbor. It is better to join only two strips at a time (Fig. 2-1B). Follow by joining two linked pairs (Fig. 2-1C) and so on. The result is less work in final leveling and trueing the joined pieces. Use a good waterproof glue—boatbuilding quality is the strongest. You do not want your work wasted by joints opening in use.

PLAIN BOARD

One or more simple boards will always have uses. They could be different sizes, but about 10 inches square is a good average. Softwood should not be less than ¾ inch thick, but hardwoods could be about ½ inch.

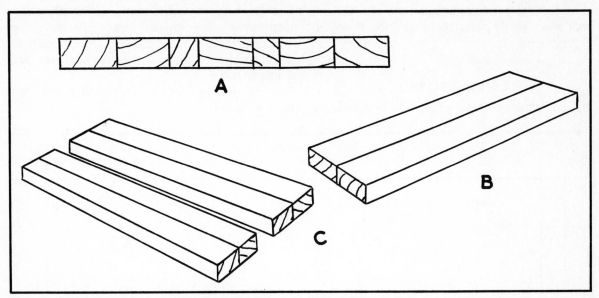

Fig. 2-1. Gluing narrow strips counteracts any tendency of individual pieces to warp.

1. If the strips are cut from one piece of wood, turn some over and reverse some to vary grain directions and counteract any tendency of one to warp (Fig. 2-2A).

2. Glue strips in pairs and then join the pairs together until you have made the width required.

3. When the glue has fully hardened, mark out and cut the shape (Fig. 2-2B).

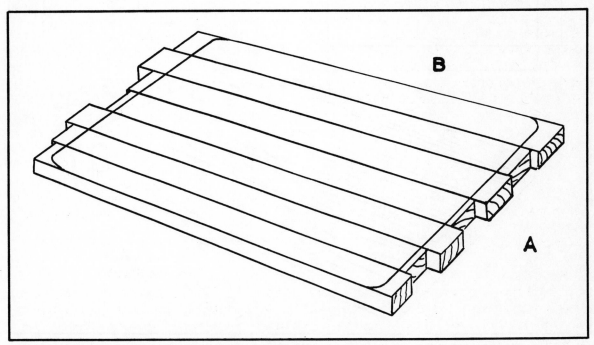

Fig. 2-2. The strips are glued and then trimmed to length.

4. Round the corners and the edges. Sand both sides thoroughly, then soak the board in vegetable oil.

LARGER BOARD

It is convenient to have a finger hole in a larger board. It helps when you want to pull it out of vertical storage, or it can hang on a peg or hook. You can make the large board in Fig. 2-3A from softwood strips for lightness, although hardwood has a longer life.

1. Glue together sufficient strips and level their surfaces.

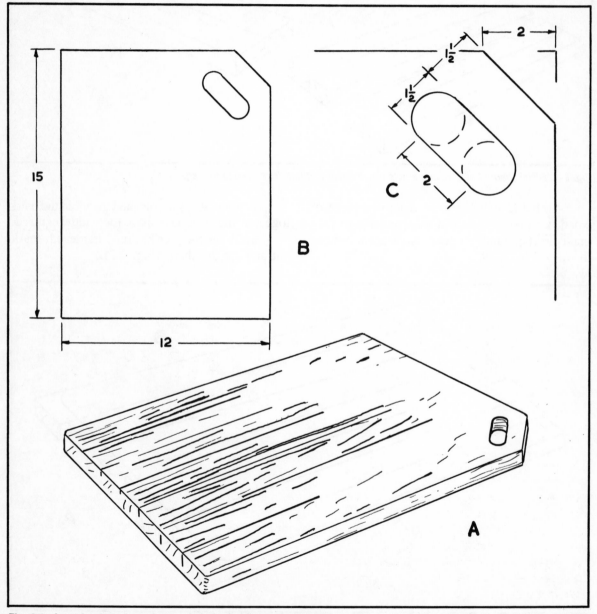

Fig. 2-3. A cutting board can have a hole for holding or hanging.

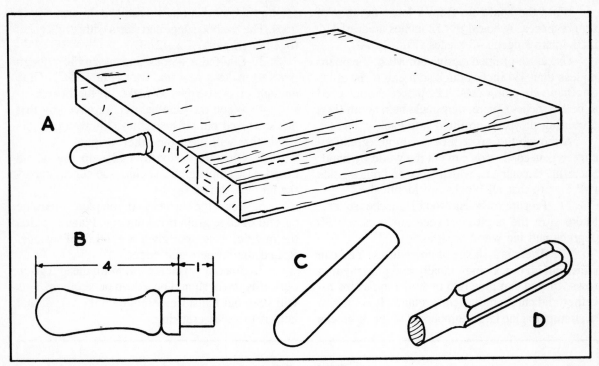

Fig. 2-4. This board has a handle that is turned, doweled, or planed.

2. Mark out the outline and the hole (Fig. 2-4B).

3. Cut the hole by drilling the ends and removing the waste (Fig. 2-3C).

4. Round the edges of the hole to make a comfortable grip.

5. Cut the board to shape, round its edges, and soak in vegetable oil.

THICK BOARD

The cook needs a thick board when using a cleaver to chop bones, for instance. The thickness provides strength as well as resistance to the blows, and spreads and deadens the shock on the supporting work top or table underneath.

To resist chopping cuts without the risk of breaking or splintering, use close-grained hardwood. Because hardwood will make the board heavy, add a handle (Fig. 2-4A) and possibly another at the opposite side, if you wish. Make the board 1½ inches thick, although 1¼ inches can be a minimum.

1. Make the board from 1½-inch square strips or join random widths to make about 15 inches square.

2. Cut the board to size with squared sides. Give the edges and corners moderate curves.

3. The handle looks best if turned (Fig. 2-4B). Make it with an end to glue into a hole. Arrange it square to the edge, then the board can be used on either side.

4. If you do not have the use of a lathe, make the handle from a dowel rod with a rounded end (Fig. 2-4C) or a square piece planed octagonal and shaped to fit a hole (Fig. 2-4D).

BUTCHER BLOCK

The finest board on which to chop food with a knife or cleaver is made like a true butcher block with end grain on the surface. It is made by gluing pieces together with their end grain upward. A butcher might use a massive assembly on legs, but for a cook's use, the board could be a similar size to other boards, but thicker.

11

Build the board up from a large number of square pieces. A board 9 × 12 inches made of 1½-inch squares needs 48 pieces (Fig. 2-5A).

Use close-grained hardwood. Make the board no less than 1¼ inches thick so it can resist splitting from chopping cuts. The pieces do not need to be 1½ inches square; they could be random sizes providing they can be fitted into each other.

Although the procedure is simple, great accuracy is needed. You can cut the wood by hand, but a fine circular saw with a fence and miter guide will ensure that all blocks are identical.

1. Prepare sufficient wood 1½ inches square. Make sure the angles between surfaces are 90 degrees and the wood is straight.

2. There is a choice of procedures. You can either cut all blocks individually and glue them in rows, or you can glue two or four long strips together and cut them into pieces later. It is unwise to attempt to glue large numbers of strips or blocks at one time as this might result in unevenness or gaps. The method suggested starts with strips glued together in pairs (Fig. 2-5B).

3. Cut these across and assemble enough pairs to make a row one way (Fig. 2-5C). Glue enough of these rows to make up the board.

4. When the glue has set, remove any that has squeezed out. If necessary, lightly plane the edges that will meet the other strips.

5. Glue the strips to make up the whole board. Use ample glue and clamp so edges, in particular, are drawn tight.

6. Level the surfaces. If you plane them, be careful of edge grain breaking out. Plane towards the middle. A scraper gives a good final surface. Round the corners and edges.

7. Soak in vegetable oil. With the end grain outwards, there should be a deep penetration. This will keep out moisture, strengthen the wood, and help it to resist cracking.

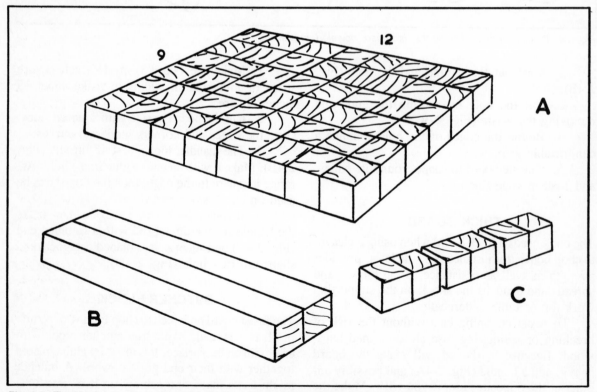

Fig. 2-5. The block is made by first gluing pairs of strips, then cutting them into pieces.

BREAD BOARD

Many of our ancestors ate off wood platters, or *trenchers*. A person with a good appetite might still be called "a good trencherman," which comes from those days. You might not want to return to using wood instead of plates, but a trencher makes a good cutting board, especially for bread. Traditional bread boards were round and very similar to trenchers.

Make both the trencher and bread board of wood at least ¾ inch thick, with several strips joined together to make up the width. Turn the boards on a lathe, if available; otherwise saw circles to make acceptable bread boards. A board of this diameter would need to be turned on a large lathe or one with a facility for using a surface plate on the outboard end of the headstock spindle.

1. The original trencher had a groove near the rim to prevent gravy and other liquid running over the edge (Fig. 2-6A). In a bread or cake board, the groove catches crumbs, which can be tipped out later. For a turned board, glue sufficient strips to allow you to cut a circle. Mount it in the lathe and turn it to about 12 inches in diameter (Fig. 2-6B).

2. Use a gouge to turn a groove. Make it ⅜ inch wide and go about halfway through the wood, ¾ inch in from the outside (Fig. 2-6C).

3. To make a similar board without a lathe, carefully saw the circle and true its edge. Use a router with a suitable cutter to make the groove, which could have a flat bottom, if you do not have a shaped cutter.

4. A traditional bread board was turned with a molded edge. Prepare wood in the same way as for a trencher, then turn it with a bead about 1 inch from the edge and a more moderate curve outside that one (Fig. 2-6D). It was customary to carve the word *bread* on the broad margin of the board. You could incise this, if you wish, or carve a name to personalize the board.

5. Both types of board were left untreated so they could be scrubbed occasionally, but your boards could be soaked in vegetable oil and allowed to dry.

ROPE-HANDLED BOARD

Rope makes a convenient handle for a board, particularly if the board is a large cutting or rolling one. You can carry the board and hang it up, and the handle falls out of the way when the board is used.

Make board any size you wish and with any number of strips. The one suggested (Fig. 2-7A) is made ⅞ inch thick from 3-inch-wide strips of softwood (Fig. 2-7B).

1. Plane the wood parallel and to size. Cut the strips and glue them together in pairs, then glue the pairs together.

2. Cut the board to size. Cut the corners off as shown or leave them square or round them.

3. The rope can be any type, three-strand or braided, and about a ⅜-inch diameter. Whip its ends tightly with a few turns of thread (Fig. 2-7C).

4. Drill a few holes in scrap wood to size the rope end. Drill the holes in the end of the board this size and about 1 inch deep.

5. Although other glues might hold the rope in the holes, an epoxy adhesive is best. Put glue into the hole with a thin piece of wood and dip the ends of the rope into the glue before pushing them in. Let the glue set. Some epoxy glue takes several days to build up its full strength—read the manufacturer's instructions.

6. Soak the board in vegetable oil.

DOWEL-HANDLED BOARD

A handle more rigid than rope can be an advantage if the cook needs to manipulate the cutting board. One way of providing a firm grip is to recess the end of the board and put a dowel across. Figure 2-8(A) shows a board 10 inches wide and ⅞ inch thick. It could be 15 inches long. It is made up of five 2-inch strips, but other sizes and widths can be used. It does not matter if the cutout comes on strip joints, but if it does, you can economize on the lengths of some pieces (Fig. 2-8B).

1. Make up the board from strips, square the ends, and mark the cutout part for the handle.

2. Corners of the cutout could be square, but

EAU CLAIRE DISTRICT LIBRARY

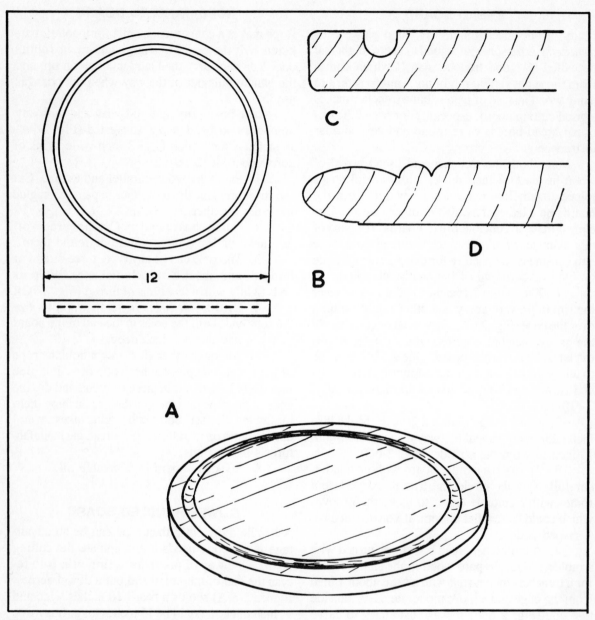

Fig. 2-6. A round board follows the design of a traditional platter.

curved is better. Round the inside corners by drilling ¾-inch holes and sawing into them.

3. Square the holes in opposite sides to the edges so the dowel rod can pass through (Fig. 2-8C). Use a drilling guide or a drill press. For the sizes of board suggested, a ½-inch dowel rod is suitable.

4. True the board to shape, remove any excess glue, and sand the surfaces. Round the corners. When you are satisfied, glue in the dowel rod and plane its ends level after the glue has set.

GROOVED BOARD

If what is being cut produces crumbs, a groove can

help catch them. The round bread board (Fig. 2-6) is an example, but the design can be taken further with a means of collecting the crumbs at one point and tipping them out. It is unwise to groove a very small board because the groove might take up too much working surface.

Make the board in Fig. 2-9A at least ¾ inch thick, and build it up from strips in any way described for earlier boards. It is a plain board with rounded corners, but you could add a handle. Form the outline suggested with a power router, using its guide to follow the edge all around.

1. Make the board from strips and finish it to size but do not round its corners yet.

2. The grooves are ⅜ inch wide and deep and ¾ inch from the edge. Pencil these lines at one corner.

3. The circular hollow at one corner (Fig. 2-9B) is to collect crumbs shaken around the grooves. It should have a 1½-inch diameter but could be slightly smaller if you do not have a bit that size. Ideally, make the hollow with a Forstner bit, which will drill a flat-bottomed hole without the deep impression from the central spur of any other bit.

4. Mark the center of the hole. Use that as

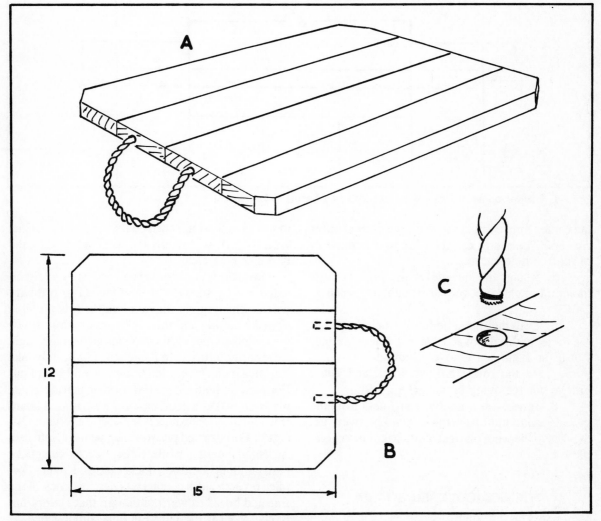

Fig. 2-7. Rope glued into holes forms a handle for this board.

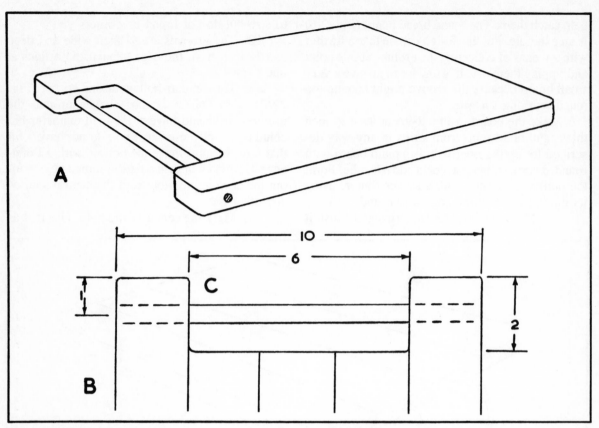

Fig. 2-8. A dowel rod across the end can be used as a handle or for hanging.

the center for a compass to mark the curved outer corners. The router can then follow it around to match the hole curve.

5. Round the outside at the hole corner, though it might be better cut straight across (Fig. 2-9C).

6. Drill the round hollow ⅜ inch deep. Set the router to this depth and distance from the edge. Cut a flat-bottomed groove all around.

7. At the round hollow, mark and cut a groove for removing crumbs (Fig. 2-9D).

8. If necessary, remove roughness from the grooves and sand inside them. Sand all over. Either leave the wood untreated or soak it in vegetable oil.

FORMICA-COVERED BOARD

Laminated plastic, such as Formica, is very good to use on a working surface that comes in contact with food. It withstands the usual knife cuts and is easily kept clean.

Because it does not expand and contract, laminated plastic should not be attached to ordinary wood, which might move in width. It is possible to make cutting and mixing boards with Formica on hardboard, but even the oil-tempered type might suffer after long use in a kitchen. It will only take Formica on its face side. A more useful board has Formica on both sides. Exterior or marine-grade plywood makes a good base for a two-sided board (Fig. 2-10). Its thickness is not very important. Off-cuts of Formica and plywood can be made into useful small boards, while larger pieces can make pastry rolling boards on thicker bases. Having Formica on both sides counteracts any tendency of the finished board to warp, although that is very unlikely, even if the board is only single-sided.

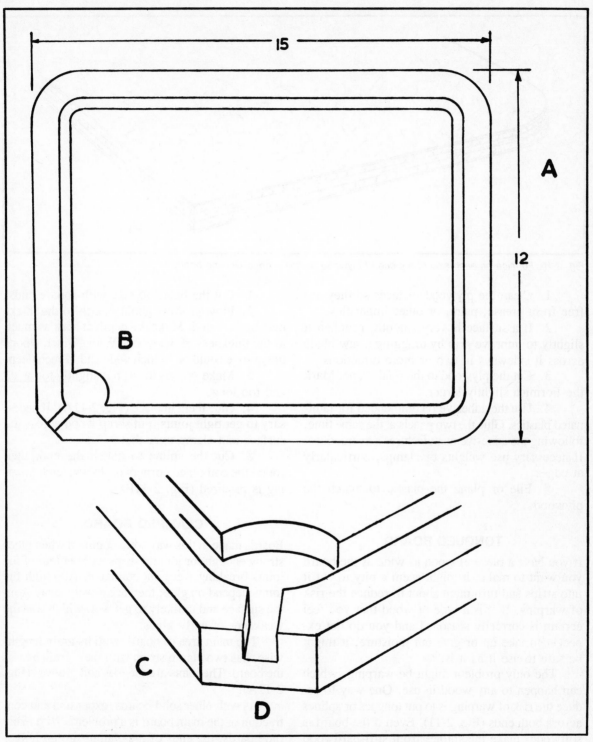

Fig. 2-9. A groove around a board collects crumbs that can be shaken out at a corner.

Fig. 2-10. Formica on each side of a piece of plywood makes a good working board.

1. Clean the plywood surfaces so they are free from grease, paint, or other impurities.

2. If a surface is very smooth, roughen it slightly to improve grip by dragging a saw blade across it sideways in two or more directions.

3. Cut the plywood to the final shape. Mark the Formica slightly larger.

4. Use the adhesive recommended for laminated plastics. Glue the two panels at the same time, following the adhesive manufacturer's instructions. If necessary use weights or clamps, particularly at edges.

5. File or plane the plastic to match the plywood.

TONGUED BOARD

If you have a piece of wood as wide as the board you want to make, it might seem a pity to cut it into strips and turn them about to reduce the risk of warping. If it is a type of wood that you feel certain is correctly seasoned and you do not expect it to take up or give out moisture, it might be safe to use it as it is.

The only problem might be warping, which can happen to any wood in use. One way to reduce the risk of warping is to put tongues or splines across both ends (Fig. 2-11). Even if the board is softwood, make the splines from stiff hardwood so they resist movement in the other piece.

1. Cut the board to size with square ends.

2. Plow grooves about one-third the thickness of the wood. Make the depth at least as much as the thickness of the wood. With ¾-inch wood, the groove could be ¼ inch wide and ⅞ inch deep.

3. Make splines to fit, but slightly too wide and too long.

4. Glue them in place (Fig. 2-11A). If necessary to get tight joints, put scrap wood across the surface and clamp over that.

5. Cut the spline to match the end, then round the combined corners or do whatever shaping is required (Fig. 2-11B).

CLAMPED BOARD

Boards made in this way were common when glues strong enough for joining strips without fear of the joints breaking were unobtainable. Although the joints depend on glue, they are mostly away from the surface and unlikely to get wet, which was the weakener of early glues.

The main area of board, with its grain lengthwise, has two clamp strips with their grain across the board. The joints are tongues and grooves (Fig. 2-12A).

As with other solid boards, expansion and contraction of the main board is a problem. With many old boards, the ends of the clamps are no longer level with the sides of the central piece, yet the

18

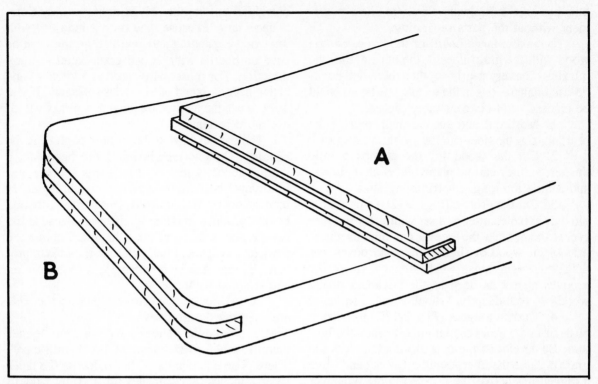

Fig. 2-11. A piece inset in the end will resist the tendency of a board to warp.

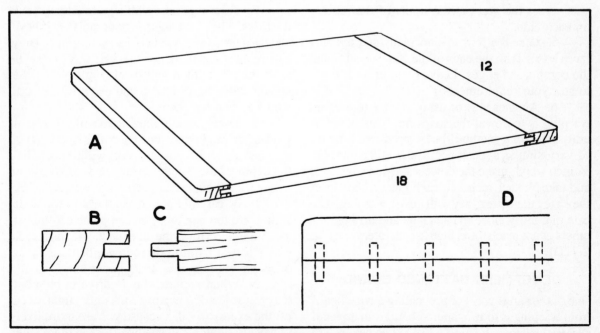

Fig. 2-12. The traditional method of preventing warping is with tongued-and-grooved joints (A-C). A doweled strip (D) can have a similar effect.

glue has been sufficiently elastic to allow movement without the parts separating.

To make a large board of this type, choose wood with the grain lines at the ends across the thickness, or very nearly so, then there will be little risk of alterations in the width. The board could be made up from two or more pieces.

1. Mark out and cut the main part of the board making the sides parallel and the ends square.

2. Cut the wood for the clamps a little thicker, so they can be planed level after fitting, and a little too long, for trimming later.

3. Cut the groove (Fig. 2-12B) first with a plow or spindle cutter at a set width. Fit the tongues to them. Make the grooves one-third the thickness of the wood or slightly more. Grooves less than this might cause weak tongues. Make the grooves almost as deep as the thickness of the wood—⅝ inch deep on ¾-inch wood is suitable.

4. Cut the tongues (Fig. 2-12C) to make a push fit in the grooves that almost reach the bottom. Be careful as the cuts are made across the grain because the fibers could break out and leave a ragged line across the finished joint. Whatever method is used to cut the tongues, make deep knife cuts across the grain at the limits of the rabbets on each side.

5. Glue the joints. Plane and sand the surfaces level. Trim the ends of the clamps and round the corners and edges. Leave plain or soak in oil to suit your requirements.

6. Another way of using clamps to prevent warping is to dowel the strips on. This is not as craftsmanlike a method, but it produces a board of very similar appearance to the other one. On ¾-inch wood, make the dowels a ⅜-inch diameter and take about 1 inch into each piece. The closer they are, the better they will resist warping. Locate one fairly close to each side and arrange the others at not much more than 2-inch intervals (Fig. 2-12D).

DOVETAILED BATTENED BOARD

One of the surest ways of preventing a wide board from warping is to use tapered battens in dovetail grooves underneath (Fig. 2-13A). The battens are not glued but can be driven tighter at any time, if necessary. Because they do not interfere with the wood expanding and contracting, they can be used on boards with an end-grain pattern in any direction. For most boards used in a kitchen, one batten near each end of a board is sufficient. If you want to use the method on longer pieces of wood, use more battens.

The battens have to be stout enough to resist bending. On a ¾-inch board, 10 inches wide, a section about ¾ inch × 2 inches is appropriate. For thinner boards, make the battens a little thicker than the board. Hardwood battens across softwood boards produce maximum stiffness. Because the battens act as feet and raise the board above the work top, keep them fairly close to the ends to prevent tipping. A 2-inch batten 1½ inches from an end is about right.

1. Make the board to size or trim the ends after cutting the grooves.

2. Make the battens 1 inch or more longer than the width of the board. Give them a taper. There is no exact amount, but reducing the taper from 2 inches to 1¾ inches for a 10-inch board should be satisfactory (Fig. 2-13B).

3. After tapering with square edges, bevel the sides. The exact angle is not crucial, but bevel all edges the same. A suitable angle is 1 in 7. Draw square lines and mark one unit one way and seven units the other, then join them (Fig. 2-13C). Set an adjustable bevel to this and use it to check all edges as you cut them.

4. Draw square lines across the board as guides for the battens but mark the slots tapered symmetrically. Because the slots will be about half the depth of the battens, measure at this position and mark the bevels and depths at each side (Fig. 2-13D). Be careful not to make the slots too wide. If they are too narrow, you can plane off the batten, but if the error is the other way, you must make a new batten. Aim to drive in the batten so most of its excess length is at its wider end.

5. When you are able to drive in both battens to project the narrow ends only slightly, cut off the excess wood. Because you are more likely to have to tighten battens than slacken them when

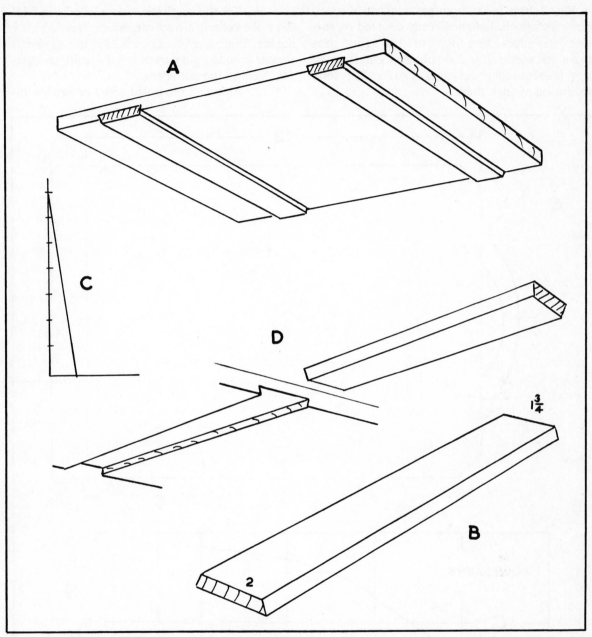

Fig. 2-13. Tapered dovetailed battens restrict warping and can be driven further to tighten, if necessary.

in use, you could leave about ¼ inch projecting at the wide end of the batten for driving in further. After the board has been in use in the kitchen for two or three months, test tightness and trim the battens level. It is improbable that there will be much later movement.

PARTICLEBOARD PASTRY BOARD
Plastic veneered particleboard (especially white) provides a good surface for rolling and mixing pastry, although the usual plastic surface is not hard enough to resist much cutting. If you want a hard surface, use Formica on thick plywood. The board

21

in Fig. 2-14 is made from particleboard ⅝ inch or ¾ inch thick, bought already covered on surfaces and edges. You might need to adjust sizes to a stock width. You also will need some narrow strip plastic to cover cut edges. The handle is solid hardwood ½ inch thick.

1. Cut the particleboard to length. In Fig. 2-14, the corners are cut off, but they could be left square. Rounding is not practical as taking plastic veneer around tight curves is not usually successful. Veneer the cut edges.

2. Although the board could be used with-

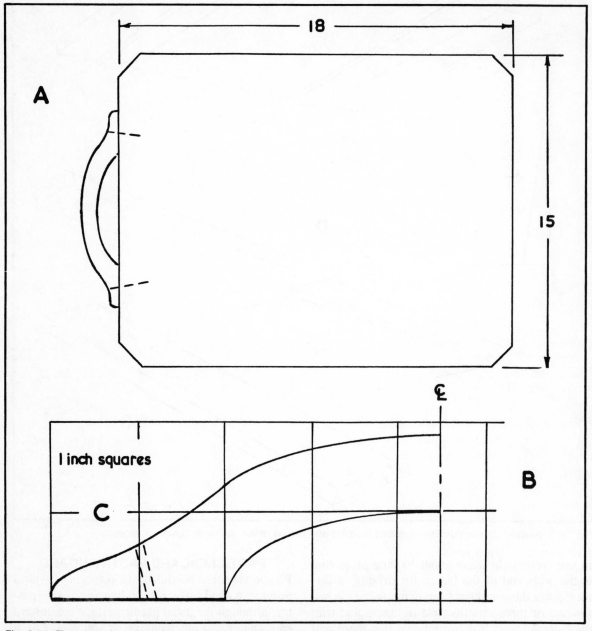

Fig. 2-14. The pastry board can have a wood handle screwed on at one end.

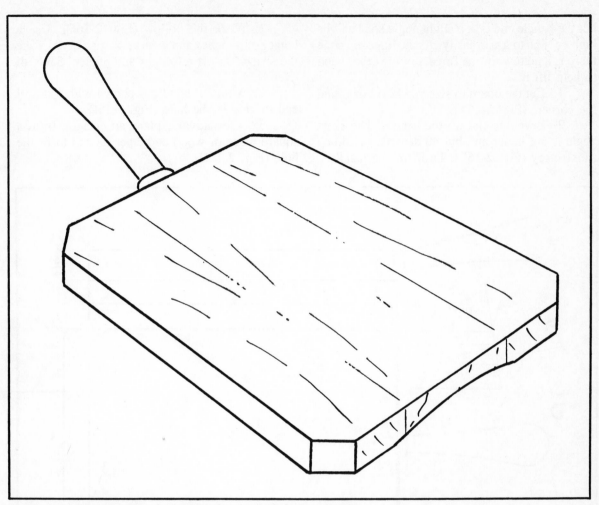

Fig. 2-15. A cheeseboard can be laminated and provided with a handle.

out a handle, a large piece of particleboard is fairly heavy, and a handle for moving it will be appreciated. This one has flat feet against the edge of the board and two screws holding it.

3. Prepare the wood with the edge that will be against the board carefully squared, or the handle will not fit accurately.

4. Mark out and cut the handle (Fig. 2-14B). Round all edges that will be held.

5. Drill for screws at an angle (Fig. 2-14C). This brings the screw heads flush with the surface and increases the strength of the joint. Allow for screws going about 1 inch into the particleboard. Varnish the handle before screwing it on.

HANDLED CHEESEBOARD

A board on which cheese is served and cut benefits from having a handle. The handle enables it to be moved around the work top or passed around the dining table. If it is thick enough to have some weight, it is less likely to move in use.

The board in Fig. 2-15 is large enough for most pieces of cheese, but it could be made any size to suit your needs or available wood. A close-grained hardwood is best, although you could use softwood if you are equipping with that kind of kitchen ware.

Make board with three edges cut square. The hole for the handle is drilled square to the edge, but the handle end is at a slight angle so it will be high enough to grasp easily. At the opposite edge there is a hollow for the fingers of the other hand to help lift it.

1. Cut the board to size and bevel or round the corners (Fig. 2-16A).

2. Bevel the end for the handle. The exact angle is not important, but 80 degrees should be satisfactory (Fig. 2-16B). Drill for the handle.

3. Work the hollow (Fig. 2-16C). Use a length of 3 inches and a curve ½ inch deep. Take the sharpness off all edges and angles. Sand all over.

4. A turned handle is shown with a dowel end to glue in the hole (Fig. 2-16D).

5. Alternatively, plane an octagon from a square piece of wood and taper its end to fit the hole (Fig. 2-16E).

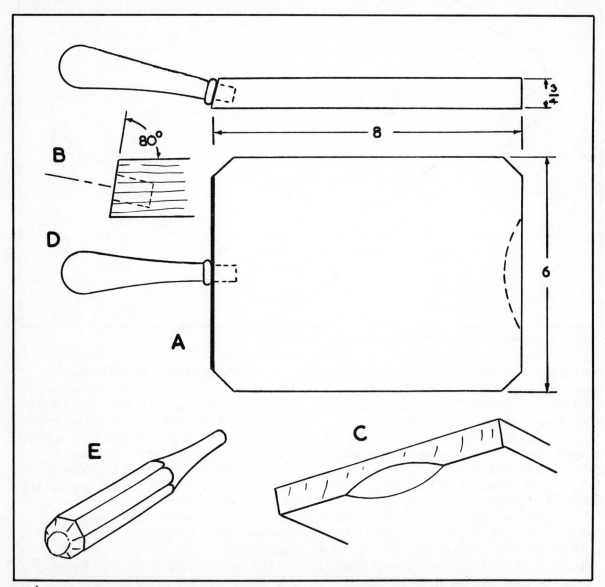

Fig. 2-16. A turned or planed handle fits into a sloping end. A notch at the other end allows fingers to be used when lifting.

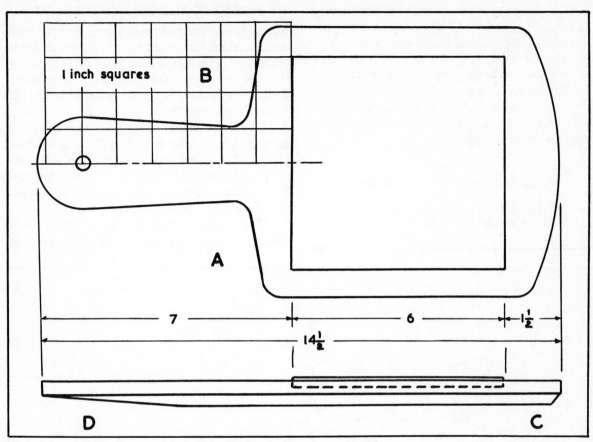

1 inch squares

B

A

7

6

$1\frac{1}{2}$

$14\frac{1}{2}$

D

C

Fig. 2-17. The tile fits in a recess. A bevel under the handle aids gripping.

Materials List for Handled Cheeseboard

1 piece $\frac{3}{4} \times$ 6×9
1 piece $1\frac{1}{8} \times 1\frac{1}{8} \times 6$

TILE CHEESEBOARD

Ceramic tiles, of the type used in bathrooms, are hygienic and suitable for use with food. A 6-inch-square one can be mounted in wood to provide the working surface of a cheeseboard. The tile can be a solid color, but a pictorial or patterned tile is attractive and could be hung on the wall as a decoration when not in use.

     The wood could be anything you wish, either a full-width piece of solid wood or several pieces glued together. Using several pieces reduces the risk of warping. Make sure the wood is dry and fully seasoned. If it dries out after assembly, it might shrink or warp enough to crack the tile.

     1. Check the tile size. The drawing in Fig. 2-17A suits a tile 6 inches square. Adjust sizes, if necessary.

     2. Prepare the wood to width and thickness. Mark the shape about a centerline (Fig. 2-17B). Mark the recess to suit the tile.

     3. Cut the recess before shaping the outside. Allow for a small amount of the tile to stand above the wood surface. Do not make the tile too tight, especially in the width, in case the wood shrinks slightly and damages the tile. If the recess is cut with a power router it can be level all over, but if you cut it with drill and chisel, level the recess around the edges. It does not matter if it goes a little deeper in the middle.

4. Shape the outside and drill the hanging hole.

5. Round or bevel the underside up to about half thickness (Fig. 2-17C). Slope the underside of the handle up to half thickness at the end (Fig. 2-17D) for a better grasp.

6. Stain and varnish or polish the wood to provide a background to the tile. Glue in the tile with an epoxy adhesive.

Materials List for Tile Cheeseboard

I piece wood	¾ × 7½ × 16
I ceramic tile	¼ × 6 × 6

BREAD BOARD WITH KNIFE SLOT

Not all bread comes already sliced, and the cook needs a board for cutting loaves. Although bread might be cut on a board used for other foods, it is better to keep a board solely for cutting bread. It can provide storage for the bread knife for added convenience.

The bread board in Fig. 2-18 has a recess for the knife handle. That might be sufficient, but there also could be a small round magnet to hold the knife in place. Some stainless steel is nonmagnetic, however, and you should check the knife you intend to use by touching it to the magnet first.

The suggested sizes in Fig. 2-18 are large enough for any loaf of bread, but you might need

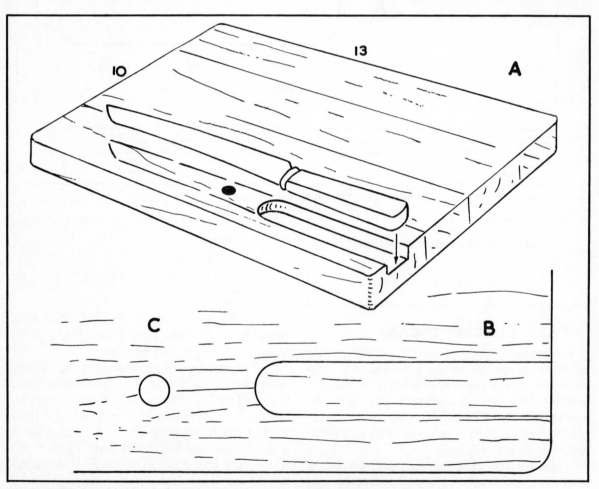

Fig. 2-18. This board holds a knife. Its handle is in a recess and a magnet grips the blade.

to adjust them to suit the length of your knife. The board could be made in any of the ways suggested for other boards. One suggestion is to use four lengthwise strips between ¾ inch and 1 inch thick, preferably a light-colored, close-grained hardwood, but softwood is acceptable. Because the cook cuts downward on the board, avoid wood that might splinter.

1. Make up the board with lightly rounded corners.

2. Measure the knife handle and mark the recess to make an easy fit around it (Fig. 2-18B). Its depth should be sufficient for the handle to fit in when the blade is resting on the surface of the board. If you arrange for the end of the knife handle to project about ¼ inch, it will be easier to lift out. Cut the recess and try the knife in position.

3. To fit a round magnet, drill a place for it a short distance from the handle recess (Fig. 2-18C). Arrange the depth so the magnet projects very slightly above the surrounding wood. Glue the magnet in, preferably with an epoxy adhesive.

4. Sand the wood and leave it untreated.

```
Materials List for Bread Board with Knife Slot

4 pieces   ⅞ × 2½ × 14
```

LEAF CHEESEBOARD

The handle of this cheeseboard (Fig. 2-19A) has a recess for the handle of a cheese knife. There also could be a magnet to hold the knife, as in the bread board. Check that the magnet will hold the knife you intend to use.

The board could be a single piece of wood or any number of strips glued together. Sizes are suggested, but adjust the length of the board handle to suit the knife handle, which should project a short distance. Make the board any convenient thickness, but too light a board might be a nuisance in the kitchen, although it still might be useful on the dining table. A thickness of ¾ inch is good for general use. A stylized leaf outline is shown in Fig. 2-19B, but the main part of the board could be square or round, if you wish.

1. Glue sufficient strips to make up the width, if you are not using a single piece.

2. With the aid of 1-inch squares, draw the shape and cut it. The top edges are best left square. The lower edges of the handle could be rounded, for ease in picking up, and this could be continued all around.

3. Mark and cut the recess for the knife handle. It could have a flat or round bottom, but when the handle is in place, the knife blade should rest flat on the board.

4. If there is to be a magnet, drill for it and glue it in so it projects very slightly above the board surface.

5. Sand the wood. Leave it bare or treat it with vegetable oil as desired.

```
Materials List for Leaf Cheeseboard

1 piece    ¾ × 6 × 13
```

KNIFE BOARD

When a knife is regularly used with the same board, the knife can be fitted into the board to store. The board in Fig. 2-20 has a carving or bread knife fitted into a slot in its edge. In addition to keeping the knife where you can find it, the arrangement protects the knife edge from damage and the cook's hands from cuts.

Adjust the board size to suit the knife. Extend the slotted part past the tip of the handle. The thickness must be more than the thickness of the blade. As shown, the board is ⅞ inch thick and about 9 × 12 inches. You can use any of the methods described for earlier boards, but it is best made of several strips glued together. At the edge with the slot, make the strip wide enough to leave solid wood behind the cut.

1. Assemble sufficient strips, glue them together, and cut the board to size (Fig. 2-20B).

2. Cut away for the handle (Fig. 2-20C).

3. Mark the slot for the blade (Fig. 2-20D). The slot has to be a push fit over the blade. Experiment with your saws in scrap wood to see

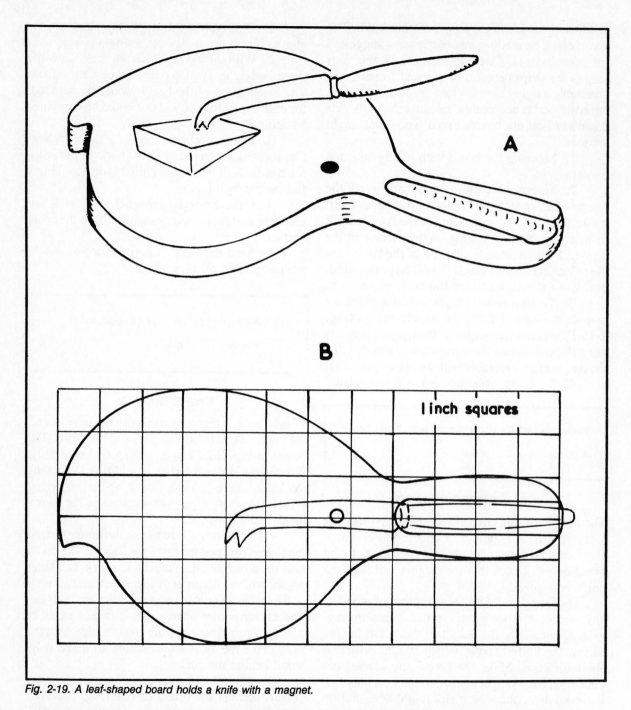

Fig. 2-19. A leaf-shaped board holds a knife with a magnet.

which produces a suitable slot. You might have to make the slot too thin at first and ease it out until the saw blade pushes in. Move a handsaw backwards and forwards, like a file, to size the slot.

The knife blade need not penetrate completely; its back can project slightly.

4. Round the corners and edges (Fig. 2-20E).

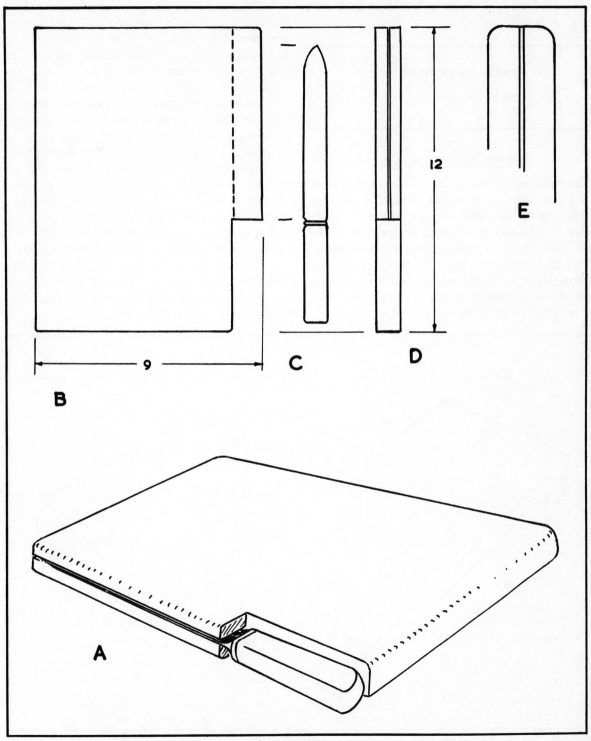

Fig. 2-20. A bread knife can fit in a slot in the edge of its board.

5. Leave the board untreated or soak it in vegetable oil.

Materials List for Knife Board

1 piece   ⅞ × 9 × 12

WIRED CHEESEBOARD

The traditional way of cutting cheese is with a wire. A large wheel of cheese is reduced to smaller chunks with a long wire stretched between two handles. The smaller chunks then are reduced to useful sizes with a wire attached to a slotted board. You might not need to cut large cheeses, but a wire cheeseboard is useful for cutting store-bought chunks. Many cheeses cut much more cleanly with a wire than with a knife.

The board in Fig. 2-21 is 9 inches square (Fig. 2-22A), but it could be made any size. Make it bigger than any piece of cheese you expect to cut since it must be held by one hand while you pull the wire with the other. Screw it down if it is to have frequent use in a regular position. There could be a strip projecting downward on the near side to hook over the edge of a table or work top; then you can press forward against it while cutting.

Get the wire before making the wood parts. It should be steel, preferably stainless, and 22 gauge or thinner. Mild steel wire tends to kink. Unhardened tool or spring steel, sometimes described as "piano" wire, is suitable. A piece 18 inches long is adequate, but it might be worthwhile getting more for replacements, if ever needed.

The wood parts are ⅝ inch thick. A light-colored hardwood is preferred to softwood, which can splinter if the wire pulls into it. You can turn the handle or use a dowel rod.

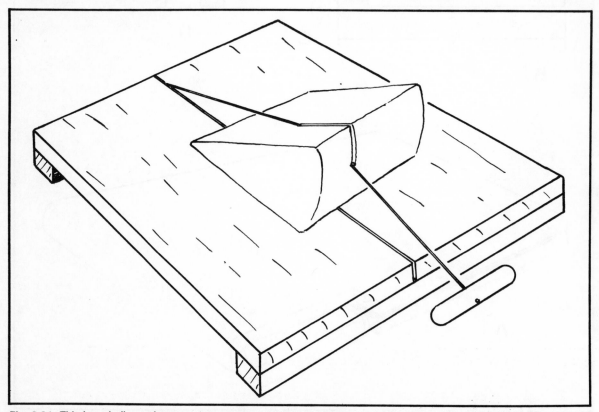

Fig. 2-21. This board allows cheese to be cut with a wire over a slot.

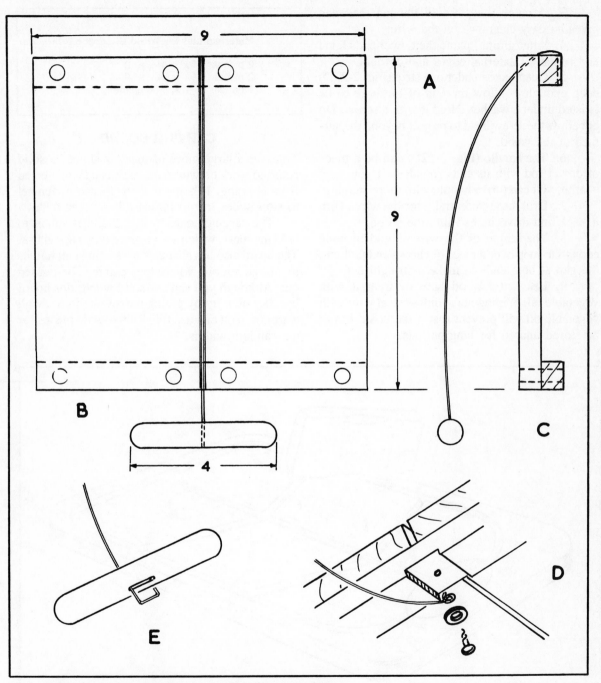

Fig. 2-22. The board is in two parts so the wire pulls between them.

1. Make the two sides (Fig. 2-22B).

2. The sides must be attached to two end strips underneath. Glue alone might not be strong enough. Brass screws could be driven upward from below, but you can avoid metal if you use ⅜-inch dowels (Fig. 2-22C).

3. Arrange the parts so the gap between gives an easy clearance on the wire.

4. After gluing, plane the dowel ends level and round all external edges and corners.

5. Cut a recess under one strip (Fig. 2-22D) deep enough to allow the end of the wire to be twisted under a washer. Hold it with a screw. Do not allow the screw head to project beyond the surface of the wood.

6. The handle (Fig. 2-22E) can be a piece of dowel rod with its ends rounded. If you have a lathe, you can turn a handle with more shaping.

7. Drill through centrally for the wire. Turn it back and drive its end into the wood.

8. The length of the wire should be long enough to loop over a piece of cheese and pull into the gap at both ends to make a straight cut.

9. Leave the wood bare or treat it with vegetable oil. Wiping nonstainless steel wire with vegetable oil will prevent rust if the board has to be stored unused for long periods.

Materials List for Wired Cheeseboard

2 pieces	⅝ × 4½ × 9	
2 pieces	⅝ × ¾ × 9	
1 handle	4 × ⅝ diameter	

CARVING BOARD

To carve a large piece of meat, you need a solid board to work on where the meat can be prevented from slipping. It helps if there is also a channel to stop juices from running all over the table.

The carving board in Fig. 2-23 has spikes to hold the meat, which are covered when not in use. The board also has channels cut to direct all liquids to a large hollow, where they can then be poured out. Although you can use solid wood, this board is better built up by gluing narrow strips to avoid warping. You can use five 2-inch-wide pieces, or use random widths.

Fig. 2-23. For carving meat, this board has grooves to take away liquids. There are points to hold the meat and a block to cover them when out of use.

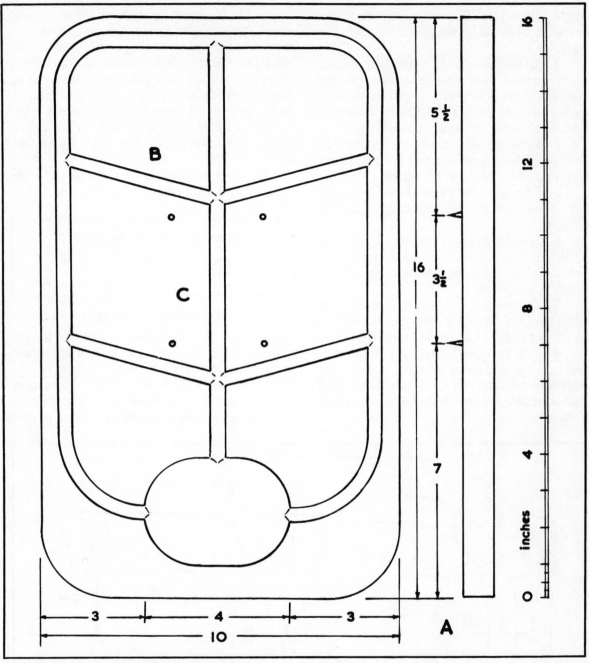

Fig. 2-24. Suggested sizes for the carving board.

1. Glue strips to make up the width, then true the surfaces and mark the wood to size (Fig. 2-24A). Mark the corners (Fig. 2-25A) and the positions and widths of the channels (Fig. 2-25B). The diagonal channels are shown at 15 degrees (Fig. 2-24B). Tilting the board will run all liquid to the bottom.

2. Cut the curved corners and square all

edges to the surface. This ensures accuracy when they are used as guides for the router cutting the channels.

3. Set the router 5/16 inch deep (Fig. 2-25C). Use the edges of the board to guide cuts at the top, sides, and center. Clamp on guide strips when cutting the other channels. Make the large hollow the same depth as the channels or slightly deeper.

4. Make sure all channels are smooth. Sand the edges of the channels and hollow, if necessary. Round the outer edges of the board.

5. Four spikes are shown (Fig. 2-24C). Add more if you think they are necessary. Mark their locations.

6. Spikes are steel projecting ½ inch above the surface (Fig. 2-25D). Stainless steel rod is best with a 7/64-inch diameter, although slightly more or less is acceptable.

7. The best way to make the spikes is to start with a long rod. Grind the point on one end, then cut off that spike. Make each in turn in this way.

8. Drill the wood to make a push fit for the spikes. Put a little epoxy adhesive in each hole. Drive each spike in, using soft metal over the point. Lead is suitable, or you can hammer over a piece of aluminum.

9. It is important that the spikes remain sharp. Because you do not want to risk anyone scratching themselves on the points, make a wood block to cover them when not in use. Tap it onto the spikes to mark their positions, then cut it to shape around them by drilling holes for a push fit on the spikes and around the outer edges (Fig. 2-25E). If the block is a tight fit, hollow finger grips in the lower edges (Fig. 2-23) for pulling away.

10. Soak the wood in vegetable oil and wipe over with oil after each use and washing.

Materials List for Carving Board

1 piece   7/8 × 10 × 17 laminated
1 piece   3/4 ×   3 × 5

SQUARE HOT STAND

Because it is unwise to put a hot pan on an unprotected table or countertop, several hot stands or pads should be available in the kitchen. A simple piece of plywood is all that is needed in most cases, but a pan direct from the oven might produce enough heat to penetrate a thin piece of ply-

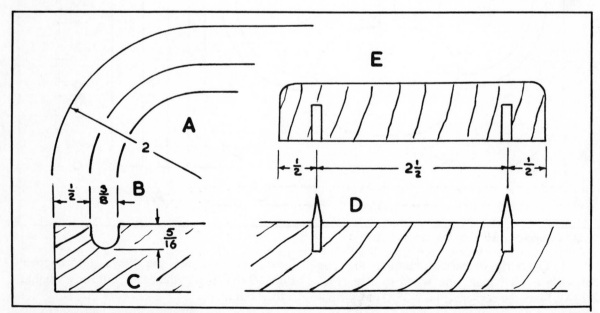

Fig. 2-25. Details of grooves and points.

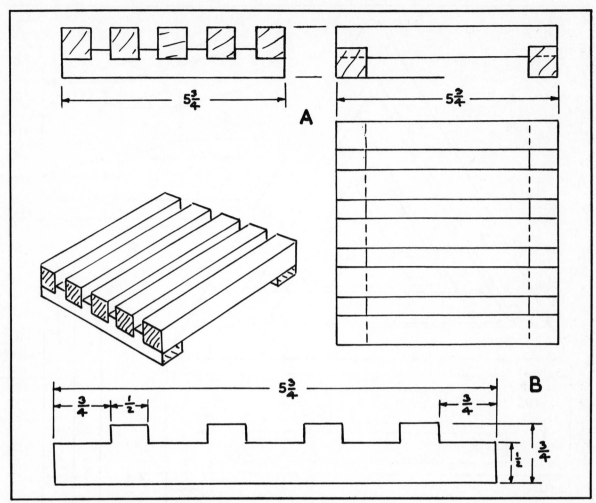

Fig. 2-26. Strips instead of a solid board allow heat to be released underneath.

wood and damage the surface below. It is better if the stand is raised and has ventilation gaps.

The stand in Fig. 2-26 is a simple assembly that lifts the pan 1¼ inches and gives plenty of space below for heat to disperse. It could be any size, but the arrangement should have an odd number of bars and an even number of spaces. The suggested measurements (Fig. 2-26A) will suit most pots and pans. All the wood is ¾-inch square.

1. Cut the five top pieces to length.

2. Make the two bottom pieces the same length but notch the other parts (Fig. 2-26B).

3. You can glue the assembly together. Drive screws upwards through each joint, if you wish.

4. Round all edges and corners.

TRIANGULAR HOT STAND

A stand for hot pans does not have to be square or round. A triangular stand is just as satisfactory under a round pan. The three triangular stands in Fig. 2-27 are made to store inside each other. The largest is about 10 inches, the next 7 inches, and the smallest 4 inches along each side. All are made of ¾-inch-square strips. The largest has a base to prevent the others from falling through, and the corners have halved joints. The triangles will be strongest if hardwood is used.

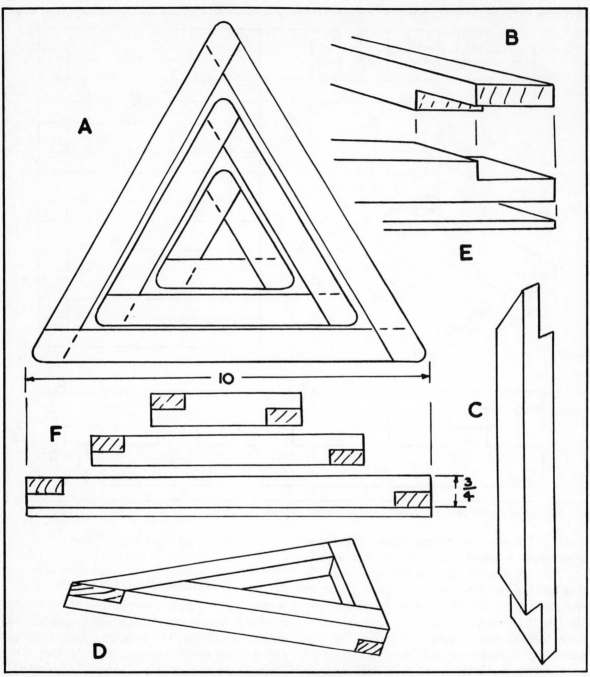

Fig. 2-27. The triangular frames fit into each other. Their corners are halved.

The shapes are equilateral triangles, meaning all sides of each stand is the same length and the corners are 60 degrees. Set out the largest triangle first (Fig. 2-27A), then fit the next after that one is completed.

1. Cut the three sides to length and mark out

and cut the halved joints (Fig. 2-27B). If you cut opposite ends from opposite sides (Fig. 2-27C), all three parts will be the same (Fig. 2-27D).

2. Have the base of the large stand ready (Fig. 2-27E). It can be hardboard or thin plywood. When you glue the corner joints, also glue on the base. Reinforce the glue with a few pins from below.

3. When the glue has set, true the edges and round the corners.

4. Make the next triangle (Fig. 2-27F) with about 1/8-inch clearance all around inside the large stand.

5. Cut the joints and assemble it in the same way, but without a base. Drive a screw from below into each corner joint.

6. Round the outer corners.

7. Make the smallest triangle to fit into middle one.

TURNED HOT STAND

With a lathe you can make stands with rims which will prevent round pots from sliding off. The stand can be a size that will take any round pot up to the stand's internal diameter. Such a stand can be useful for coffee and tea pots, as well as cooking pots and pans.

The round hot stand in Fig. 2-28 is intended for a pan with a handle that comes close to the base; therefore there is a notch in the rim. The whole stand is made from 1/2-inch plywood glued together. The sizes (Fig. 2-28A) are typical, but can be adjusted to suit your needs. If the parts are sawn with reasonable accuracy, work on the lathe will be simplified.

1. Saw two pieces for the rim (Fig. 2-28B) and a disc for the base, keeping saw cuts only a little way outside the lines.

2. Glue the parts with clamps or under weights to ensure close joints.

3. Draw the size of the lathe faceplate on the base using the same center as for the disc outline to keep it true. Screw the disc to the faceplate and turn the shape. Be careful to avoid cutting into the base plywood when turning the inside of the rim.

4. Round the top of the rim. Use scraping

tools with sharp edges as some plywood can tear out at end grain.

5. Finish by sanding with progressively finer grits.

6. If a recess for a handle is needed (Fig. 2-28C), cut it across the rim with a shape that will clear the handle.

7. Glue a cloth disc under the base (Fig. 2-28D). Besides preventing slipping, it hides the holes left by the screws through the faceplate.

8. Glue a disc of Formica inside (Fig. 2-28E). Paint the rim to hide the plywood construction.

BREAD BOARD/CRUMB BOX

You cannot cut bread into slices without producing crumbs, and those crumbs, which might be useful in cooking, can scatter across the tabletop. If you cut the bread on a slatted surface, the crumbs can fall through and collect in a box below.

This combined slatted bread board and crumb box (Fig. 2-29) consists of a box into which loosely fits an assembly of six slats with gaps between. After you cut the bread, lift the top and tip out the accumulation of crumbs.

Because the slats and the top edge of the box are a cutting surface, make them of close-grained hardwood that will not splinter. The bottom could be plywood, although solid wood the same as the rest of the box would look better.

When assembled, the slatted top rests on strips that bring its top surfaces level with the top edges of the box. Supports inside the ends of the box are sufficient, but if the slats tend to flex, fix small blocks under the ends of the central strip as well. Join corners of the box any way you wish, from simply overlapping the parts and nailing or screwing to cutting comb joints or dovetails. Screw on the bottom.

1. Prepare six lengths of 5/8-inch-square wood (Fig. 2-30A) and three notched crosspieces to fit them (Fig. 2-30B). Glue the parts together, place strips across at the ends (Fig. 2-30C) and one at the center. See that the assembly finishes square and without twist.

2. Prepare and mark the strips for the sides

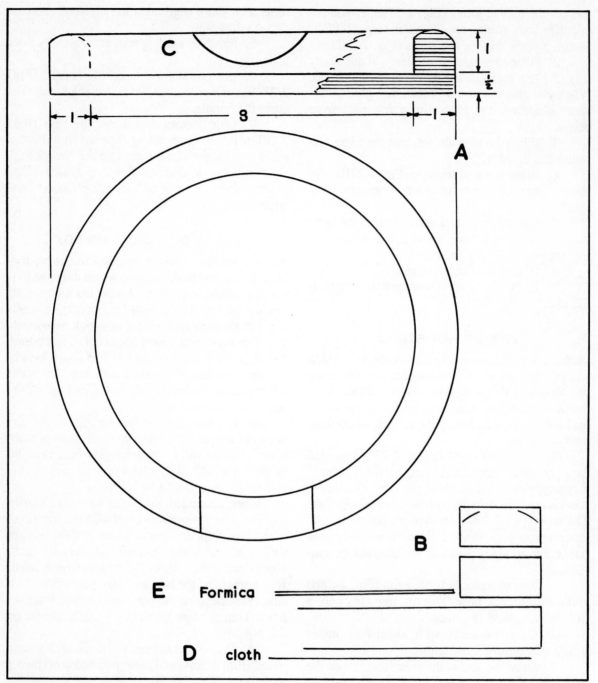

Fig. 2-28. Sizes and construction of the round stand.

and ends of the box (Fig. 2-30D) to allow ample clearance for the slatted board. About ¹/₁₆ inch all around should be sufficient.

3. Cut the corner joints and fit the sides and ends together. When the glue has set, true inside and out and add the bottom.

4. Check the fit of the top and make supports across at the ends (Fig. 2-30E) to bring top surfaces level.

5. Leave all wood untreated or varnish or polish all but the working top surfaces.

Materials List for Bread Board/Crumb Box

6 strips	⅝ × ⅝ × 11	
3 strips	⅝ × ⅝ × 7	
2 supports	⅝ × ⅝ × 7	
2 sides	⅝ × 2 × 13	
2 ends	⅝ × 2 × 8	
1 bottom	⅜ × 8 × 13	

CARVER TRAY

For carving meat, you need a substantial solid board, but it would also be useful if you could lift the board like a tray. The carver tray in Fig. 2-31 is a solid block that is hollowed enough to retain meat juices and has the ends shaped as handles to carry board and meat. The board is laminated in butcher block form, which allows preforming some sections. Most of the shaping is done with a router, but all of the curves are a ⅝-inch radius, and one cutter should do almost everything.

The carver tray is 10 inches wide, 14 inches long, and 1¼ inches deep, and it can be built up with eight, 1¼-inch square laminations (Fig. 2-32A). Other sizes are possible but allow for two outside solid strips in the first construction.

1. Prepare eight, straight 1¼-inch-square strips. Leave two square for the outside edges and cut away six pieces for the intermediate strips (Fig. 2-32B). In the finished tray, the inner edges will be 2 inches from the outer edges at the ends, and the bottom will be ⅝ inch thick. Saw the pieces so there is a little wood left for finishing to these sizes later.

2. Glue all pieces together. To avoid movement and twist, it is best to glue in pairs, then in fours, before making up the full width.

3. Level the underside. Square the ends.

4. Use the router to cut the inside across the ends, then ⅝ inch in along the sides (Fig. 2-32C) to the full depth all around. Level the remainder

Fig. 2-29. This bread board has slots between strips for crumbs to fall through.

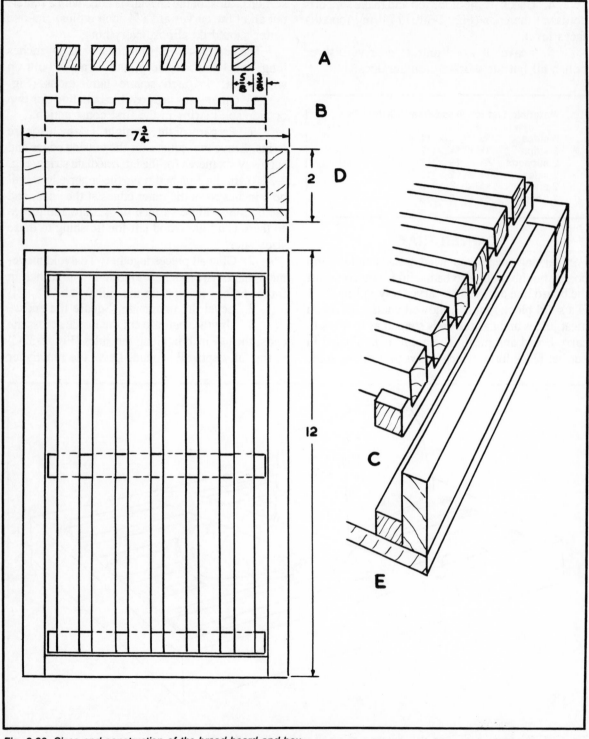

Fig. 2-30. Sizes and construction of the bread board and box.

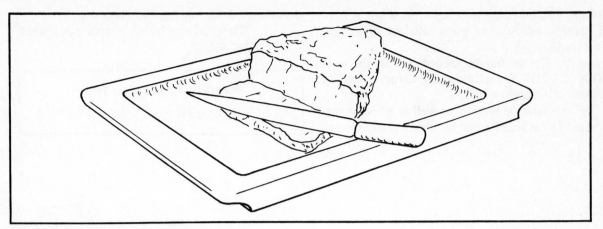

Fig. 2-31. A meat carving board shaped as a tray.

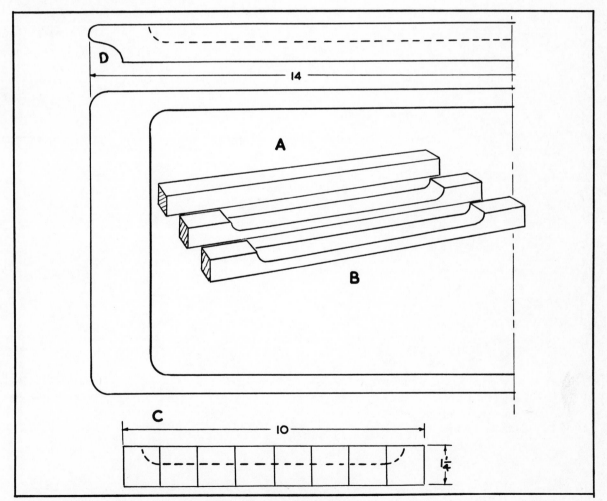

Fig. 2-32. Sizes and method of construction of a meat carving tray.

41

of the inside to the same depth. You might have to scrape and sand to get a satisfactory surface within the hollow.

5. Cut the handle sections across the ends (Fig. 2-32D). Round the outer corners. Lightly round all straight edges.

6. Sand the bottom, as well as all other surfaces, as the board could be inverted and the underside used for cutting and chopping.

7. The wood may be left untreated or soaked in vegetable oil.

Materials List for Carver Tray

8 pieces 1¼ × 1¼ × 15

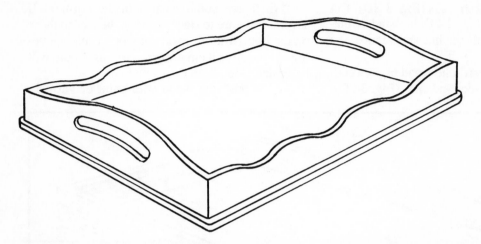

3

Trays

Trays are useful anywhere that food is prepared. A tray allows the cook to keep things together and pick them up. They can take many forms, but fitness for purpose is often more important than appearance. Any kitchen tray should be strong enough to stand up to hard use, of the right size for its purpose, and able to be easily carried.

The trays in this chapter provide ideas, and most can be adapted to suit your needs. As with other kitchen equipment, you can make your tray to suit available spaces—to fit on a shelf or stand in a recess for instance. It can be a special size to prevent a large dish sliding about, or it can hold a particular load of dishes.

You can use almost any wood, but hardwoods stand up to harder use than softwoods, although they can be heavier. Much depends on circumstances, and you might want to match trays to other wood in the kitchen.

BOX TRAY

One of the simplest trays is just a shallow box with

hand holes in the ends. It can be used for many things in the kitchen, not just for utensils or cutlery. It could carry potatoes, vegetables, and other garden produce. Trash could be gathered in it. Unless it is given a quality finish, this is not intended to be a tray for taking food to the dining table. It is utilitarian, and the cook can turn to it when she wants to collect and transport almost anything.

Several similar trays could be arranged to stack. Even with only one tray, its flat top will allow other things to be on top. One or more trays could fit on a shelf. They then serve the same purpose as drawers, with the hand holes providing a grip for pulling out.

You can make the box tray in Fig. 3-1 to almost any size, but measurements are suggested in Fig. 3-2A. Several methods of construction are possible, from nails to fitted joints. You can use almost any wood. If plywood is included, it ought to be exterior or marine grade to withstand damp conditions.

1. Prepare the wood for the sides and ends.
2. Mark and cut the hand holes in the ends

(Fig. 3-2B) by drilling the ends and cutting away between. Round the edges of the holes. The size of the hole suggested should suit any size tray as hands do not vary very much.

3. Decide on the corner joints. For simple nailing, drive in dovetail manner (Fig. 3-2C) for maximum strength in the end grain. For nails or screws, there is an advantage in rabbeting one piece so they can be driven both ways (Fig. 3-2D). Cut comb or finger joints (Fig. 3-2E) by hand or machine. For the most craftsmanlike appearance, use through dovetails (Fig. 3-2F).

4. Make the bottom solid wood or plywood. Make it level with the sides and ends (Fig. 3-2G), as it should be if it is to fit on a shelf, or project it (Fig. 3-2H). You could also arrange it within the sides and ends (Fig. 3-2J) for a neat appearance. Attach the bottom with glue and nails or screws.

5. For general purposes, the wood surface inside might be adequate. You could also cover the bottom with Formica, cork, or rubber.

6. There could be feet in the corners. If several trays are to stack, arrange the feet so those on the upper tray fit inside the top of the one below. If you give them a slight taper, assembly will be easier (Fig. 3-2K).

7. Finish the wood with paint or varnish.

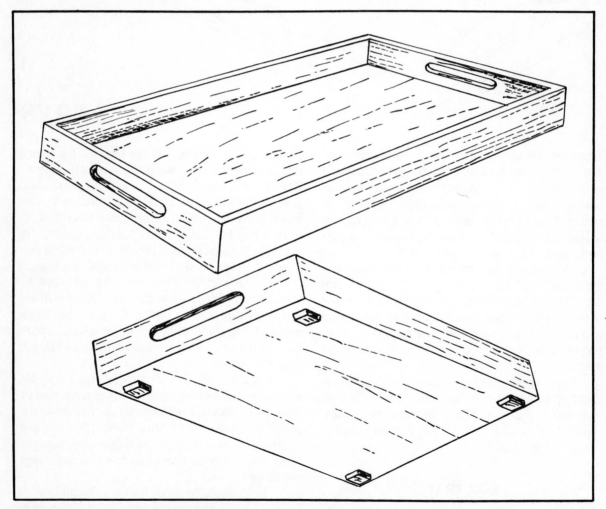

Fig. 3-1. A kitchen tray with slotted handles.

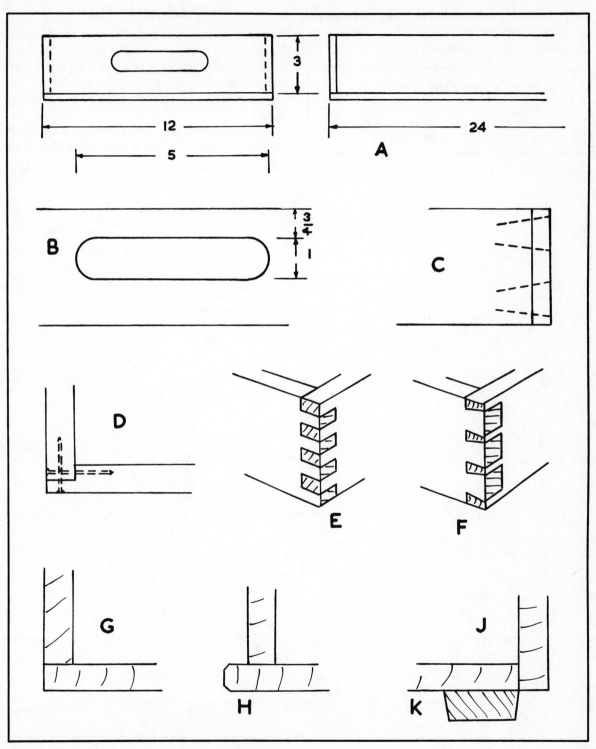

Fig. 3-2. Details of the tray and alternative corner joints.

45

Even if you think appearance is not important, one or two coats of varnish will seal the grain and reduce any tendency to absorb dirt.

Materials List for Box Tray

2 sides	$\frac{3}{8} \times 3 \times 25$
2 ends	$\frac{3}{8} \times 3 \times 13$
1 bottom	$\frac{3}{8} \times 13 \times 25$

MOLDED-GRIP TRAY

An attractive tray can be made with a molded edge that provides a grip for thumbs and fingers at any point. The molding must be made with fairly deep hollows on each side. It could be cut with a suitable router cutter, a spindle molder, or a molding plane.

The suggested tray in Fig. 3-3A has the molding mitered and attached to the base with screws

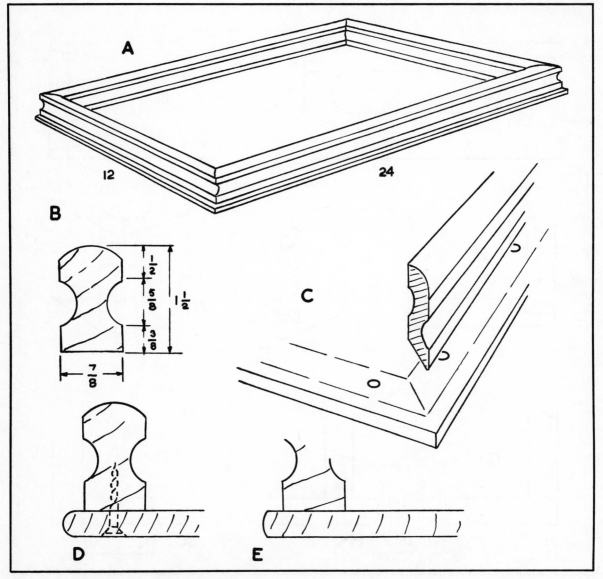

Fig. 3-3. The molded edges of this tray form handles.

driven upward. If made of a good quality hardwood and polished or varnished, the tray can be used to serve meals. In a more basic form, it can be suitable for general kitchen purposes.

1. Make the molding in one long piece, but if it is to be worked by a hand-held router or molding plane, use a shorter, wide board that can be clamped to the bench while the hollows and rounding work is done. When one piece is satisfactory, cut it off and repeat the process on what is left until you have enough for the tray. Make the hollows reasonably deep leaving enough between for the points of screws to grip without the risk of breaking out (Fig. 3-3B).

2. Cut the wood for the bottom slightly too big; trim it parallel with the molding later. Glue several strips together or make a single piece. You can use plywood if the exposed ply edges are acceptable.

3. Lightly mark out the positions on the moldings on the bottom. Use these lines as guides when marking and cutting the mitered moldings. Gluing the miters should be sufficient. Screws through the bottom can hold the parts close.

4. Mark out for screw holes. Arrange two fairly close to each corner (Fig. 3-3C) and others at 4-inch intervals. Countersink sufficiently underneath for the screw heads to be below the surface.

5. Glue and screw the parts together.

6. Trim the edges of the bottom parallel with the molding. The edges could be left square, fully rounded (Fig. 3-3D), or given a slight curve (Fig. 3-3E), which is neat.

7. Sand thoroughly. Take sharpness off corners. Finish in any way you wish. Glue strips of cloth around the bottom to prevent slipping or marking a polished surface.

Materials List for Molded-Grip Tray	
2 sides	7/8 × 1 1/2 × 24
2 ends	7/8 × 1/2 × 12
1 bottom	3/8 × 12 × 24

MOLDED-HANDLE TRAY

Ends of a tray shaped to provide a grip look attractive and are practical. The tray in Fig. 3-4 has straight sides, but the ends are swept outward so fingers can grip below them. This is suitable for a small tray and a light load. For a heavy load, it is better for the fingers to go through holes or

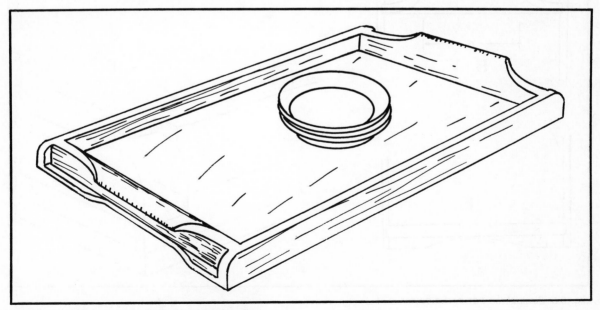

Fig. 3-4. The shaped ends of the tray form handles.

around handles. The corners can be level with the handles to let the tray stand on its end against a wall or in a rack below a countertop. If this is not required, the bottom and sides can finish level with the lower part of the ends.

The sizes shown (Fig. 3-5A) are for a small tray, but the same section ends and other parts could be used for larger trays. It is better to use hardwood to provide strength in the outswept handles than to rely on softwood. If you are using softwood because it is easier to work, choose wood with straight grain across the part that will be gripped.

1. Prepare sufficient 1½-×-2½-inch wood for the ends. Make sure the inner and bottom surfaces are square to each other.

2. Reduce a handle to half thickness for the depth of the sides, then cut the upper half to curve outwards (Fig. 3-6A). Cut the hollowed part first. You can remove much of the waste by cutting one rabbet, then another into that (Fig. 3-6B), which does not leave much waste to be removed to get the finished curve.

3. Bring the outside curve near to size with ordinary planing. Finish both surfaces with thorough sanding.

4. Mark a width of 6 inches at the center (Fig. 3-5B) and cut curves down to the depth of the sides (Fig. 3-5C). These shapes are shown flat across, but they could be rounded if you wish. Leave the parts that fit into the sides with flat tops.

5. The sides are straight strips (Fig. 3-5D) with their ends extending the same amounts as the handles (Fig. 3-6C).

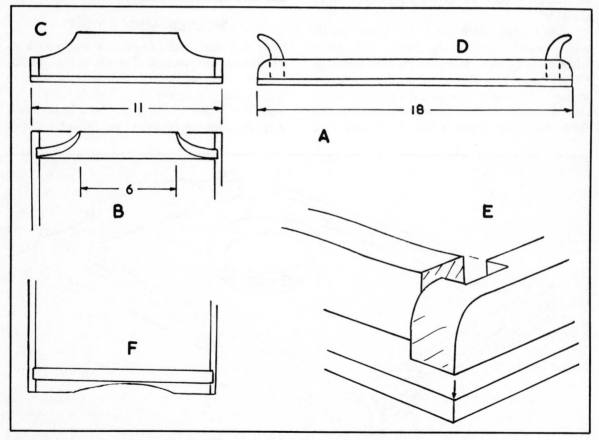

Fig. 3-5. Sizes of the tray and a corner joint.

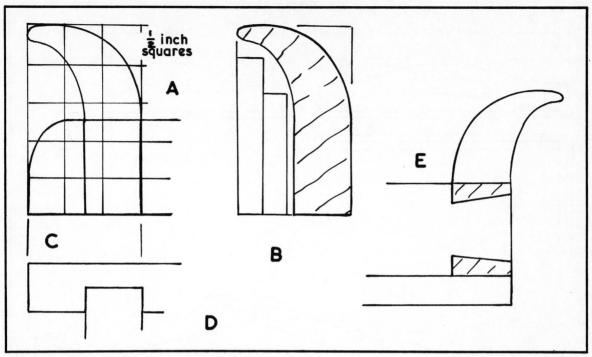

Fig. 3-6. Section of the tray end (A-C). Two corner joints (D, E).

6. Cut dado grooves to half thickness to fit the ends (Figs. 3-5E and 3-6D). Round the extending sides.

7. If the tray is to be made without the sides and bottom extending, the neatest corner joint is a dovetail (Fig. 3-6E).

8. Join the sides and ends. Glue is sufficient, but if your joints are not a good fit, use thin nails punched below the surface and covered with stopping.

9. Make the bottom the same width as the framework when finished, but leave a little for planing level. At the ends the bottom reaches the limits of the sides, but it can be hollowed to the ends for about the same width as the handle (Fig. 3-5F). This gives extra clearance for the fingers and allows the tray to stand on three points when it is up-ended.

10. Screw and glue on the bottom. Sink screw heads below the surface.

11. Finish the tray with paint or varnish and glue cloth strips underneath, if you wish.

Materials List for Molded-Handle Tray

2 ends	1½ × 2½ × 11
2 sides	⅝ × 1¼ × 19
1 bottom	⅜ × 11 × 19

WAVY-EDGED TRAY

Putting curves on the edges of a tray breaks up the rather stark and boxlike appearance. When you want to make something that is not purely utilitarian but has a pleasing appearance, such as a serving tray, adding curves can be the answer.

The tray in Fig. 3-7A has the finger holes as well as the tops of the ends curved. The tops of the sides are given a deckle edge. If sizes are altered, choose a length that allows curves to be arranged evenly. The tray has 3 inches between the tops and bottoms of curves, which are ½ inch deep.

Use hard or soft wood, but for the best appearance, choose a hardwood and finish it with var-

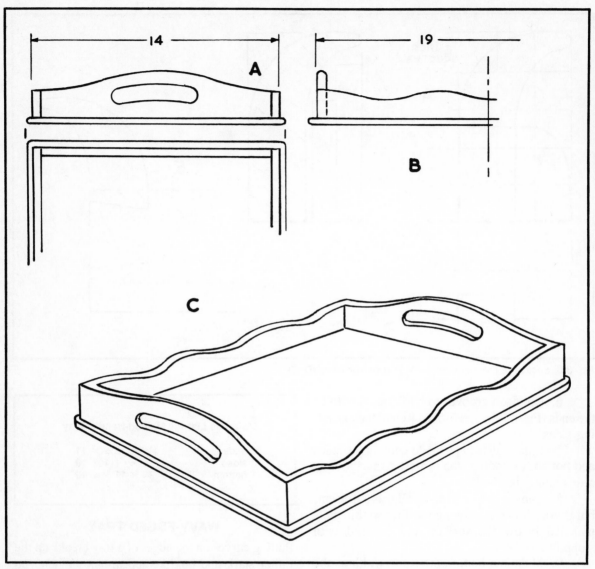

Fig. 3-7. A tray with shaped hand holes and edges.

nish or polish. If the base has an attractive grain pattern, this finish will look good. Apply a decal between coats of varnish on a plainer wood, if you wish.

    1. Make the ends and sides ½ inch thick. Decide on the corner joints. Any of those described earlier could be used (Fig. 3-2C to F). Cut the wood to length to allow for the joints.

    2. Mark the ends to shape using the half

drawing (Figs. 3-7A and 3-8A). Check that each end is symmetrical and the two match. The curve of the hand holes should match the curve of the top.

    3. Drill the ends of the hand holes and cut away the waste between. It is easier to do this before cutting the outside to shape. When you are satisfied with the outlines, round the top edges and the edges of the hand holes.

    4. Cut the corner joints in the ends and sides.

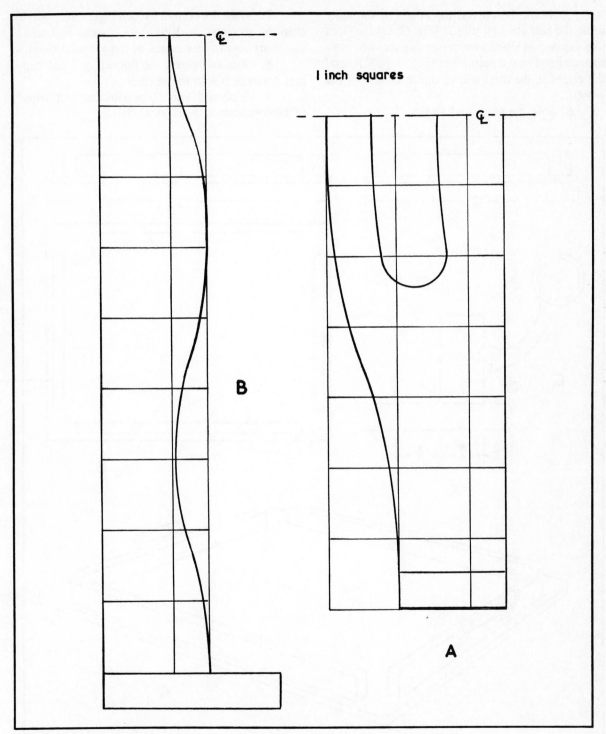

1 inch squares

B

A

Fig. 3-8. Details of the shaping.

5. Mark the curved top edges of the sides using the half drawing (Fig. 3-8B). Check the sides together as you shape them to see that they are symmetrical and match each other (Fig. 3-7C). Round the edges in the direction of the thickness of the wood.

6. Join the sides and ends.

7. Make the bottom ¼ inch bigger all around than the framework. Round its corners and take the sharpness off its edges or fully round them.

8. Glue and screw the bottom on. Sink the screw heads below the surface.

9. Finish with varnish or polish and put strips of cloth underneath, if you wish.

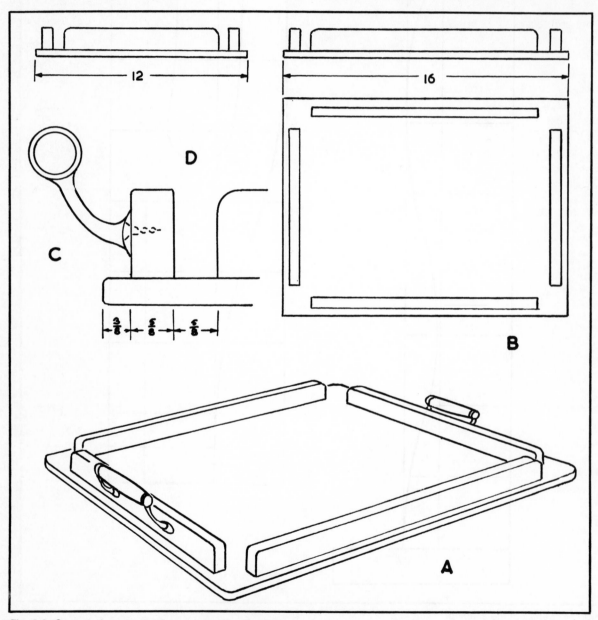

Fig. 3-9. Gaps at the corners of a tray simplify cleaning.

Materials List for Wavy-Edged Tray

2 ends	½ ×	2½ × 15
2 sides	½ ×	1½ × 20
1 bottom	⅜ ×	15 × 20

OPEN-CORNER TRAY

One problem with the closed, boxlike tray is cleaning out crumbs and dirt that tend to accumulate in corners. One way of avoiding this problem is to make a tray without angular corners. It can be extremely simple, with four pieces that do not meet on a base (Fig. 3-9A). With the open corners, loose particles can be shaken or brushed out without trouble.

Since there is no frame with corner joints to hold a bottom flat, make the bottom of plywood, which will not be liable to warp as thin, solid wood might. The sides and ends can be any wood. The handles are metal or plastic screwed on.

1. Start with the bottom (Fig. 3-9B). Square it carefully, take the sharpness off edges, and round its corners. Mark on it where the strips will come, allowing the same gaps at each corner (Fig. 3-9C).

2. Make the strips. Round down their ends and round the cross sections (Fig. 3-9D).

3. Glue and screw the strips to the base parallel to the edges.

4. Mark and drill for the screws that will hold the handles. Apply the chosen finish to the wood before screwing them on, however.

Materials List for Open-Corner Tray

1 bottom	⅜ ×	12 × 16
2 ends	⅝ ×	1¼ × 10
2 sides	⅝ ×	1¼ × 14

4
Small Storage Items

In any kitchen there are large built-in or free-standing cabinets and cupboards for storing equipment and food, but there is also a need for many smaller racks, bins, boxes, and containers to take care of other storage. Some of these can be attached to a wall or countertop, although many are better if portable. Some can be fitted into drawers or on the insides of doors to be brought out when needed. Others can have fairly permanent places on tables or worktops, yet be movable to suit your needs.

Metal or plastic might be more appropriate for a few things, but wood is suitable for many small storage units. Wood has character and gives a sense of quality to the surroundings. It is not as harsh on the contents as are metal and plastic. If you wish to give your kitchen a traditional appearance, wood is the obvious choice.

What wood to use depends on several considerations. Your kitchen will look smarter if the same wood is used for the majority of things you make. You can protect most wood with varnish or polish, but even then you would be wise to avoid very resinous or oily woods in case bare wood comes into contact with food. Light-colored woods have a clean appearance, but a darker finish can be attractive when it forms a background to lighter contents or surroundings.

Although most hardwoods are stronger than softwoods, for many of these smaller projects any wood will have adequate strength. Most softwoods are lighter and might be better for anything that must be carried. Since softwoods mostly are light in color, you can choose them for the sake of appearance. For anything with a thin section, however, light-colored hardwood would be a better choice.

When anything must be built up, you often have a choice of joints (see Chapter 1). Modern, waterproof glues have considerable strength, but none are very effective on end grain. Any plain joint on the end of a board also will require nails or screws. Nail heads sunk and covered with stopping might be satisfactory, but you can show your skill by cutting dovetails or other appropriate joints.

CUTLERY BOX

The box or tray in Fig. 4-1 is suitable for table cutlery or the many knives, forks, and other tools needed in the kitchen. It can be put in a drawer because it does not have a raised handle that will interfere with closing. Instead of a handle, there are two finger holes in the center partition.

The sizes suggested (Fig. 4-2) can accommodate knives, forks, and spoons of several sizes. If you wish to fit in other items, measure the intended contents and design your own box to suit. As shown, there is one crosswise division slightly off center to suit different lengths of small spoons. If you alter sizes, keep the main partition central so the lifting holes will be at the point of balance (Fig. 4-2A). Wood can be hard or soft. The bottom is plywood or hardboard.

1. Prepare all the wood to width and thickness.

2. Mark out the ends (Fig. 4-3A) and sides (Fig. 4-3B) with corner details and partition positions.

3. The corners are shown notched (Fig. 4-2B), so thin nails can be driven both ways. Several other joints are possible; the best would be dovetails.

4. Make the partitions. Drill finger holes with ¾-inch or ⅞-inch diameters. Round the hole edges for a comfortable grip. Round all top edges and sand all inside surfaces.

5. Cut all joints. The partitions can go halfway through the outside pieces.

6. Assemble the box and check squareness.

7. Glue and nail the plywood or hardboard bottom directly onto the other parts. Covering it with cloth makes an attractive interior, however (Fig. 4-2D). Varnish all interior parts before putting the cloth-covered bottom in place. Finish the outside after planing the bottom edges level.

Materials List for Cutlery Box	
2 sides	⅜ × 2½ × 13
2 ends	⅜ × 2½ × 10
3 partitions	⅜ × 2½ × 13
1 partition	⅜ × 2½ × 3
1 bottom	10 × 13 × ⅛
	plywood or hardboard

CUTLERY CARRIER

A box with a handle can be used to carry cutlery into the dining room or to take cooking knives, forks, and other tools about the kitchen or outdoors to a barbecue. The unusual modern shape of the carrier in Fig. 4-4 has two compartments with sloping sides for easy access, and a central division with a slotted handle.

Make all parts ⅜-inch hardwood. If you use softwood, make them slightly thicker, either 7⁄16

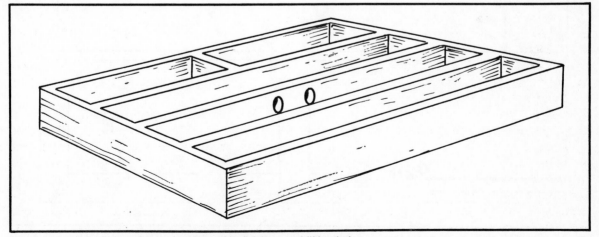

Fig. 4-1. A tray to fit in a drawer is a box with divisions and lifting holes.

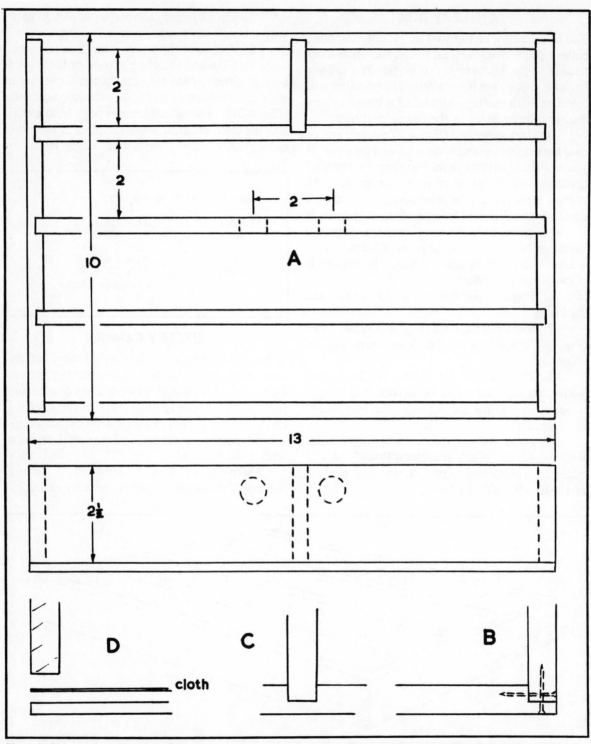

Fig. 4-2. Sizes and construction of the tray.

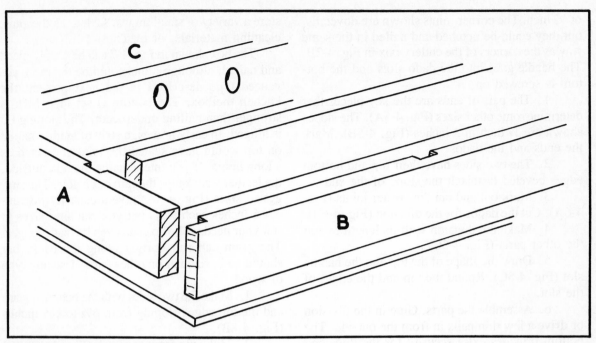

Fig. 4-3. Joint details and lifting holes.

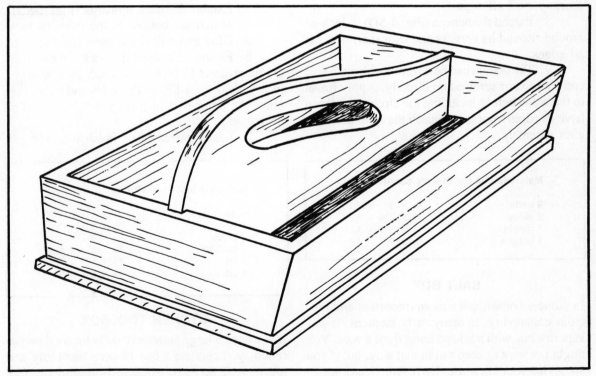

Fig. 4-4. A cutlery box with a shaped handle.

or ½ inch. The corner joints shown are dovetails, but they could be notched and nailed in the same way as the corners of the cutlery box in Fig. 4-2B. The handle goes into the dado slots and the bottom is screwed on.

1. The pair of ends are the key pieces that determine some other sizes (Fig. 4-5A). The slopes shown are ⅜ inch in 3 inches (Fig. 4-5B). Mark the ends and the dados.

2. The two sides have their top and bottom edges beveled to match the slope of the ends.

3. Mark out and cut the corner joints (Fig. 4-6A). Cut the dados for the division (Fig. 4-6B).

4. Make the division with its length to suit the other parts (Fig. 4-5C).

5. Draw the shape of the top and the handle slot (Fig. 4-6C). Round the top and the edges of the slot.

6. Assemble the parts. Glue in the division or drive a few thin nails in from the outside. The bottom provides extra security for the division.

7. Level the outsides of the joints. Take sharpness off all edges.

8. Extend the bottom (Fig. 4-5D) ¼ inch all around. Round its corners and take sharpness off all edges.

9. The bottom can be covered with cloth (see cutlery box) or screwed on directly. Apply finish to the wood before including the cloth, which can have its edges trimmed to match the sides and ends after assembly.

store a variety of small things, such as clothespins, cleaning materials, or matches.

The box shown in Fig. 4-7 can be simply glued and nailed, although joints could be the more advanced type described in the next project, the kitchen toolbox. The bottom is set in, which is stronger than nailing underneath. The sloping lid is hinged. In early homes, a strip of leather nailed on top would have sealed the joint and acted as a long hinge. If you intend using the box outside, the leather strip keeps the rain out better. The suggested sizes (Fig. 4-8A) give a capacity just under 6 inches each way, but you can alter sizes to suit your needs. The box can even be made longer. The grain can run upright along the back, but should be horizontal on other parts. Use any type of wood.

1. Make the two sides with the bottom square and the top edges sloping from 6½ to 5½ inches (Fig. 4-8B).

2. Make the front to match (Fig. 4-8C) and bevel its top edge.

3. Extend the back upwards (Fig. 4-8D).

4. Match the bottom to the other parts.

5. Glue and nail these parts together.

6. Fit the lid against the back but overhang the other parts ⅜ inch all around. Nail a strip 1 inch wide (Fig. 4-8E) to the sides and back, then hinge the other part to it (Fig. 4-8F). Round all lid corners.

7. Leave untreated or finish with varnish.

Materials List for Cutlery Carrier

2 ends	⅜ × 3 × 10
2 sides	⅜ × 3¼ × 12
1 division	⅜ × 5½ × 12
1 bottom	⅜ × 9 × 13

Materials List for Salt Box

1 back	⅜ × 5¼ × 9
1 front	⅜ × 5¼ × 6
2 sides	⅜ × 6 × 7
1 bottom	⅜ × 5¼ × 6
1 lid	⅜ × 1 × 7
1 lid	⅜ × 5¼ × 7

SALT BOX

In pioneer homes, salt was an important and precious commodity. In many early kitchens, it was kept in a box with a lid and hung from a wall. You might not want to keep salt in that way, but if you are giving your kitchen an Early American appearance, you can include a typical salt box. Use it to

KITCHEN TOOLBOX

If you have a large number of tools for food preparation, you can use a box to keep them tidy and together. If they are wood, it is appropriate that they should stand in a box made of wood, although

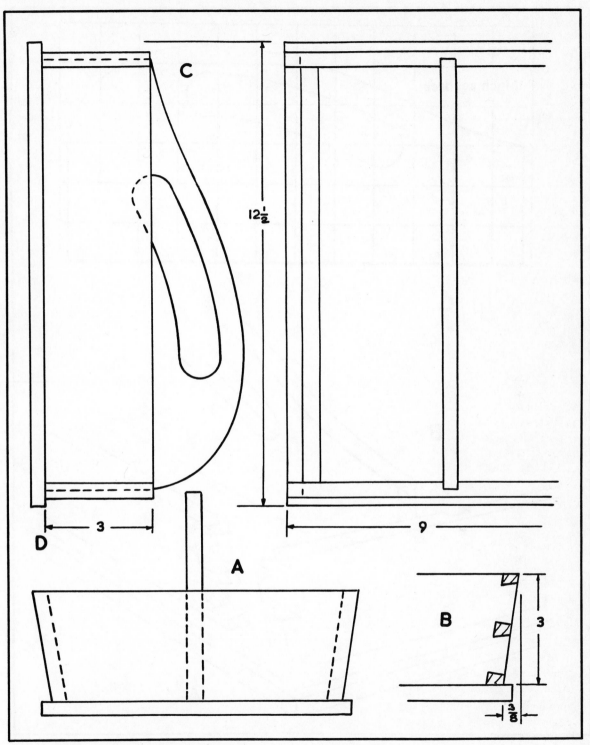

Fig. 4-5. General arrangement of the cutlery box.

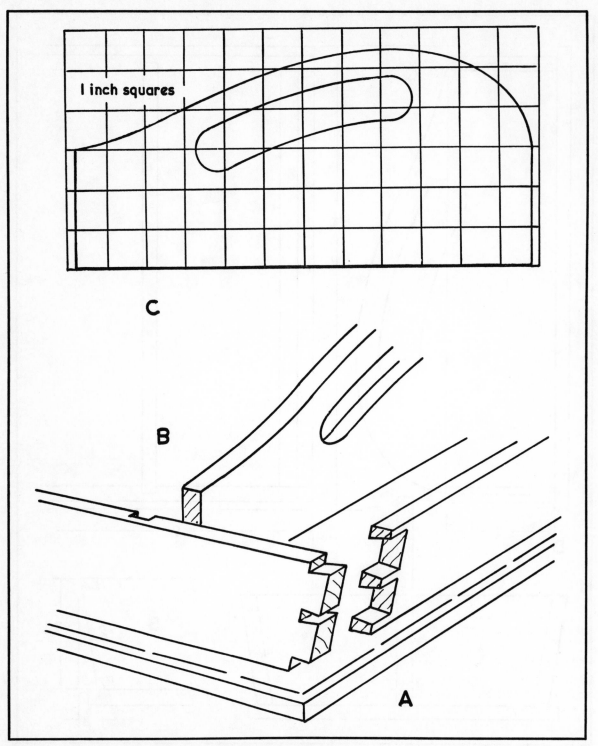

Fig. 4-6. Handle shape and method of construction of the cutlery box.

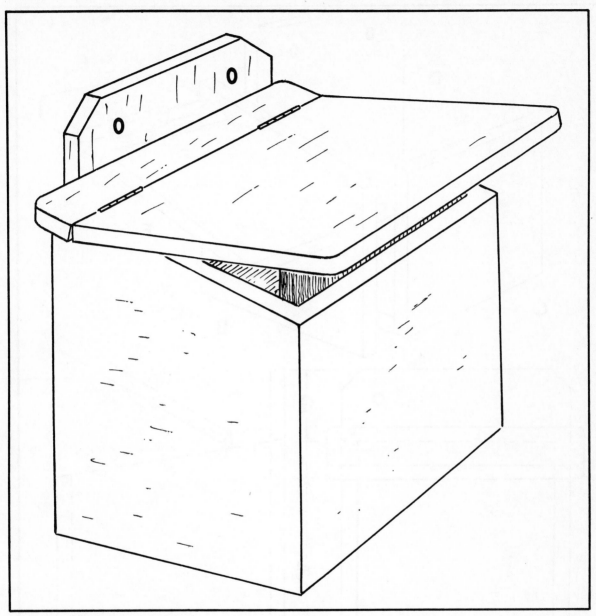

Fig. 4-7. A wall-hanging box with lid.

the box in Fig. 4-9 is just as suitable for metal or plastic tools and implements. The box's back extends to screw to the wall, but it also can stand on a countertop.

If this box and the salt box are made in the same way and to similar sizes, they could be hung on the wall as a pair. This box is shown with dado

joints, but you could use simpler glued and nailed joints.

The sizes given (Fig. 4-10) suit ⅜-inch-thick hardwood, but if softwood is used, it can be ⁷⁄₁₆ or ½ inch thick. All parts have their grain upright.

1. Make the back and mark on it the position of the sides (Fig. 4-10A). Bevel the top corners

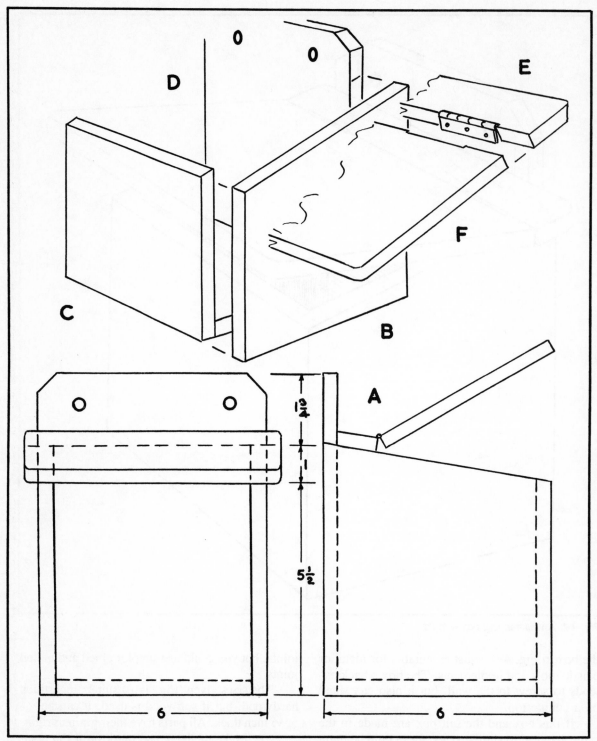

Fig. 4-8. Sizes and parts of the box.

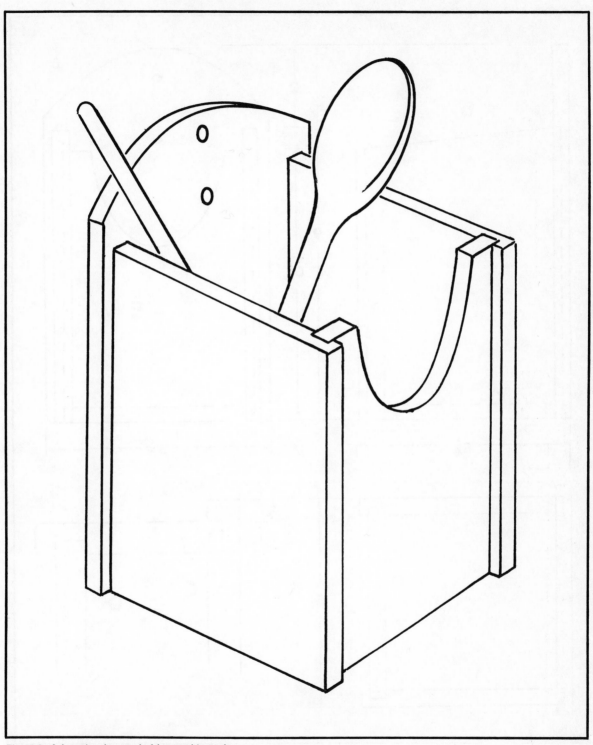

Fig. 4-9. A hanging box to hold a cook's tools.

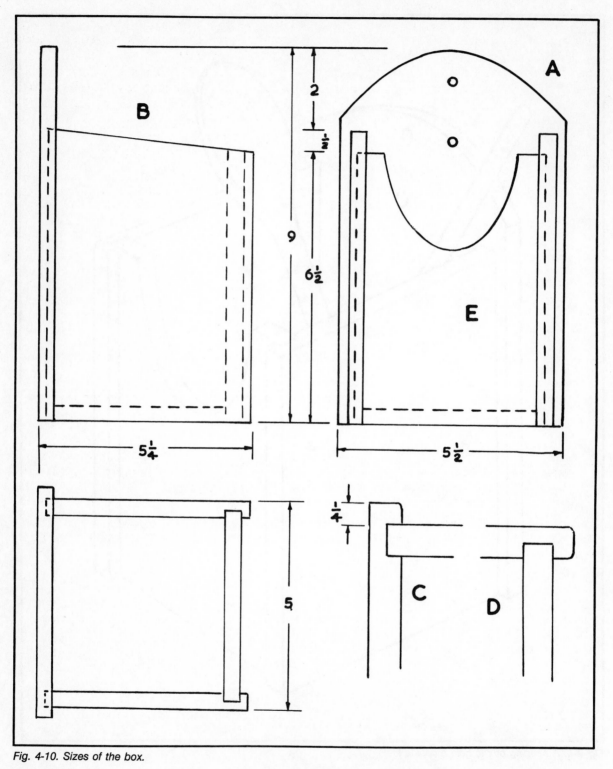

Fig. 4-10. Sizes of the box.

or curve them (Fig. 4-11A). Mark two holes for screwing to the wall.

2. Make the pair of sides (Fig. 10B). Slope them at the top and go halfway through the back (Fig. 10C). Overlap the front by ¼ inch where there is a similar joint (Fig. 4-10D).

3. Make the front (Fig. 10E) with a hollow in the top edge (Fig. 4-11B).

4. Cut the dados (Fig. 4-11C and D) a tight fit on the other parts. When you assemble, gluing these joints should be sufficient, but you could also screw through the back into the sides because the heads will not show.

5. Make the bottom to fit inside the other parts. Hold it with glue and a few fine nails punched below the surface and covered with stopping.

6. Round all exposed edges and corners before assembly.

7. Finish with varnish or leave the wood untreated.

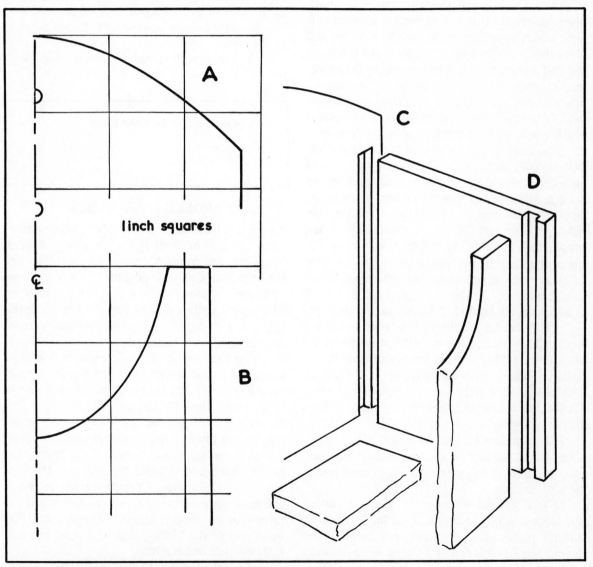

Fig. 4-11. Shaped parts and assembly details of the box.

Materials List for Kitchen Toolbox	
1 back	⅜ × 5½ × 10
2 sides	⅜ × 5¼ × 8
1 front	⅜ × 5 × 7
1 bottom	⅜ × 4¼ × 5

KNIFE BLOCK

Kitchen knives should be sharp if they are to do all the cook wishes satisfactorily. Once they have been sharpened, do not store them with other cutlery, which would rub against the knife edges and blunt them. It also could be dangerous if a hand is thrust into the box. It is better to store the knives so their blades are sheathed. Individual sheaths are possible, but a wood block with slots can accommodate several knives, protecting both blades and hands while keeping the knives ready for use.

The knife block in Fig. 4-12 holds six kitchen knives, with blades up to 9 inches long, as well as a sharpening steel. The same construction can hold a different number of knives or different lengths of blades. Two methods of forming the block are described. The block is intended to stand on one end, and it is reversible. It should be stable enough as it is, but you could screw on a base of greater area, if you wish. You can use any wood to match existing furniture or equipment. Softwood is adequate, but hardwood is heavier and steadier.

1. To make the block from solid wood, use a piece 3 × 4 inches and mark the positions of the slots (Fig. 4-13A). Check the widths and thicknesses of blades. Slots shown are 3/16 × 1½ inches. The blades fit loosely and these sizes suit most knives, but you might need to adjust them for very heavy chopping knives.

2. Cut the slots the full length of the wood. One method would be to use a wobble circular saw in a saw table. It might be possible to use a router or a plow plane.

3. If you do not have facilities for cutting the slots in solid wood, laminate the block with several pieces glued together. For most of the block, use 5/16-inch pieces 3 inches wide alternating with 3/16-inch pieces 1½ inches wide (Fig.

4-13B). Use a thicker piece for the side with the round hole.

4. Square the ends of the block.

5. Measure the maximum diameter of the sharpening steel. Drill a hole that allows it to drop in easily, probably ⅝ or ¾ inch. Drill from opposite ends, even if you have a long drill, to reduce the risk of the drill being deflected by the grain.

6. Prepare ¼-×-1-inch strips to go across the slotted sides (Fig. 4-13C). Place strips level with the ends of the block and others midway. Glue them and hold with pins punched and covered with stopping or use a few brass screws. Round the ends of the strips.

7. Finish with varnish or treat the wood with oil.

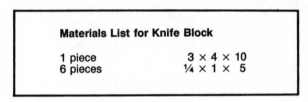

Materials List for Knife Block	
1 piece	3 × 4 × 10
6 pieces	¼ × 1 × 5

ANGLED KNIFE BLOCK

An upright knife block stores knives using a minimum of table or shelf space. In a busy kitchen where the cook frequently reaches for a knife, there is an advantage to arranging the block at an angle so knives are more easily withdrawn or replaced. The angled knife block in Fig. 4-14 holds seven knives at a 45-degree angle to the base and occupies an area of 6 × 9 inches.

You could make the block wider to take more knives or include more slots or holes for a sharpening steel or other cook's tools. The sizes shown (Fig. 4-15) allow for knives with blades up to 9 inches long in the top row and blades up to 7 inches long in the lower row. The drawing shows four knives in the top row and three in the lower row, but the arrangement could be reversed. The slots are 3/16 × 1¼ inches. Check your knives for fit and alter some slots if necessary. Any wood can be used to match other furniture or equipment. The main part of the block could be a solid piece or built up with laminations.

1. If the block is to be solid, prepare a piece

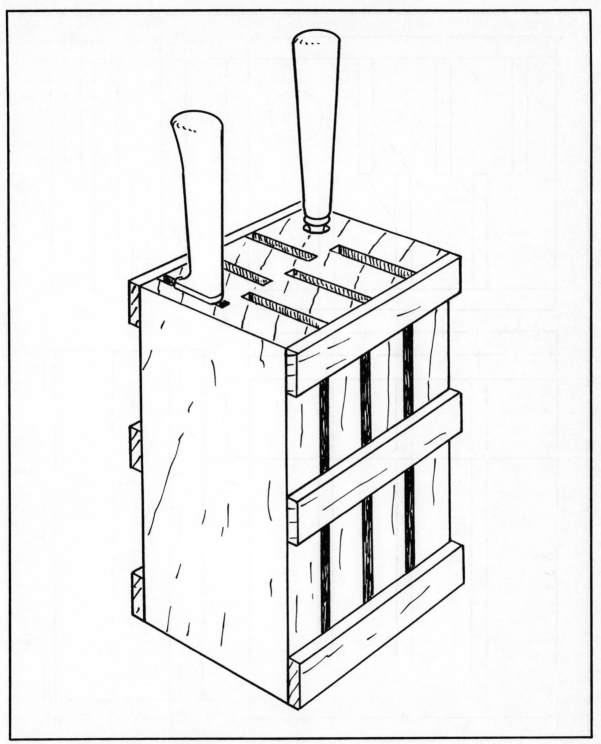

Fig. 4-12. A knife block to stand vertically.

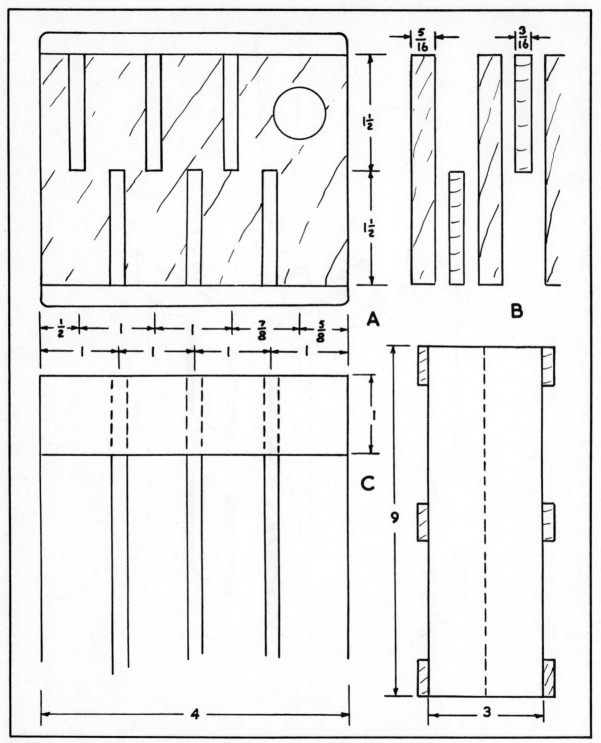

Fig. 4-13. Suggested sizes for the knife block.

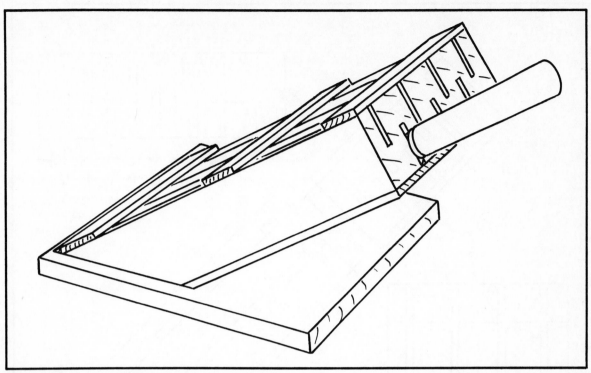

Fig. 4-14. A sloping knife block on a base.

2¼ × 5 inches and at least 9 inches long. Level the bottom after the slots have been cut. Mark the slots (Fig. 4-15A) and cut them with a wobble saw or other means.

2. If the block is to be built up, prepare strips as you did for the knife block in Fig. 4-13B. Make the strips ½ × 2¼ inches and ³⁄₁₆ × 1 inch. Glue the strips together to make the assembly similar to the solid block.

3. Square the top of the block and cut its bottom at a 45-degree angle (Fig. 4-15B).

4. Cut a single piece of ¼-inch wood to cover the slots on the underside (Fig. 4-15C). Glue it to the block and bevel its lower edge to match.

5. Cut three, ¼-×-1-inch strips to fit across the upper surface (Fig. 4-15D). Glue and pin or screw them to the block, with the bottom one beveled to match the block.

6. Make the base (Fig. 4-15E) large enough to keep the whole knife holder steady.

7. Sand sharpness off all exposed edges and corners.

8. Join the block to the base with glue and screws upwards. Be careful that the screw holes avoid the knife slots and see that the assembly is square.

9. Finish the wood with varnish or treat it with oil.

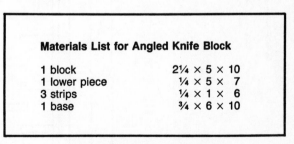

Materials List for Angled Knife Block

1 block	2¼ × 5 × 10
1 lower piece	¼ × 5 × 7
3 strips	¼ × 1 × 6
1 base	¾ × 6 × 10

COOKBOOK STAND

When a cook is following a recipe, she usually props open the book or magazine, often not very successfully, somewhere on the countertop. A stand to hold the pages open would be convenient. The cookbook stand in Fig. 4-16 has two arms that fold

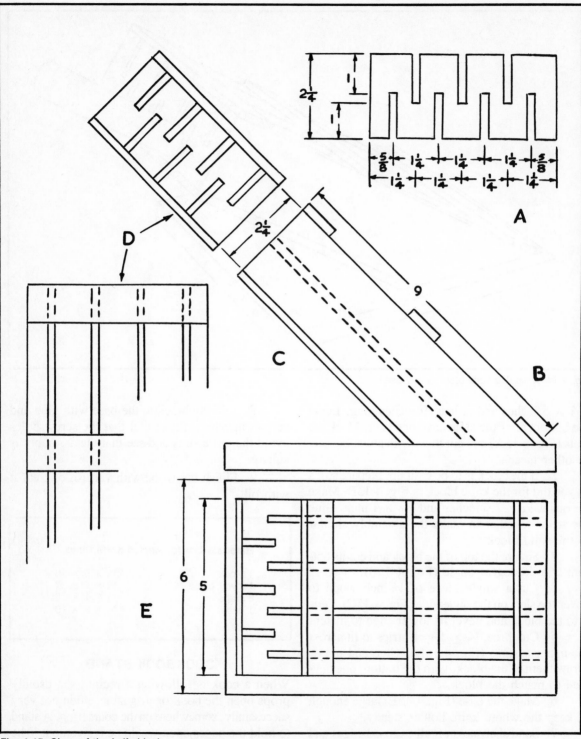

Fig. 4-15. Sizes of the knife block.

flat when out of use and open to support a book at a convenient angle with the pages held back.

The two parts are identical and hinged together on their vertical edges. The forward sloping edges are about 9 inches long, but they will support a deeper book. The arms can be set at any angle to suit the size of the book (Fig. 4-16A). The hooks at the bottom hold the pages of any normal book.

1. Set out the shape on a grid of 1-inch squares (Fig. 4-16B) and make two pieces to this

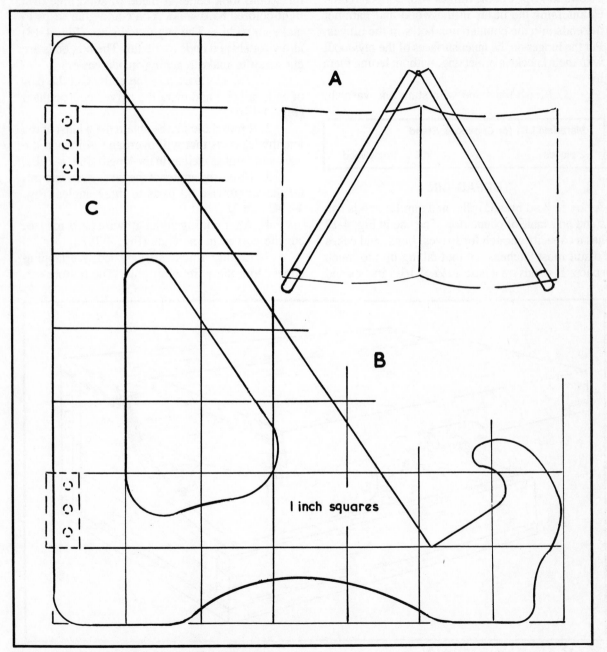

Fig. 4-16. The arrangement and shape of easel parts.

size from ¼-inch plywood. Leave the vertical edges and the bottom straight edges square, but round all other edges.

2. Use small brass hinges (Fig. 4-16C) because the plywood isn't thick enough for wood screws to grip. Fix the hinges with copper rivets. Countersink the heads in the wood and hammer the ends into the countersunk holes in the hinges. Put the hinges on the inner surfaces of the plywood, with their knuckles projecting, without letting them in.

3. Finish the stand with stain and varnish.

Materials List for Cookbook Stand	
2 pieces	7 × 8 × ¼ plywood

BREAD BIN

A box to hold bread, rolls, and similar foods can stand on a table or countertop. The one in Fig. 4-17 has a capacity enough for loaves, buns, and cakes to suit most kitchens without taking up too much space. It stands on a base 11½ × 16½ inches and

is 7 inches high. Its sloping lid is hinged to lift for access.

All of the parts are ½ inch thick. They could be thicker, but it would be unwise to reduce the thickness. Plywood might be used, but the bread bin would look better if made of solid pine or a light-colored hardwood. You could glue strips to make up widths. The suggested sizes (Fig. 4-18) allow for shaped ends to the lid. The box ends are cut away to make reaching inside easier.

1. The key parts are the ends. Cut the pair of ends full size and mark the curved cuts on them (Fig. 4-19A).

2. From these pieces obtain the widths of the lengthwise parts that will overhang ¼ inch at the back and front as well as in the length (Fig. 4-19B).

3. Bisect the angles at the lid corners and miter the lengthwise lid parts to these angles (Fig. 4-19C and D).

4. After cutting all lengthwise parts to size, cut the curves in the ends (Fig. 4-19E).

5. Lightly round all exposed overlapping edges. Join the parts with glue. The bottom can

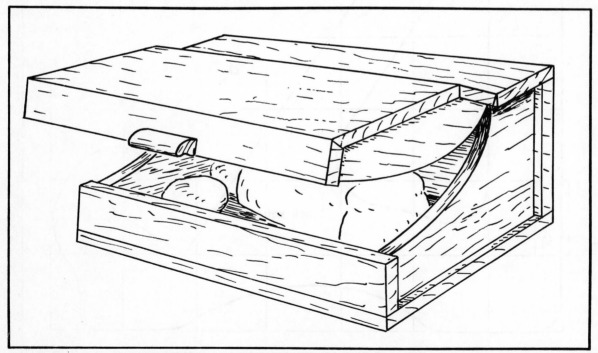

Fig. 4-17. A bread box with hinged lid.

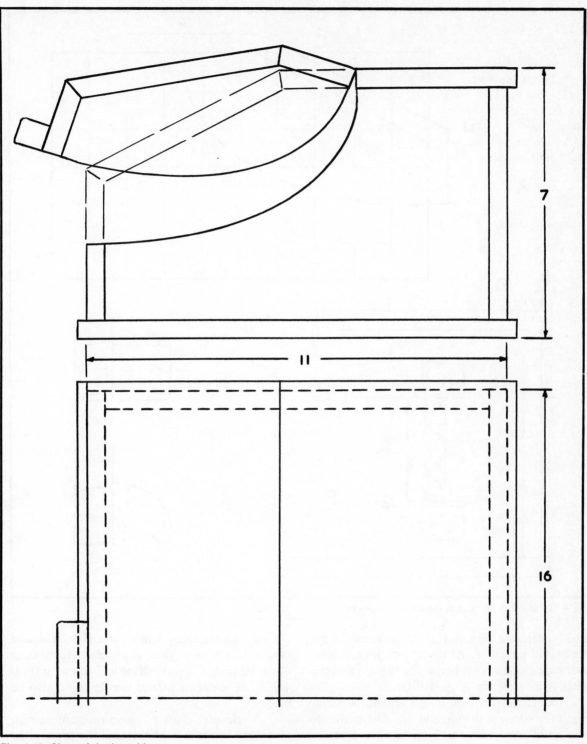

Fig. 4-18. Sizes of the bread box.

73

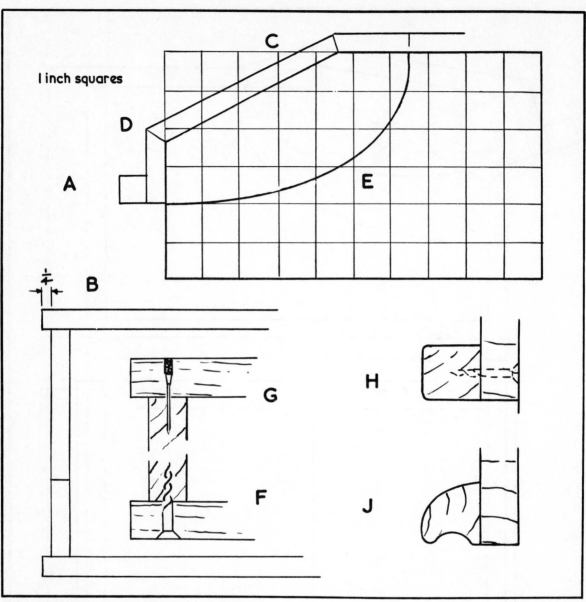

Fig. 4-19. Shaping, joints, and handle of the bread box.

also be screwed (Fig. 4-19F) because the screw heads will not show. At the visible joints, however, use fine nails set below the surface and covered with stopping (Fig. 4-19G).

6. Three, 1½-inch hinges should be suitable at the edges of the top and lid. Alternatively, you could use ornamental hinges on the surface. Brass would be best. Steel should be plated.

7. The simplest handle is a ¾-inch square block 4 inches long, glued and screwed to the edge of the lid (Fig. 4-19H). Shape it if you wish (Fig. 4-19J). A metal or plastic handle could also be used.

8. Several coats of damp-resistant varnish provides a hygienic finish that could be wiped clean with a damp cloth.

Materials List for Bread Bin

2 ends	½ × 6 × 11	
1 bottom	½ × 11½ × 17	
1 top	½ × 3¾ × 17	
1 front	½ × 2 × 17	
1 lid front	½ × 2 × 17	
1 lid top	½ × 2 × 17	
1 lid	½ × 5¾ × 17	
1 handle	¾ × ¾ × 5	

ROLL-BACK BREAD BIN

A door or lid that disappears into the body of the container is sometimes called a *tambour fall* and was a particular feature of old-time rolltop desks. It is also appropriate for a bread bin; the lid can slide back under the top to give easy access to the contents.

A bin could be the same size as the bread bin in Fig. 4-19. This one has a drawer for cutlery, kitchen tools, or books (Fig. 4-20). The roll-back front is made of a number of strips of wood glued to a canvas backing with their ends sliding in grooves in the bin ends. When the bin is closed, they fill the curved part but can be lifted to slide in a groove straight under the bin top.

All parts are ½ inch thick, except the ends that are ⅝ inch, and the lid strips are ¼ inch. The bin is shown on a base 11¾ × 16 inches with a total height of 9 inches. If sizes are varied, the roll-back assembly's rear edge must be under the top when closed and slide back sufficiently to give the maximum space when open. Make the bin of softwood or a light-colored hardwood. Glue strips to make up width. Some of the lengthwise parts could be

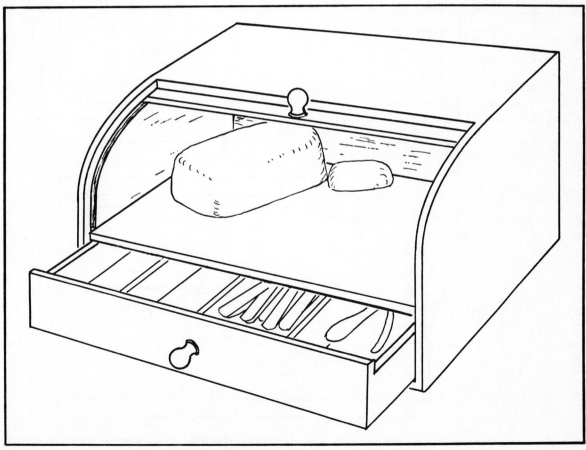

Fig. 4-20. A bread box with sliding lid and drawer.

plywood. Choose straight-grained wood for the narrow strips that make up the lid to reduce risk of warping.

1. The ends govern the sizes of several other parts. Set them out (Fig. 4-21A). The drawer compartment is made with a shelf 3 inches above the

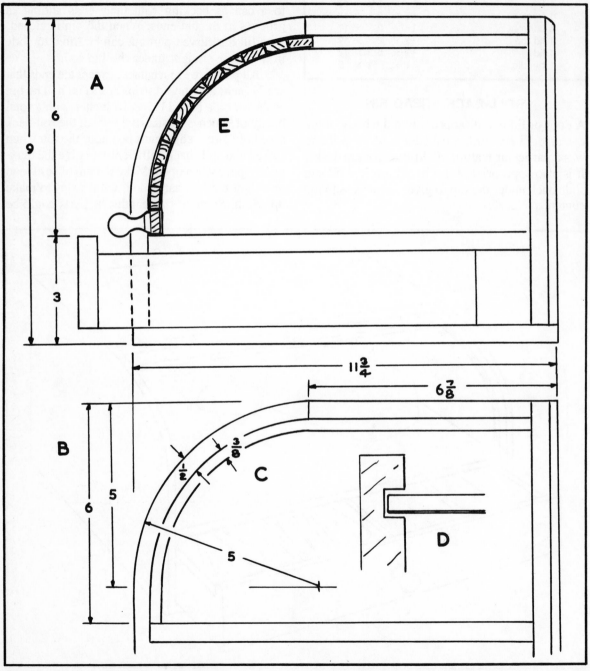

Fig. 4-21. Sizes of the bread box with drawer.

underside of the bottom. Mark the curved outline (Fig. 4-21B). Cut the pair of ends to this shape. True the outsides of the curves smoothly, since they will control the cutting of the grooves.

2. The grooves must provide easy-fitting guides for the roll-back lid. Use a router guided around the edge to cut the grooves (Fig. 4-21C) to half the thickness of the wood (Fig. 4-21D). At the top the grooves go as far as the back position,

and they go down to the shelf top. Use a chisel to square the ends of the grooves.

3. Cut the strips for the roll-back lid. Twelve ⅝-inch-wide pieces are shown (Fig. 4-21E). If other widths are used, make up the same total width. The strips could be simple rectangular sections with the outer corners rounded (Fig. 4-22A), but if you have the equipment to work a rounded front (Fig. 4-22B), that will look neat. You

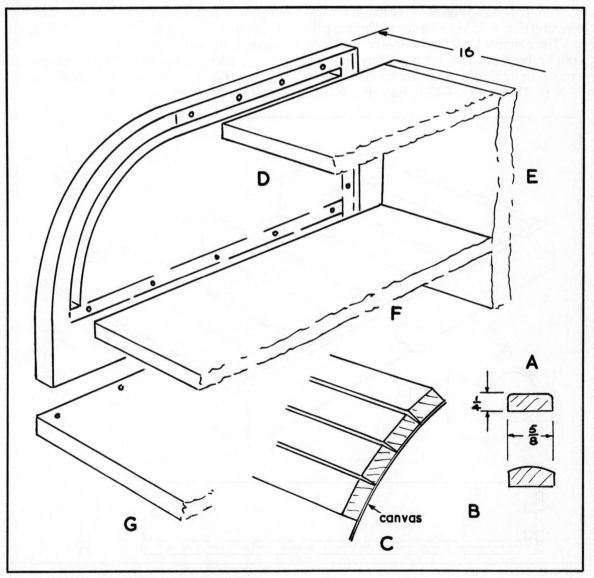

Fig. 4-22. Details of the sliding lid of the bread box.

could make the lower strip thicker to provide a stiff edge, then reduce its ends to fit in the grooves.

4. Use a piece of canvas or stout cloth to back the strips. Leave the ends of the strips projecting without canvas for a sufficient distance to go into the grooves, but cut the canvas so it will come not more than ⅛ inch inside the ends when the lid is in use. Glue the strips to the canvas (Fig. 4-22C) and clamp under weights until the glue has set. Trim off any surplus canvas.

5. Provide a knob at the center of the bottom strip (Fig. 4-23A) for raising and lowering the lid. Use a similar knob for the drawer. Turn your own knobs, if possible, but if you buy them, the one on the lid should not be thicker than ⅝ inch.

6. The top (Fig. 4-22D), back (Fig. 4-22E),

and shelf (Fig. 4-22F) are all the same length, and they fit between the bin ends. Make the length to hold the ends at a distance to allow the lid strips to move easily in the grooves. The neatest joints are with ¼-inch dowels arranged about 2 inches apart. Simpler joints are nailed or screwed through the ends. You could also rabbet the back and dado the shelf. It might be advisable to make a dry assembly of the parts made so far to check the action of the lid. If it is satisfactory, join the lengthwise parts between the ends with the lid in its grooves. Set back the front of the shelf by the thickness of the drawer front.

7. Make the bottom to fit below the ends and the back (Fig. 4-23G). Glue it and screw upwards; the screw heads will not show.

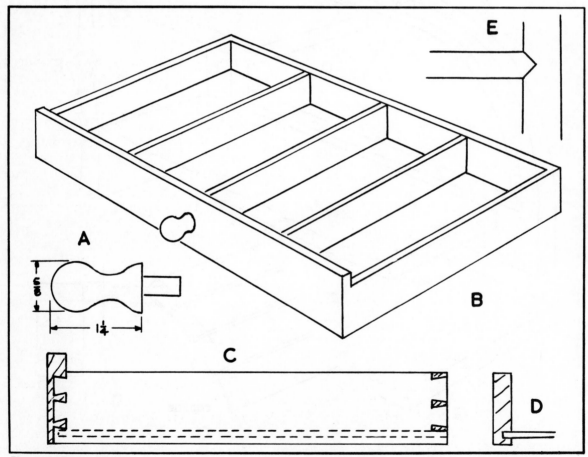

Fig. 4-23. Drawer details.

8. The drawer is made as a shallow tray (Fig. 4-23B) with its front high enough to overlap the front edge of the shelf. It might have the divisions shown for cutlery, or others might be arranged to suit your intended contents. Dovetailed corners are suggested, but other corner joints could be used.

9. Make the drawer sides (Fig. 4-23C) to slide between the bin shelf and bottom. Make the lengthwise parts to fit easily between the bin ends. Avoid excessive slackness because the drawer might twist out of line and stick in use.

10. Groove the sides and front for the bottom (Fig. 4-23D), which could be ⅛-inch hardboard. The drawer back will be above the bottom.

11. Allow for the joints and make the length of the sides so they will not quite reach the bin back when the drawer front is stopped by the shelf edge.

12. Cut the joints and assemble the parts, with the bottom slid in last, after the action of the other parts has been tried in the bin. Screw the drawer bottom to its back. Fit a knob.

13. Finish the bin with several coats of damp-resistant varnish.

14. You can fit divisions into dados, but it is simpler to use V grooves (Fig. 4-23E).

Materials List for Roll-Back Bread Bin				
2 ends	⅝	×	9	× 12
1 top	½	×	6⅛	× 16
1 back	½	×	8½	× 16
1 shelf	½	×	10½	× 16
1 bottom	½	×	11¾	× 16
12 front strips	¼	×	⅝	× 16
1 drawer front	½	×	2½	× 15
1 drawer back	½	×	1¾	× 15
2 drawer sides	½	×	2	× 11
			hardboard	
1 drawer bottom	11½	×	15	× ⅛
3 drawer divisions	½	×	1¾	× 11

CARD INDEX/NOTEPAD

Recipes are sometimes published on cards. More often the cook jots down notes of recipes she wishes to keep. To be tidy and to keep all these details where they can be found when needed, it helps to use cards of a standard size and to store them together. The index in Fig. 4-24 is a drawer in a box intended to take cards 4 × 6 inches or less. On top is a clamping arrangement to hold a pad of paper, loose sheets, or spare cards, as well as coupons and the many odd papers that accumulate in the kitchen.

The drawer is large enough to hold more than 100 cards. There are two removable divisions to separate recipes and to prevent cards from falling over if the drawer is not full. The clamp on top is a strip of wood across the back with two long wood screws through springs to press the strip onto the paper. There could be any number of pieces of paper, possibly up to 50, depending on the lengths of screws and springs. Papers could be any size up to 7 × 10 inches.

You can use any wood. Most parts are ½ inch thick, but the drawer front is ⅝ inch thick. Make the drawer bottom ⅛-inch hardboard. The two divisions could be hardboard, but thin plywood is better.

Start by making the drawer instead of the more usual sequence of fitting a drawer in after making the case. The sizes given suit cards 4 × 6 inches with plenty of clearance all round. If you use different cards, make the inside measurements to suit with at least ¼ inch extra for ease of handling.

The drawer has a front that overlaps the case top to about half thickness, but at its lower side it is level with the rest of the drawer, so it will stand level if pulled out. The drawer sides are low and prevented from tilting when being moved by strips on the case sides. Examine Fig. 4-25 before you cut any wood.

1. Make the drawer front (Fig. 4-26A and B) and the pair of sides (Fig. 4-26C and D). Groove them to take the bottom hardboard.

2. Make the drawer back (Fig. 4-26E) to fit above the grooves in the sides.

3. Dovetails are shown, but other corner joints could be used.

4. Mark the positions of grooves for the divisions (Fig. 4-26F). They are shown at a 15-degree angle and arranged with two broader compartments and a space for spare cards at the back (Fig. 4-26G), but you could make other arrangements.

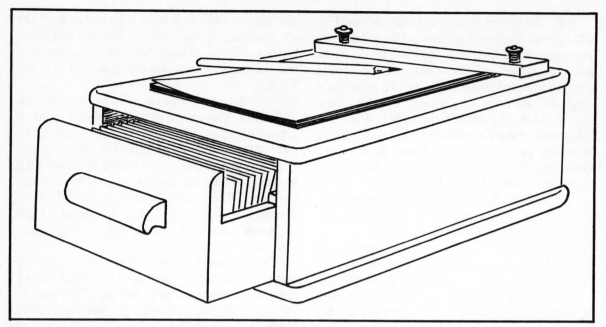

Fig. 4-24. A box for filing recipe and other cards, with a pad on top.

5. Make the divisions to stand almost as high as the cards. Round their top corners (Fig. 4-26H). Cut the grooves so the divisions can be slipped in and out easily. Do the final trimming of the divisions to length after the drawer has been assembled.

6. The drawer front needs a handle. Shape a block of wood and drive screws from inside. You could also buy a metal or plastic handle.

7. Assemble the drawer. Check squareness, but if the bottom has been cut squarely, it should hold the other parts true. Screw the bottom upwards into the back.

8. The case (Figs. 4-25A and 4-27) is made with the top and bottom overlapping the sides and back ¼ inch all around. The bottom is screwed upwards, but the top is held down with glue and fine nails set below the surface and covered with stopping.

9. Make the pair of sides (Fig. 4-27A). The length should reach the inside of the drawer front but extend to allow a little clearance inside the back (Fig. 4-25B). When the drawer front closes tightly against the case front, the drawer back should not touch the case back.

10. Allow for the thickness of the back and glue and pin drawer guides (Figs. 4-25C and 4-27B) to the case sides. The drawer should slide below them but without excessive clearance.

11. Make the back to fit between the sides and hold them just far enough apart for the drawer to slide easily.

12. Top (Fig. 4-27C) and bottom (Fig. 4-27D) are the same. Make them level with the other parts at the front but overlap ¼ inch elsewhere.

13. Fit the back between the sides and join on the top and bottom. Use the drawer to check the assembly. If the bottom is put on before the top, you can see if it fits the drawer properly and make adjustments if necessary.

14. Round all exposed edges and corners. Round the top edge of the drawer front.

15. The notepad clamp bar (Figs. 4-25D and 4-27E) is a ¼-×-¾-inch section. Even if the rest of the project is softwood, make this part of a close-grained hardwood.

16. The notepad clamp bar is pressed down by springs under washers on screws long enough to go through the case top into the sides (Fig.

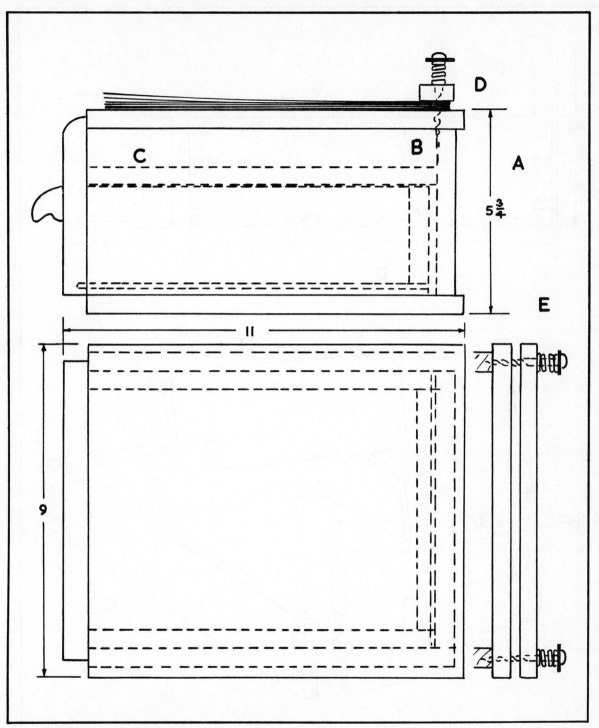

Fig. 4-25. Sizes of the filing box.

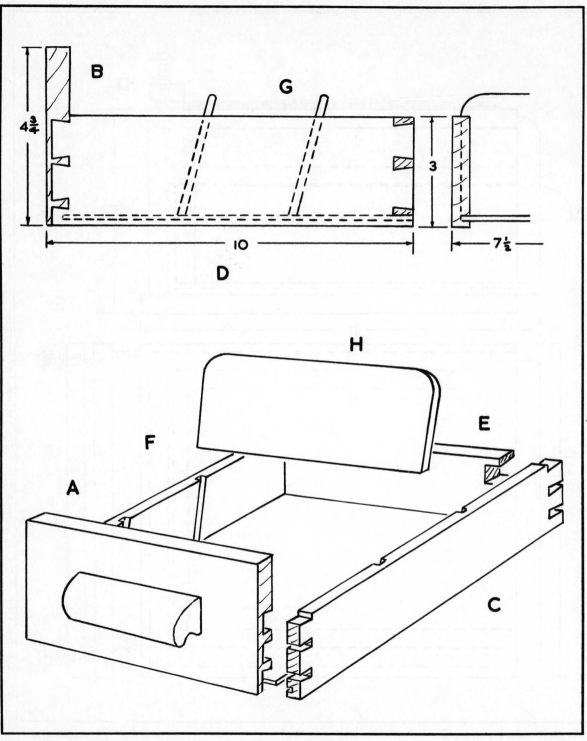

Fig. 4-26. Details of the filing drawer.

4-25E). Roundhead 8-gauge screws, 2 or 2½ inches long, and small coil compression springs that slide on and are about ¾ inch long when expanded should be suitable.

17. Drill clearance holes in the clamp bar above the centers of the sides. Make a trial assembly with several thicknesses of paper under the bar.

18. If this and the drawer action are satisfactory, sand all parts and finish inside and out with stain, if you wish, followed by polish or varnish. Cloth might be glued to the underside of the case bottom to prevent slipping or marking on a table surface.

Materials List for Card Index/Notepad	
1 drawer front	⅝ × 4¾ × 8
2 drawer sides	½ × 3 × 10
1 drawer back	½ × 2¾ × 8
1 drawer bottom	8 × 10 × ⅛ hardboard
2 drawer divisions	3½ × 8 × ⅛ hardboard
1 drawer handle	⅞ × ⅞ × 5
2 case sides	½ × 4¾ × 11
2 drawer guides	½ × ½ × 11
1 case back	½ × 4¾ × 8
1 case top	½ × 9 × 11
1 case bottom	½ × 9 × 11
1 clamp bar	¼ × ¾ × 10

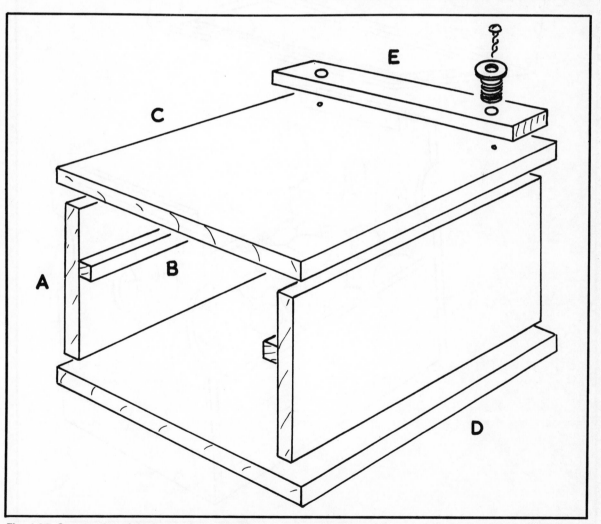

Fig. 4-27. Construction of the box and paper holder.

Fig. 4-28. Stacking storage boxes.

STACKING VEGETABLE BOXES

Storage boxes can be for vegetables in particular, but they are suitable for many other loose foods, or even cans and bags that are needed within reach. The design in Fig. 4-28 is for a box with raised ends that allow several boxes or bins to be built up into a stack. Three would be as high as a countertop, but the stack could be even higher.

You can alter the suggested sizes. You can arrange sizes to make the best use of available space. The method of construction allows for all parts being ½-inch plywood, preferably exterior or marine grade for water resistance.

For uniform boxes that stack in any order, make a set at one time. Mark out and cut all parts that must be identical before moving on to other parts. Work through the same assembly stage with each box in turn. There is some tolerance, but make the boxes as identical as possible.

For clarity, the construction of only one box is described. Repeat the stages in step for other boxes.

1. The box ends are the key parts (Fig. 4-29A). Mark them out with the positions of other parts shown (Fig. 4-30A). The curves in the edges improve access, and the 2-inch holes serve as handles. Round the edges of all the curves.

2. Cut the strips for the sides (Fig. 4-29B). In the simplest construction, nail the corners, but it is better to cut finger joints (Fig. 4-30B). If the depth is divided into 1-inch parts, drive thin nails both ways to lock the glued corners (Fig. 4-30C). Check squareness as you make the corner joints. When the glue has set, level any projecting ends and remove excess glue inside.

3. Put ½-inch-square strips inside the sides (Fig. 4-29C) to support the bottom. Make the bottom to fit inside and secure it with glue and a few nails.

4. So the top of one box will take another stacked on it, arrange strips inside the top edges (Fig. 4-29D) to project enough to fit below the upper box bottom (Fig. 4-29E). Make the length to fit easily between the strips under the bottom (Fig. 4-30D). Round or bevel the top corners to help when stacking.

Materials List for Stacking Vegetable Boxes

(Quantity for one box—all ½-inch plywood)

2 ends	10	× 13
2 sides	6	× 15
1 bottom	9	× 14
2 bottom strips	½	× 14
2 locating strips	1½	× 8

TOTE BOX

A container that can be carried about has many uses in and around a kitchen. It can hold cleaning materials or gather all the ingredients ready for mixing. It can carry the knives, forks, and other utensils to set a table. Most of the things needed for a meal in the yard or on the patio can be taken in one load.

The tote box in Fig. 4-31 has four compartments and a pair of handles that can swing down out of the way to give full access to the interior. You can simply use nailed joints and softwood, or make it to a better standard with cut joints in an attractive hardwood. The instructions assume that you will use cut joints, but you can modify the techniques for nailed or screwed joints. You can modify sizes (Fig. 4-32) to suit needs, but you must arrange the handles to swing over the ends.

1. Prepare the wood for the sides and ends, and mark to length. Notch the corners (Fig. 4-33A) to allow thin nails to be driven both ways for simple, strong joints. Comb joints can be cut (Fig. 4-33B), but dovetails (Fig. 4-33C) look attractive and show your skill.

2. Four compartments are shown (Fig. 4-32A). You might prefer no divisions or another arrangement. Notch the compartments where they cross (Fig. 4-33D). You could nail or screw the ends from outside, but stopped dados are better (Fig. 4-34E).

3. Assemble the box parts and screw on the bottom, which can be hardboard or thin plywood. Thin, solid wood will match the other parts. If necessary, you can add a joint in the bottom along the central division.

4. The two handles are the same (Fig. 4-32B). Make the arms with the screws and dowels

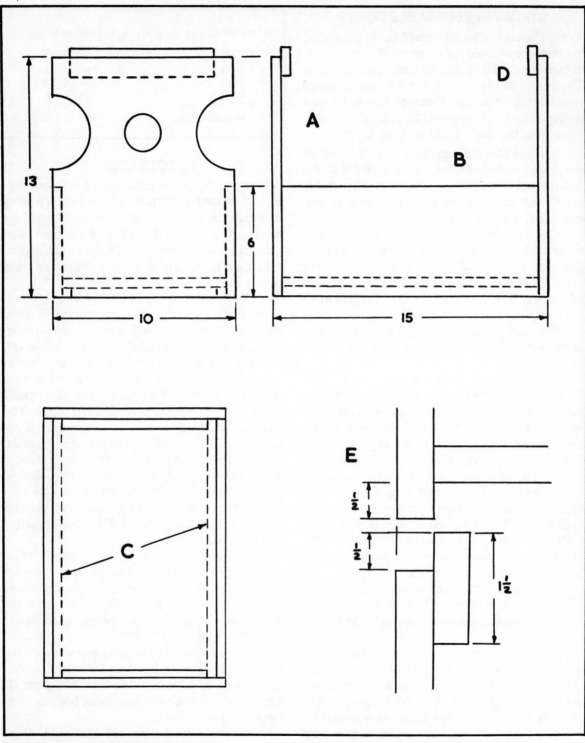

Fig. 4-29. Sizes of a stacking box.

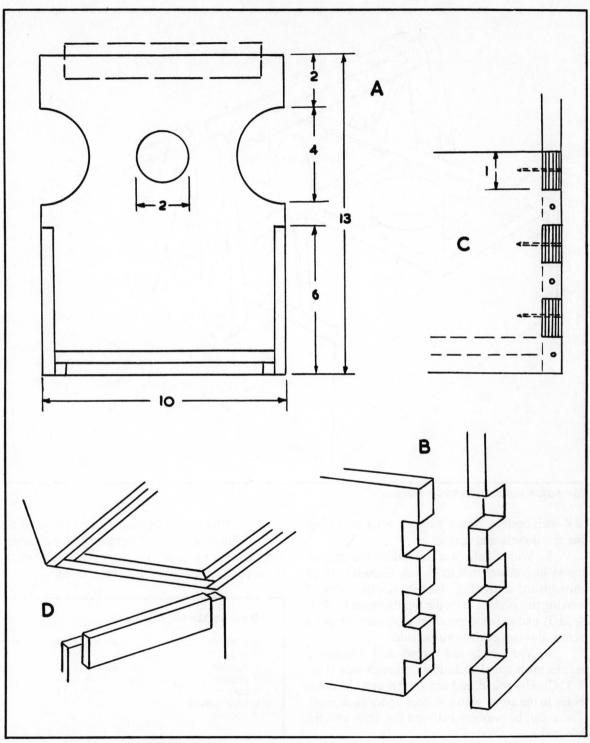

Fig. 4-30. Details of a stacking box.

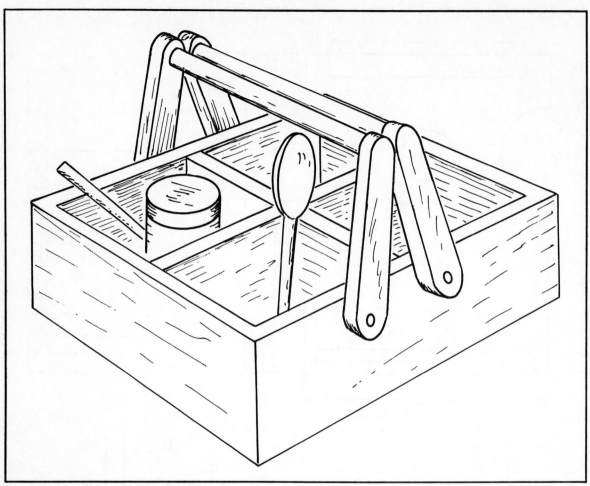

Fig. 4-31. A tote box with folding handles.

at 4-inch centers. Shape the ends after preparing for the dowels and screws.

5. With a lathe you can reduce the ends of the ⅝-inch dowel rods to ⅜-inch diameters to go through the arms (Fig. 4-33F). Another way of making the joints is to let the full diameter in (Fig. 4-33G) and either depend on glue only or put a screw through each from outside.

6. The pivots are screws and washers 3 inches apart and 1 inch down on each side (Fig. 4-32C). Use roundhead screws through clearance holes in the arms, with a washer under each head. There can be washers between the arms and the box sides.

7. After a trial assembly, take the handles off and finish all parts of the tote box with stain and varnish or polish. Alternatively, use a bright color paint to make the box easy to find.

Materials List for Tote Box	
2 sides	½ × 4 × 11
2 ends	½ × 4 × 9
1 division	½ × 4 × 11
1 division	½ × 4 × 9
1 bottom	¼ × 8 × 11
4 handle arms	½ × 1 × 6
2 handles	11 × ⅝ diameter

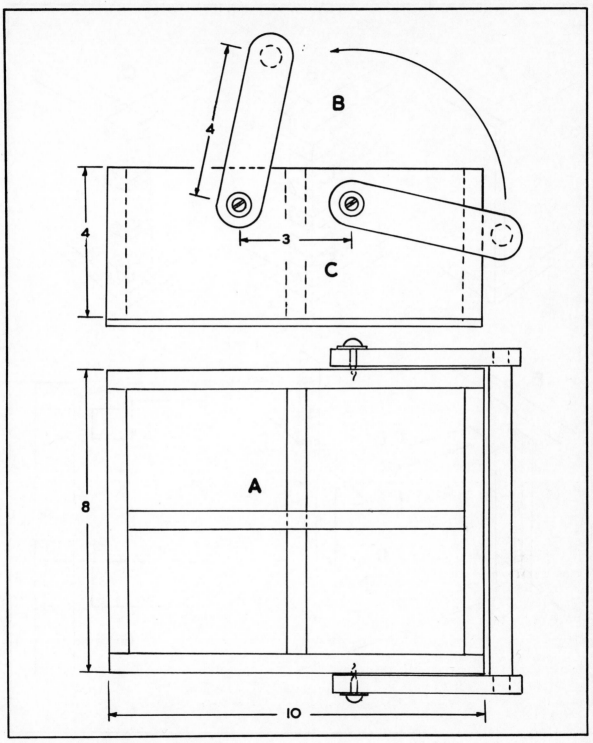

Fig. 4-32. Sizes of the tote box and handles.

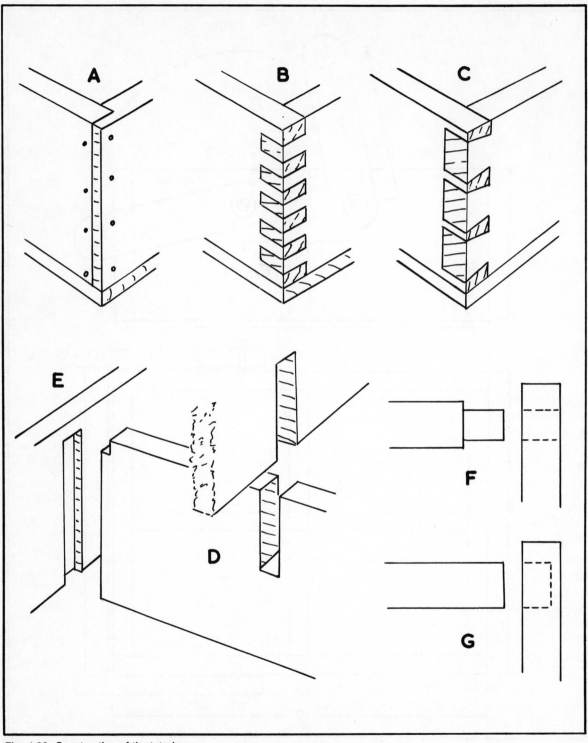

Fig. 4-33. Construction of the tote box.

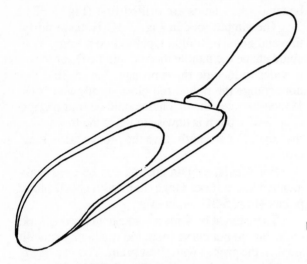

5
Tools and Utensils

A large number of tools and utensils that a cook uses are better made of wood than metal or other materials. Wood tools and utensils are less likely to damage containers than metal or hard plastic, particularly if they are treated or coated with nonstick material. Many of them are quite simple, and the home woodworker can produce a variety in a range of sizes unavailable from a store.

As with other wood articles to be used with food, avoid resinous or naturally oily types. Softwoods have some uses, but if the tool will have thin edges, it should be hardwood since softwood can break or splinter. Splinters must be avoided. In most kitchens a light-colored, close-grained hardwood is preferable. Where it is available, beech is a good choice. The light color is chosen largely because of its appearance. A dark-colored wood can be just as hygienic, and you can choose it if you are giving your kitchen a distinctive appearance. Where weight is an advantage or strength and cleanliness are required in a small size, one of the very hard woods, such as box, is better. Tools that are used on the dining table might look

better if they are made of a furniture wood, such as teak or cherry.

For spoons, spatulas, and other tools that are sometimes handled with pressure and power, choose wood with reasonably straight grain, particularly near edges and along handles. Avoid knots or even places where the grain curves around where a knotted part has been cut away.

Be careful when finishing. In nearly every case, round edges and corners. Sand with progressively finer abrasive. Where the wood will be used in wet conditions, it is a good idea to moisten the wood and allow it to dry before final sanding. This process lifts any tiny pieces of wood fiber that were bent in earlier sanding so you can rub them off, instead of leaving them to rise during the first use of the tool.

SPATULAS

You can use a piece of wood with a broad, thinned edge for mixing and scraping. You can modify the basic form to suit your preferences and needs. The form is usually spadelike with the end cut diagonally and thinned almost to a cutting edge (Fig. 5-1A). One edge could be straight (Fig. 5-1B). If the primary use is mixing, round the end (Fig. 5-1C) or cut square across. The cook might prefer the end to have fine grooves cut along one or both sides of the blade (Fig. 5-1D). Sand well into the grooves to avoid roughness.

Lengths can vary, but 11 inches suits most needs. Different widths are also desirable. Two widths could be included in one double-ended tool (Fig. 5-1E); make the length longer—14 inches—to allow for the hand being at the middle.

For stirring or draining, perforate the end of the spatula. Drill one large hole (Fig. 5-1F) or a pattern of smaller holes (Fig. 5-1G), or cut slots (Fig. 5-1H)

When the spatula might be required to scrape on its side as well as the end, shape it more like a knife (Fig. 5-1J) with its edge and end thinned. If it is to be just a mixer, the end need not be thinned but can have a hole. Project one corner so it can get into angles (Fig. 5-1K).

Drill a hole in all handles for hanging directly or to take a cord for hanging. This might not be necessary if the spatulas will be kept in a container.

With a lathe, you can make some spatulas with round handles, either parallel or with some shaping. The handles could have a ½-inch diameter (Fig. 5-2A). Leave the wood at the blade end long enough to allow for adequate tapering.

For an attractive effect, you can use two woods of different colors. Make the handle ends darker than the working ends (Fig. 5-2B). With modern waterproof glues, secure splices can be made, but to avoid end grain, give them long tapers—1 in 7 is satisfactory (Fig. 5-2C). The joint in a ¼-inch handle should be 1¾ inches long. Plane the two slopes together (Fig. 5-2D). For the same two-color effect with a turned handle, drill a hole in one part and turn a dowel to fit on the other (Fig. 5-2E). Do final turning of the outside after the parts have been glued. Alternatively, make a splice, as with the flat handle, then turn after joining for an unusual effect (Fig. 5-2F).

Make small spatulas for mustard and similar foods or pastes in exactly the same way as normal spatulas. Make them 3 or 4 inches long in harder wood.

FORKS

A wooden fork is made like a spatula with prongs. The gaps can be cut to a point (Fig. 5-3A), but shaping is easier and sanding inside can be done better if small holes are drilled first (Fig. 5-3B).

The simple fork in Fig. 5-3C is made fairly thin and given a straight taper to two prongs. You could shape the handle more (Fig. 5-3D) or make it wider to include three prongs (Fig. 5-3E). Do not arrange the points too closely; allow at least ⅜ inch between them. There could be four prongs (Fig. 5-3F), but it is unwise to make the fork wider than that. For strength, give the prongs fairly long tapers.

For salads, a plain spatula can be used with another like a fork. Make them with short, blunt points (Fig. 5-3G), however.

There might be some advantage in curving fork ends, but do not curve them too much or you will weaken the prongs with short grain. You can make a modest curve in the end (Fig. 5-3H) before you mark and cut the prongs (Fig. 5-3J).

SPOONS

Next to spatulas in usefulness and ease in making are wooden spoons. A busy cook will welcome spoons of many sizes and patterns, especially in woods similar to the spatulas. Many spoons have long, round handles that you can turn on a lathe. Without a lathe you can cut the handles square and plane the corners to an octagonal shape for most of the length, which gives a very distinctive appearance.

Most spoons can be quite shallow. For deep spoons, you need to start with thicker wood and cut away much of it. Start with wood ⅝ inch thick. Make the spoon with a bowl about 2 inches across and a full ⅝-inch round or octagonal handle. The standard spoon bowl (Fig. 5-4A) can serve as a pattern for others.

Draw the outline on the wood (Fig. 5-4B). Work the hollow before doing other shaping. It

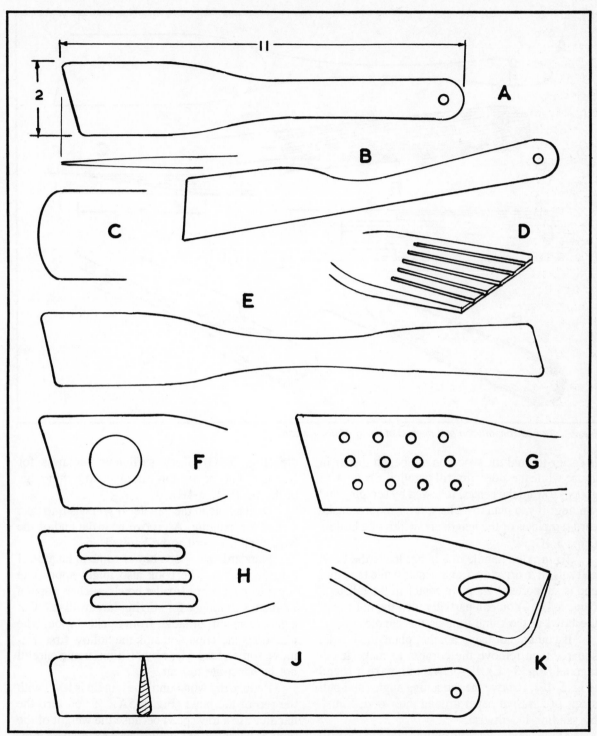

Fig. 5-1. Many spatula shapes.

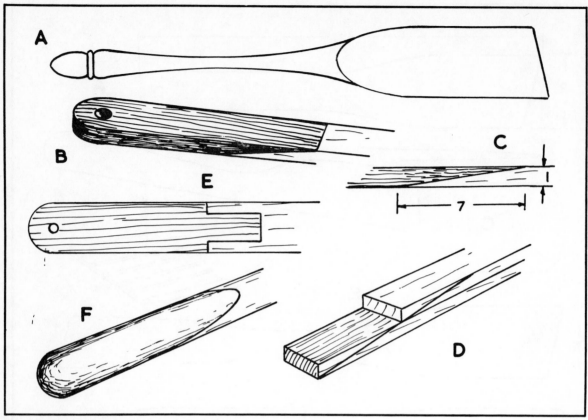

Fig. 5-2. Turned construction and method of using different woods.

is easier to hold the wood on the bench top or in a vise while the sides are still parallel. Shape with gouges toward the center, followed by scraping and sanding. If you plan to make several spoons, make card templates of the length and width of a hollow (Fig. 5-4C).

To turn the handle in a lathe, leave the bowl end square to drive on a spur center while the other end is supported by a plain center in the tailstock (Fig. 5-4D). You can partially turn the outline of the bowl at the same time as the handle.

If you are not using a lathe, plane the handle square, then remove the corners to make it octagonal (Fig. 5-4E). If you want to make it round (Fig. 5-4F), remove the remaining angles and pull strips of abrasive paper around the wood. Finish by sanding lengthwise.

At the bowl, work the outline close to the hollow, then round the back, blending into the handle (Fig. 5-4G). Keep sufficient thickness for strength, but the section can taper to a thin edge at the tip (Fig. 5-4H).

Drill a hole in the handle, if you wish, to take a cord for hanging. A groove near the end of the handle allows cord to be knotted on.

Standard-size spoon bowls come in lengths of 8 to 16 inches. The cook also might appreciate some with bigger or smaller bowls, such as a spoon 18 inches or longer for stirring larger mixes. Cut a deeper spoon, or ladle, from thicker wood. The method is the same, but sink the hollow first. Remove some of the waste by drilling, being careful not to penetrate too far.

Reduce the wood until the handle is level with the top of the bowl (Fig. 5-5A). If you turn the handle, use a low speed because the weight of the bowl is eccentric and could cause excessive vibration at high speeds.

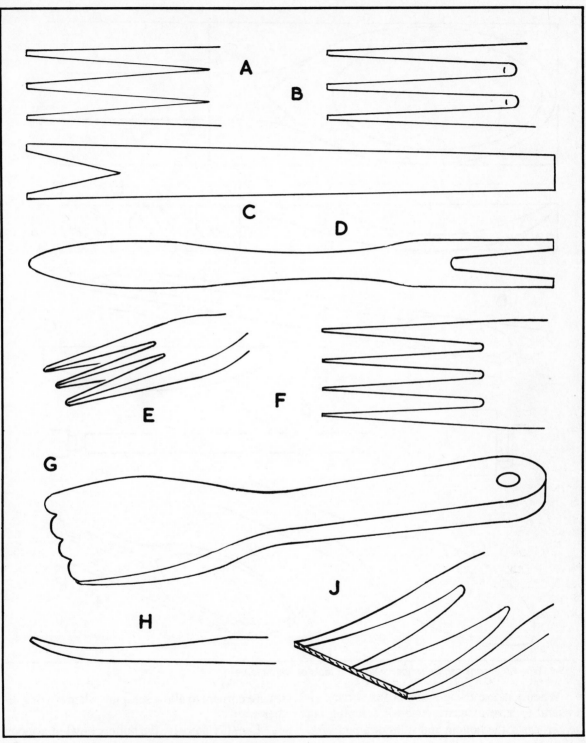

Fig. 5-3. Forks can be made in a similar way to spatulas.

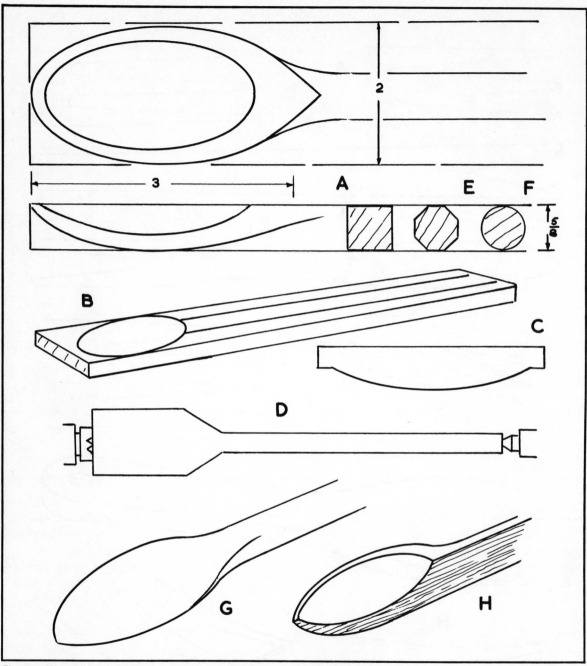

Fig. 5-4. Wooden spoons can be shaped with hand tools or with a lathe.

When you are using a spoon for stirring, it is useful to have a square edge for scraping out the corners at the bottom and sides of a pan (Fig. 5-5B). Make a pair of these spoons with opposite square corners to allow scraping when stirring either way.

For stirring only, the hollow bowl of a spoon isn't necessary, and the tool becomes more of a

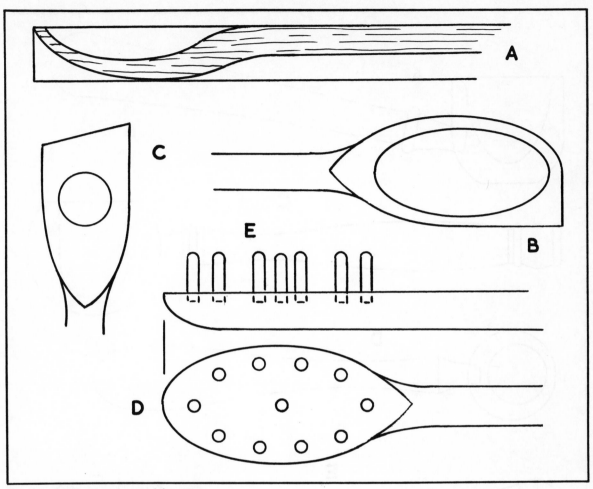

Fig. 5-5. Details of some special spoons.

paddle, like a heavier spatula. The shape could follow the outline of a spoon or have an end like a spatula. The one shown in Fig. 5-5C has a hole through it. Keep the end the full thickness and make the handle round or octagonal.

Another flat-bladed spoon is used for spaghetti. This has an outline like a spoon but has pegs or prongs (Fig. 5-5D). Make the prongs from pieces of 1/8-inch dowel rod with rounded tops and glue them into holes (Fig. 5-5E). The pegs can be taken through to project on both sides, but one side is more usual.

You can make spoons with deep bowls on a lathe in two parts. They are useful as measures to dip out a standard amount. The bowl is turned like

an eggcup (Fig. 5-6A), then the handle is doweled into it (Fig. 5-6B), either square or at a slight angle.

Smaller spoons of this construction can be turned of harder wood and the handles ornamented. An example is a pickle or olive spoon about 9 inches long (Fig. 5-6C). One about 5 inches long might be made to use with salt (Fig. 5-6D).

For spoons to be used at the dining table, use furniture woods. They will look good with darker ends to the handles spliced on, as suggested for spatulas.

A honey dipper is not a spoon, but it is used for a similar purpose. It makes an interesting turning project. The one in Fig. 5-6E is about 6 inches long with a slender knob handle and a deeply-

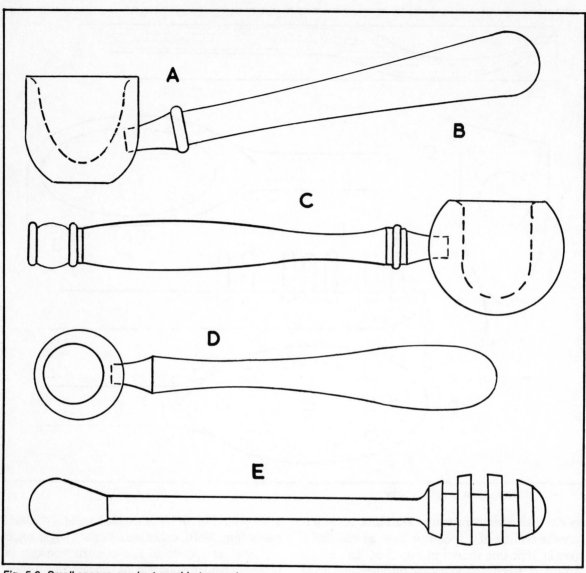

Fig. 5-6. Small spoons can be turned in two parts.

grooved end to retain honey when it is dipped.

TENDERIZER

A wood mallet or hammer can be used to beat meat to increase its tenderness. Because a weighted head is an advantage, a fairly dense hardwood is advisable. Softwood is unsuitable, not only because of its lack of weight, but because of the risk of splintering. It is usual to give one or both faces a pattern of points.

The mallet in Fig. 5-7 has a square head, but you could turn a round one, if you wish. Alternative handles are suggested. You could use malacca cane to provide spring and reduce any shock on the hand. The handle could be dowel rod or you could turn one. Because the amount of tenderizing in an average kitchen is not much, the shock on the gripping hand is not considered much of a problem.

1. The head shown is 2¼ inches square (Fig.

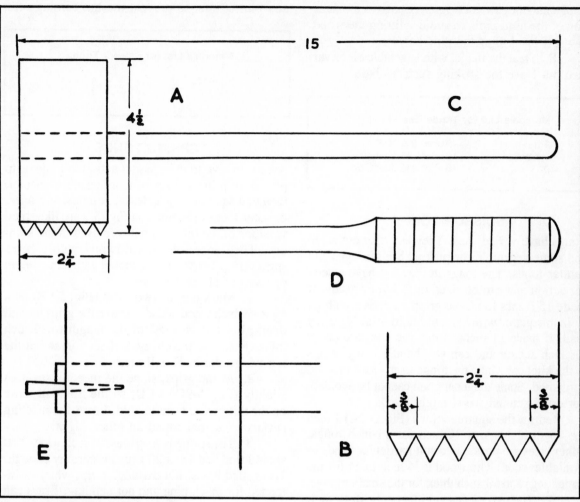

Fig. 5-7. Suggested sizes for a mallet.

5-7A) but make it any size to suit your needs or the available wood.

2. Square the ends and mark both sides for drilling through to finish the hole true.

3. Mark out the points on two opposite faces. They are shown as 60-degree triangles ⅜ inch wide (Fig. 5-7B). Whatever the width, divide it equally. Although ⅜ inch is a good size, the points can be slightly larger or smaller. Watch the lines on both faces as you saw the hollows to keep the pattern even.

4. Mark the same arrangement the other way and saw across to form the points. Smooth the surfaces of the square conical points with a half-round file or abrasive paper wrapped around an acutely angled piece of wood.

5. For a simple handle, prepare a length of ⅝-inch or ¾-inch dowel rod or malacca cane (Fig. 5-7C).

6. You could turn a handle with a neck diameter of ⅝ inch. A thickened grip is worth having, however, and you could increase the grip to 1⅛ inches with lines cut around (Fig. 5-7D). Whatever the handle, make sure the part that goes through the head is parallel and of a size to suit one of your drill bits.

7. Drill the head. Make a saw cut across the end of the handle. Glue it in and drive a glued

wedge into the saw cut (Fig. 5-7E) across the direction of the head grain to avoid splitting the wood. Saw off level after the glue has set.

8. Treat the mallet with vegetable oil or varnish but leave the striking surfaces bare.

```
Materials List for Tenderizer

1 head        2¼ × 2¼ × 5
1 handle      16  × ⅝ diameter
or            16  × 1⅛ diameter
```

SCISSOR TONGS

Tongs have varied uses. They can dish out salad and some vegetables or pick up hot sausages and similar foods. The tongs in Fig. 5-8 have a scissor action and can be sized to suit your needs. If made 15 inches long, the gripping ends are about ¾ inch square, which should hold a fairly heavy load. If made 11 inches long, the ends are about 9/16 inch square and can still handle many things in the kitchen. Make the tongs from close-grained hardwood. Some diagonal grain cannot be avoided, but open-grained wood might break.

Redraw the squares shown (Fig. 5-8A) 1 inch for 15-inch tongs or ¾ inch for 11-inch tongs. Other sizes are possible to suit particular needs or available wood. The wood is ¾ inch thick for the large tongs and 9/16 inch thick for the smaller tongs.

1. The two pieces are identical. Mark their shapes (Fig. 5-8B).

2. Drill the finger and thumb holes before doing any shaping, then cut the outlines.

3. Reduce the handle ends to half thickness at the diagonal cuts (Fig. 5-8C). As drawn, the cuts allow the ends to open to about 4 inches or 3 inches according to size. Cut in on the diagonal lines.

4. Mark the pivot holes and drill small holes so a piece of wire can be pushed through to check the action. If this is satisfactory, enlarge the holes for a 3/16-inch brass bolt.

5. Round the edges well but leave the gripping ends as large as possible.

6. Assemble with a brass bolt and washers (Fig. 5-8D). Cut the screwed end close to the nut

and burr it over to prevent the nut coming off.

```
Materials List for Scissor Tongs

2 pieces          ¾ × 4 × 16
or                9/16 × 3 × 12
```

SPRING TONGS

An alternative to the scissors action in tongs is to provide a spring to keep the tongs open sufficiently, then you squeeze to grip leaves, onions, sausages, or other foods. The tongs in Fig. 5-9 are like small versions of the tongs sometimes used in the laundry. They are made of hardwood with a brass spring (Fig. 5-9A) and are shown with a maximum opening of about 2 inches.

1. Mark out the two sides (Fig. 5-9B) on a ¾-×-⅞-inch wood section. Leave the grips the full depth, but reduce most of the length to ½ inch thick. Round at the changes of section and at the top where the ends will meet.

2. At the grips, slope the meeting surfaces slightly (Fig. 5-9C and D) so the tips will close on the things you want to hold. Leave the meeting surfaces flat, but round all other edges.

3. The spring is strip brass ¾ inch wide. You should find that 18 or 20 gauge is springy enough. Use rolled brass, not extruded strip, which is intended for machining and not bending. Brass can be hardened and made springy by hammering. Hammer your strip well on an iron block with a flat-faced hammer. You can give it a pattern by hammering with a ball-faced hammer, as used for riveting.

4. Bend the spring to shape (Fig. 5-9E). The flat sides are set at about 15 degrees to each other with the bends 1¼ inches apart. Drill and fix to the wood with roundhead brass wood screws.

```
Materials List for Spring Tongs

2 pieces wood     ¾ × ⅞ × 11
1 piece brass     ¾ × 10 × 18 or 20 gauge
```

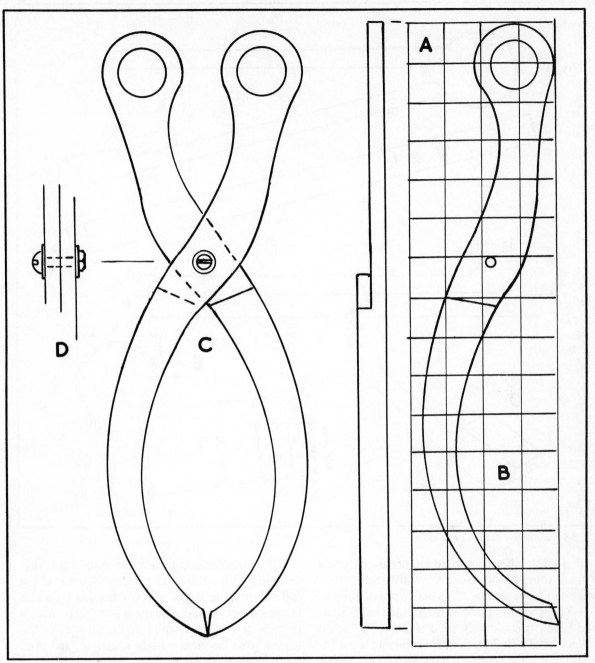

Fig. 5-8. Scissorlike tongs can be used for picking up leaves.

ROLLING PINS

Pastry can be rolled with almost anything round, such as a bottle, and there are glass and ceramic rollers, but the most popular rolling pins are wood.

Designs were stabilized a long time ago, and most cooks will want a traditional rolling pin. Sizes can be made to suit, but there is an advantage in size and weight. It is easier to roll an even thickness

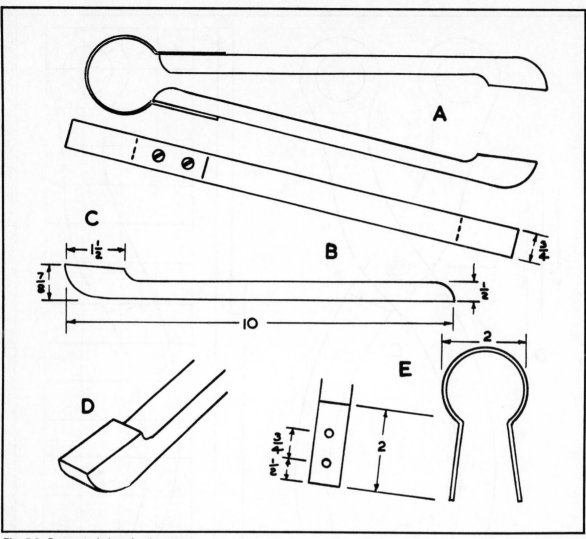

Fig. 5-9. Suggested sizes for the tongs.

with a large roller, but there are occasions when a small roller has its uses. A woodworker with a lathe can make several sizes and types of rollers.

The wood should be close-grained hardwood, and beech is commonly used if available. Some rollers have a slightly domed shape and are a little thicker at the center than the ends. This allows for the rocking action that many people apply and is believed to result in a more even thickness of pastry. It is probably wiser, though, to make rollers parallel to form a true cylinder. The working length should certainly not be hollow.

A professional chef favors a simple cylindrical roller with no shaping at the ends; some of his rollers are quite large. If you want this type in a home kitchen, a 15-inch length should be enough (Fig. 5-10A). Check with calipers throughout the length, give the ends a slight rounding, and sand thoroughly all over.

Most home cooks prefer a handle at each end (Fig. 5-10B). A maximum of 1¼ inches is the thickest most hands can comfortably grip. The parallel part should be between a 2-inch and 3-inch diameter. Its length should be at least 9 inches and

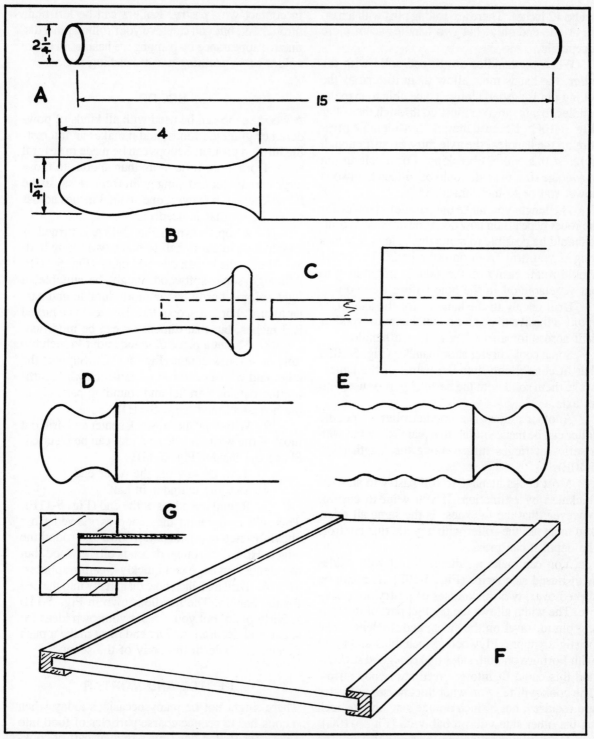

Fig. 5-10. Pastry rollers can be plain or have handles (A-E). A special board will control thickness (F, G).

can be 12 inches. There are rolling pins with a handle at one end only, but two handles seem more acceptable.

When the handles are turned solid with the roller, the hands must allow them to turn as the rolling pin is pushed along. To be able to grip the handles firmly, an axle must go through the roller (Fig. 5-10C). Because there is considerable pressure on the handles, the axle must be stiff enough to resist this without breaking. For a rolling pin of average size, the axle could be ½-inch hardwood dowel rod or ⅜-inch brass rod.

The length you make the parallel cylinder for the roller depends on how deep you are able to drill. It should be possible to make this at least 9 inches long if you drill from opposite ends. The roller should rotate easily on the axle. It might help to put vegetable oil in the hole before assembly.

Drill deeply in the handles for the axle. Use epoxy adhesive to secure a metal axle to wood or drill across for a metal pin in each handle.

Some cooks prefer short handles (Fig. 5-10D) that fit comfortably into the palms of the hands. Make them solid with the parallel part or use with an axle.

Another project is a noodle roller. A noodle roller can be made similar to a plain roller but with a series of ridges turned along the length (Fig. 5-10E).

Most cooks manage to roll pastry to an even thickness by estimation. If you want to ensure, however, that the thickness is the same all over, you must use the roller with a guide that controls the depth it can press.

You can make a suitable board with guides with raised side strips (Fig. 5-10F). If it can be turned over, two thicknesses of pastry are possible. The width allows the parallel part of the rolling pin to travel on the sides, and the length can be slightly more. Plywood ½ inch thick and faced with Formica on both sides makes a good surface, and this could fit into grooved hardwood strips. The cook will tell you what thicknesses of pastry are required, but ¼ inch on one side and ³⁄₁₆ inch on the other side will probably do (Fig. 5-10G).

Do not treat rollers on the parts that will be in contact with pastry. Rollers can be left plain throughout, but you can give your rolling pin a distinctive appearance by painting the handles in bright colors or by staining and varnishing them.

SCOOP

A wood scoop can be used with all kinds of powdered or granuled foods, and it makes an interesting turning project. Scoops can be made in several sizes, from those little more than spoons to those large enough for scooping grain from sacks. In the home kitchen, however, one about 3 inches across might be all that is needed.

The scoop shown in Fig. 5-11A is turned as a cylinder and cut in half to make two scoop bodies. The handle is then doweled into it (Fig. 5-11B). Although some softwoods might be suitable, a light-colored hardwood is more durable and easier to turn. For this scoop, the diameter to be turned is 3 inches, but that dimension can be modified.

1. Mount a piece of wood about ¾ inch too long on a screw center (Fig. 5-11C). Support the other end with a center in the tailstock while turning the outside parallel and rounding partially at the headstock end (Fig. 5-11D).

2. Withdraw the tailstock center and drill out most of the waste inside so a tool can be inserted. Shape the inside (Fig. 5-11E).

3. Turn or saw off the other end.

4. Saw the cylinder in half.

5. Round the edges at the end (Fig. 5-11F). This will also round the scoop as viewed from above. Match opposite sides. Thin and round the edges. How thin you go depends on the wood, but too slender an edge can quickly wear or splinter.

6. Drill a ½-inch hole diagonally into the end for the handle. The handle shown in Fig. 5-11B is fairly plain, but you can use your own ideas for shape and decoration. The end must make a push fit into the hole in the body of the scoop.

PESTLE AND MORTAR

There might not be many occasions today when a cook has to reduce coarse particles of food into finer ones, but at one time a regular part of cook-

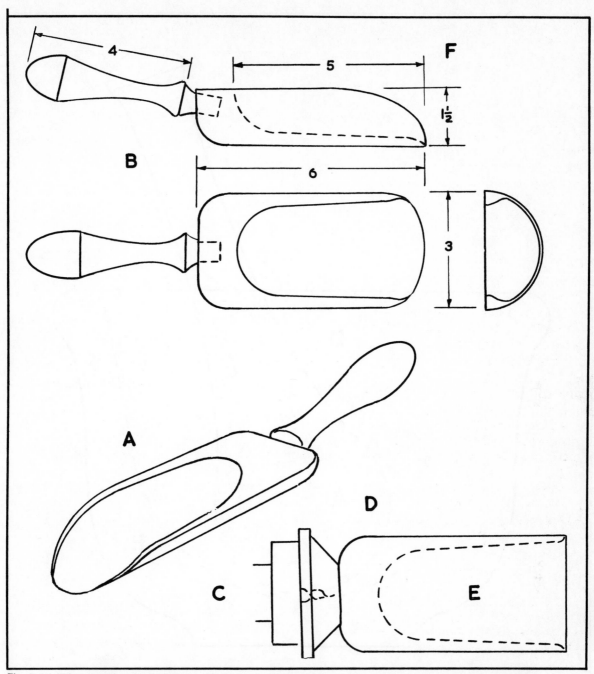

Fig. 5-11. This scoop has turned parts with the main piece turned for two scoops and cut along the middle.

ing was pounding grain to make flour or breaking up other granules into powder. The tools for doing this are a pestle and mortar, the mortar being the bowl into which the clublike pestle is pounded on the particles of food (Fig. 5-12).

This pair of items makes an interesting wood-turning project. The bowl should be a hardwood unlikely to fracture when hammered. The pestle

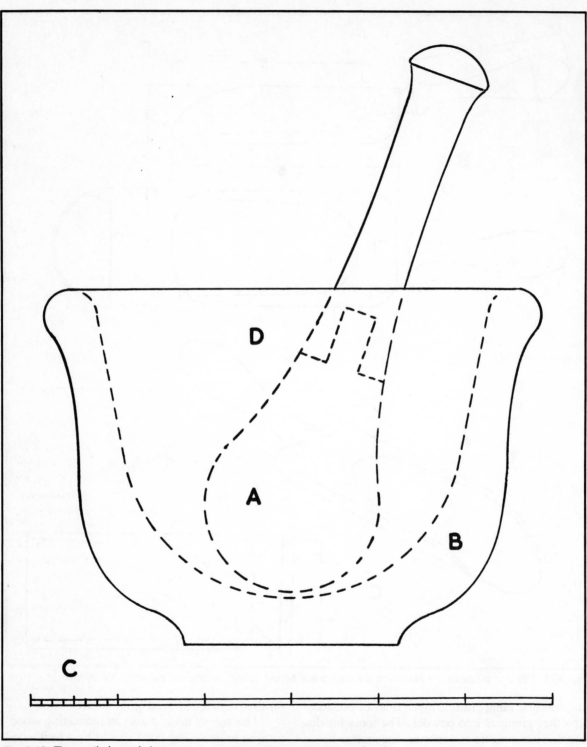

Fig. 5-12. The pestle is made in two parts, and its mortar is turned like a bowl.

could be one piece of hardwood, or the working end might be hard while a lighter handle is attached.

The important considerations are the curves of the meeting surfaces. The end of the pestle is part of a sphere (Fig. 5-12A). The inside of the mortar must be as near part of a sphere as possible (Fig. 5-12B). There must be no flattening toward the center, as is often the case with turned bowls. The pestle will be worked up and down at various angles within the limit of the bowl top. Whatever the angle, the pestle and mortar should make good contact, or some coarse particles will be missed.

The scale (Fig. 5-12C) represents inches as drawn, but it can be used as a guide to making the parts in other sizes. If the scale is used as inches, the mortar has a 6-inch diameter and a 4-inch depth and the pestle has a 2-inch diameter and 6½-inch length.

1. Turn the bowl on a faceplate starting with the inside. A card semicircular template will help shape it correctly.

2. When you are satisfied with the inside, shape the outside. Make it any pattern you wish but do not make the walls too thin, or they will weaken.

3. If the pestle is to be made in one piece, mount the wood between centers and turn it with the bottom towards the tailstock, where it will be easier to check the shape. Leave a short piece where the lathe center engages to cut off as the last stage. Shape the other end to make a comfortable grip. Give the body a slender curve.

4. If two pieces of wood are to be joined for the pestle (Fig. 5-12D), allow ample length and turn both cylindrically. Square the end of one and drill a hole in it. Turn a dowel to fit on the other and make sure the shoulder fits closely when glued and clamped. Turn the joined parts in the same way as the one-piece pestle.

5. Leave the wood untreated or soak it with vegetable oil.

BUTTER PATS

In the days when the housewife churned her own butter, she kept a pair of spadelike pats or "hands" to knead the butter into blocks of various shapes. You might want to work butter or margarine into squares, circles, octagons, and other shapes. A pair of pats can be used for picking up and shaping other foods when you do not want to use your hands and the size is too big for tongs.

The butter pats in Fig. 5-13 have ridged blades, but they could be made plain. The ridges provide grip and leave a pattern on butter or other soft food. Choose a close-grained hardwood, particularly if the ridges are to be cut. Suitable sizes are shown (Fig. 5-13A).

1. Prepare enough wood for two pats.

2. Mark to size and draw the outlines of the handles (Fig. 5-13B). One handle could be completed and used as a pattern for the other.

3. Cut ridges (Fig. 5-13C) not more than ³⁄₁₆ inch wide for most of the length of the blade. The cook might prefer to have one plain and one ridged pat.

4. Bevel the backs of the blades (Fig. 5-13D) and curve towards a thin end (Fig. 5-13E).

5. Round the edges of the handle.

6. Leave the wood untreated so it can be washed after use.

SKEWERS

A busy cook will find plenty of uses for wooden skewers, and a woodworker can use up odd pieces of dowel rod satisfying this need. Some skewers might not last long, so spare plain ones are always needed. Normally plain skewers are ¼ inch in diameter and about 6 inches in length, but others can be made thicker or thinner and to different lengths using hardwood dowel rods. Skewer points are usually round, but square points (Fig. 5-14A) are easier to make without a lathe and will penetrate meat easier.

Because it is often difficult to withdraw a plain skewer, a cook will appreciate a knob on the top. This could be a round wood head glued on (Fig. 5-14B). If you make your own, glue on a roughly shaped piece of wood, then hold the dowel in the lathe chuck while the knob is turned.

An interesting alternative is a cube with its corners trimmed off (Fig. 5-14C). This has the ad-

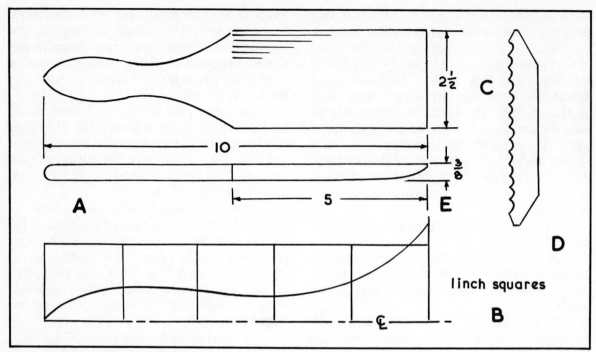

Fig. 5-13. Sizes and shape of a butter pat.

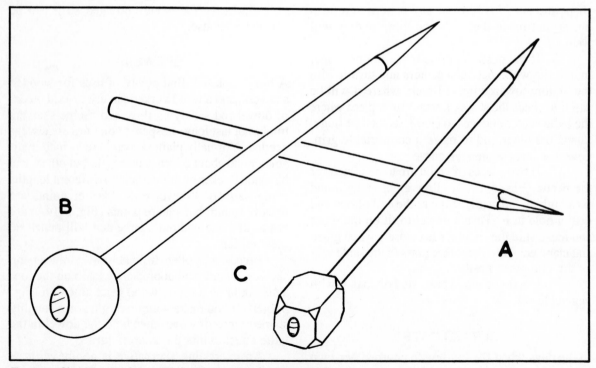

Fig. 5-14. Skewers are sharpened dowels that can be given knobs.

vantage of preventing the skewer from rolling when placed on a table. You could put a similar end on a pencil.

VEGETABLE PRESSER

A circular presser of sufficient area to cover most of the contents of a pan or colander can compress and squeeze out water from vegetables and other foods. It makes an interesting project if you have the use of a lathe. The disk should be a light-colored, close-grained hardwood. The handle could be the same or a wood of contrasting color.

The handle has a dowel to fit centrally into the disk (Fig. 5-15A). The important part is the smoothly domed surface of the disk (Fig. 5-15B). That could be turned while the disk is in a screw center in what will be the hole for the handle dowel.

1. Plane the flat back of the disk and saw the circle.

2. Mount the disk on a screw center and turn

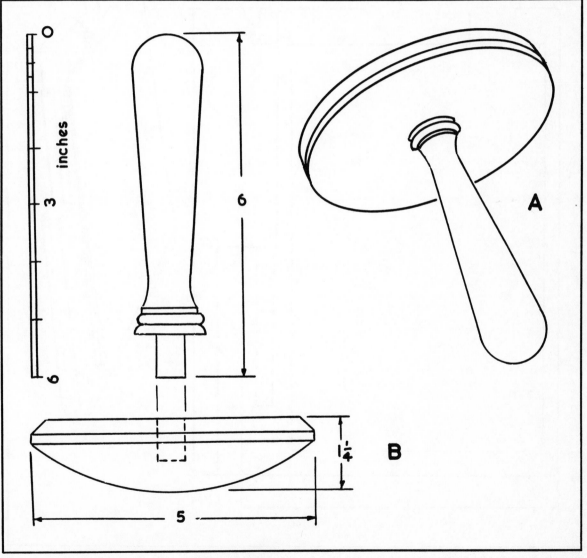

Fig. 5-15. This vegetable presser is turned in two parts.

the domed surface and beveled edge. Sand thoroughly to make the end that will be in contact with food as smooth as possible.

3. Remove from the lathe and drill the hole.

4. Turn the handle between centers, with the dowel end toward the tailstock to test its fit in the hole. Because the presser is used with a hand thrusting on the end of the handle, make that a spherical curve and a smooth surface.

5. You can stain and polish the handle be-

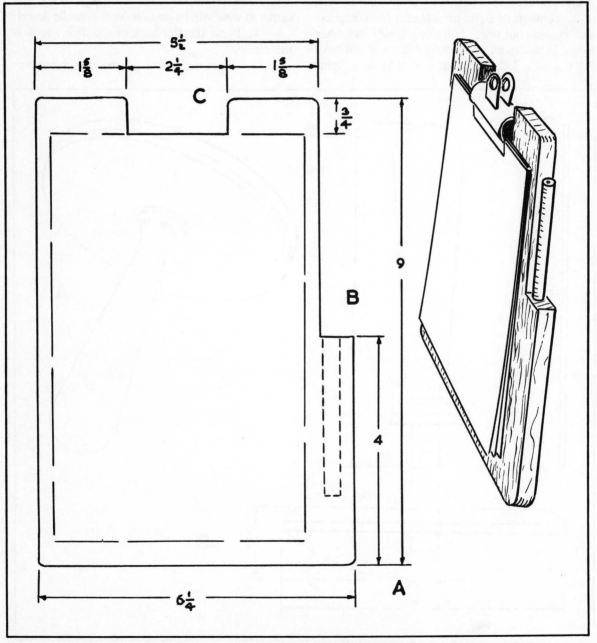

Fig. 5-16. This board for holding papers has a slot for a clip and a hole for a pencil.

fore you glue it to the untreated disk, if you wish.

COOK'S CLIPBOARD

A clipboard of modest size lets the cook make notes and hold coupons and recipe cards together. If the board is made stout enough, it can double as a chopping board or a hot pad.

The board in Fig. 5-16 is drawn to suit papers 5 × 8 inches, but you can choose sizes for whatever papers you regularly use. It should not be less than ½ inch thick, and would be better ⅝ inch if a standard pencil is to fit into a hole.

1. For the butcher block construction, glue together sufficient strips to make up the width (Fig. 5-16A).

2. If you have a long drill, the pencil hole can be drilled in the notched edge. Otherwise, drill a strip separately and glue it to the long side (Fig. 5-16B). Drill so a standard pencil will slip in easily.

3. At the top, the notch is intended to take a 2-inch paper clip (Fig. 5-16C). If the chosen clip will not open sufficiently to grip paper and the thickness of the board, cut a recess in the back of the board to reduce it sufficiently.

4. Round the corners and edges. Sand all over both sides.

5. If the board will also be used for chopping or standing hot pans on it, leave the wood untreated. If not, stain and varnish or polish it or paint it a bright color, if you wish.

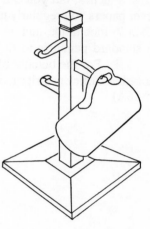

6

Racks

Much of the equipment in a kitchen is better stored on racks than enclosed in containers. You might reach for the item frequently, or you might need to keep it visible. Some things need to be kept open so they can dry after use. Certain kitchen contents might be decorative or attractive to you, and you prefer not to hide them away.

It is always a good idea to have a place for everything, even those that are not needed very often. If these objects are on a rack rather than in a drawer or other enclosed container, you can find them without searching.

Some racks are better made of metal. For nearly all things that are best kept on racks, however, wooden structures are at least as good as their metal counterparts. Wood racks also give a traditional and individual look to your kitchen. The racks you make are specially prepared and fitted to the surroundings and the needs of a particular cook. One advantage is that you can make your rack to fit into spaces a few inches bigger or smaller rather than making do with an ill-fitting, mass-produced rack.

Racks can be fitted to their contents, although such things as mugs, eggs, and wine bottles do not vary much. With many of the projects in this chapter, measure what you wish to store in case there is an advantage in altering some measurements.

For most racks you can use whatever wood seems appropriate to match other furniture, but for parts of light section or with fine detail, a close-grained hardwood is advised. Where the rack is not in direct contact with food, you can give it a furniture finish of stain and polish. Some items will look well if painted in bright colors.

PLATE RACK

Plates can be stood on edge between dowel rods. A wood rack is less liable to damage delicate china than a metal one. Because plates vary in size, any rack is a compromise, but the rack in Fig. 6-1 should take anything from saucers to large dining and serving plates. Mugs can be inverted over the posts.

The posts are ⅜-inch-diameter dowel rod mounted on ¾-inch-square strips, which could be

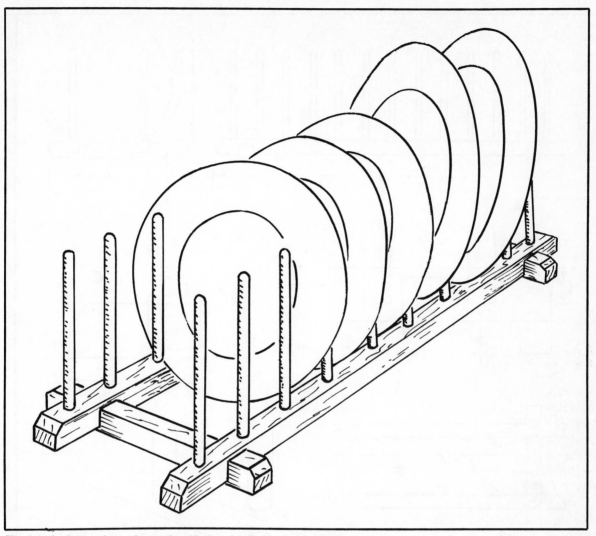

Fig. 6-1. A plate rack can be made with dowel rods in a halved base.

hardwood or softwood. An alternative folding version is suggested, and that would be better made of hardwood throughout. The sizes suggested (Fig. 6-2) take 12 plates, but any length is possible.

1. For neatness, all posts should be exactly the same length. Cut them with a jig. Round their tops.

2. Mark out the lengthwise pieces and drill for the dowel rods, using a stop to get all the holes the same depth (Fig. 6-2A). Mark the positions of the feet midway between the end posts (Fig. 6-2B).

3. Mark out the feet (Fig. 6-2C) and cut the

halved joints (Fig. 6-2D); keep the slots in the long parts shallow so the feet will be ⅛ inch below the bottoms of the long parts. The rack will then stand firm even if there is any unevenness in the supporting surface. Bevel the ends of the ¾-inch-square pieces.

4. Glue all the parts together. Check squareness.

5. The rack can be made to fold flat (Fig. 6-2E) if the feet are arranged to pivot on screws.

6. In this case, make the feet ⅝ inch thick so they do not lift the rack excessively. At each

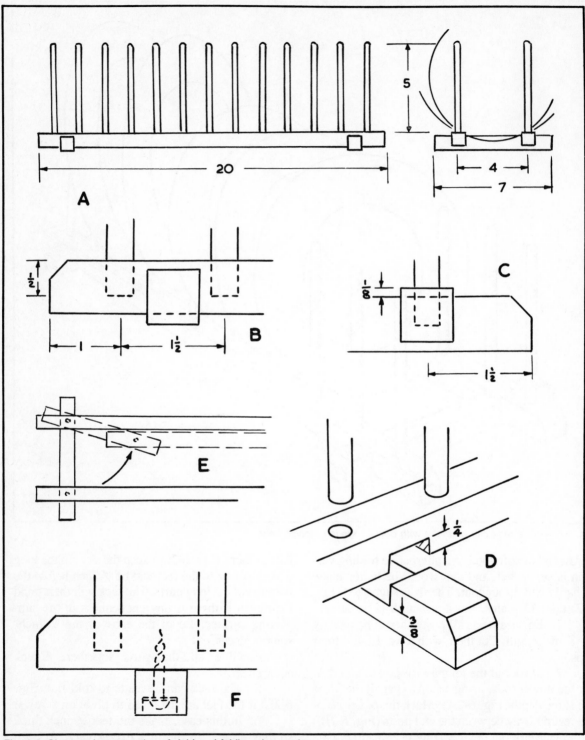

Fig. 6-2. Sizes and construction of rigid and folding plate racks.

Materials List for Plate Rack		
26 posts	6	× ⅜ diameter
2 strips	¾	× ¾ × 21
2 feet	¾	× ¾ × 8
or	⅝	× ¾ × 8 for folding

crossing drill for a screw (Fig. 6-2F). Counterbore so a metal washer and each screw head will be below the surface. You can probably let the wood parts bear against each other, but you could put thin washers between. Too free movement, however, is not required as you want there to be enough friction to hold the parts when ready to be folded.

SIMPLE MUG RACK

Mugs and cups can stand on a shelf, but those in constant use are better hung on hooks or pegs. There are several types of mug racks, but the important design considerations are the size and spacing of pegs. This requirement is common to most racks. Mugs are usually bigger than cups, but it is unusual for their diameter to be more than 3½ inches. That settles the amount of side clearance. Mugs all hung the same way tend to match each other and will hang with minimum clearance if the hooks or pegs are 4½ inches apart. This settles lengthwise spacing. Handles must admit a first finger, and the hole is not less than ¾ inch in diameter. Therefore, pegs must pass through a hole that size. Usually the handle is shaped and the clearance is more than that.

Mugs or cups can be hung from metal screw hooks driven into a board, but wood pegs look better and appeal to a woodworker. The type of pegs depend on whether a lathe is available or not. Both types, as described, are equally satisfying. The mug rack in Fig. 6-3 is a basic design for four mugs and is intended to be screwed to a wall or other vertical surface. It could be made other sizes and the back shaped, but the important parts are the pegs and their spacing. If you make a number of pegs, you can arrange them to suit your own ideas or to fit a certain space in any arrangement from a single peg upward.

1. The row of pegs (Fig. 6-3A) is shown at minimum spacing (Fig. 6-3B). Prepare and mark out the back to the size you want, marking the peg positions.

2. If you wish to make flat pegs, either make one and use it to mark others or make a template, which is advisable if you expect to make several racks. The outline (Fig. 6-4A) is intended for wood ⅜ inch thick and allows for a ½-inch-wide tenon into the back. Cut the pegs to shape. Clean saw marks from the outline and round all edges on the extending parts. In particular, round the edges of the knobs to give them a matching curved appearance.

3. You could buy turned pegs such as "Shaker" pegs, from the practice of that sect to hang furniture as well as clothing from turned pegs. Most bought pegs are too thick for mugs, however. Because the knob at the end must pass through a mug handle, it should not be much more than a ⅝-inch diameter. If you turn your own pegs (Fig. 6-4B), make the outside diameter ⅝ and the dowel end diameter ⅜ inch. Make one and use it as a pattern or make a template of the profile to produce a matching set.

4. Cut mortises for the flat peg tenons or drill holes for the dowel ends. Chamfer or round the board edges. It does not matter if the ends project at this stage. Put saw cuts across them so wedges can be used for tightening. Arrange the cuts across the grain of the back. Glue in the pegs and drive in glued tenons (Fig. 6-4C and D). Cut off level after the glue has set.

5. Drill for screws to the wall near each end of the back.

6. Give the wood a stained and polished or painted finish. The pegs could be a different color from the back.

Materials List for Simple Mug Rack		
1 back	½ × 2 × 17	
4 pegs	⅜ × ¾ × 4 flat	
or	¾ × ¾ × 4 turned	

SQUARE MUG TREE

Mugs or cups can be hung around a square pedes-

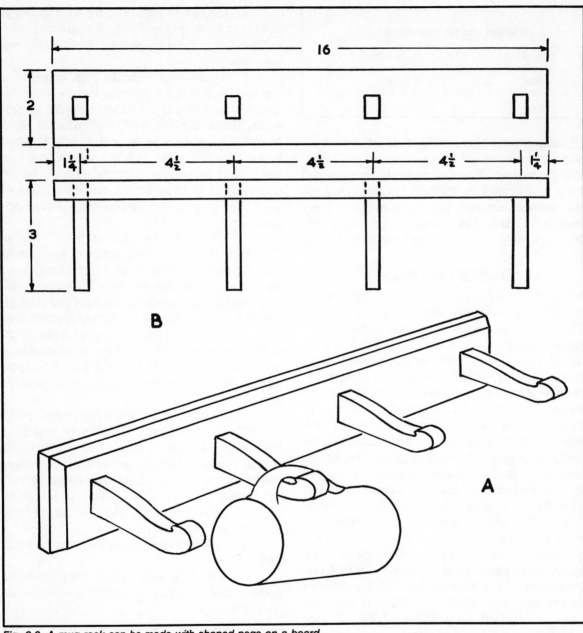

Fig. 6-3. A mug rack can be made with shaped pegs on a board.

tal, which can stand anywhere convenient and form a colorful display. The mug tree in Fig. 6-5A is intended for four mugs hung at different levels. Check the sizes of your mugs to see if they clear each other, but do not make the pedestal too high or the assembly might become unsteady. As drawn (Fig. 6-6), the pegs are arranged at 1½-inch vertical intervals.

The pegs are the same as in the simple rack (Fig. 6-4A). Make them and the other parts of the same wood, preferably a hardwood of reasonable weight for steadiness.

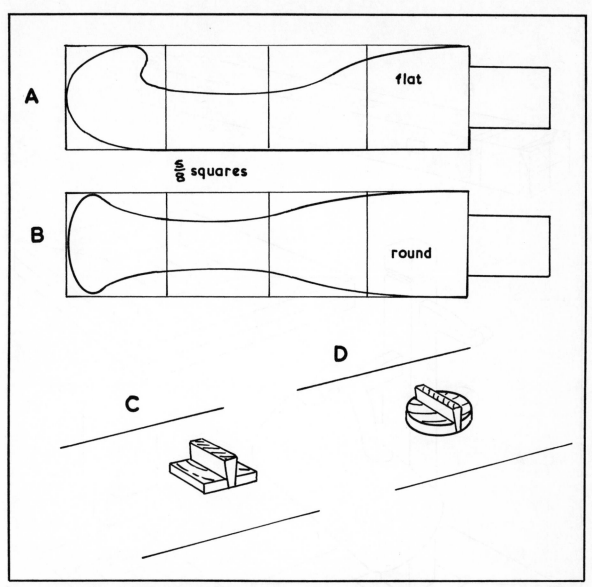

Fig. 6-4. Mug pegs can be flat (A) or round (B) and can be wedged at the back (C, D).

1. Make the four pegs completely, with well-rounded edges and tenons cut to fit in the pedestal.

2. Mark out the wood for the pedestal (Fig. 6-5B) with the positions of the pegs and details of the ends (Fig. 6-6A). There is one peg on each face and a decorated top (Fig. 6-6B), which can also serve as a knob for lifting.

3. Cut the mortises before doing other work on the pedestal.

4. AT the bottom, cut a tenon (Fig. 6-5C) for fitting into the base.

5. At the top, mark for a notch and cut this in a shallow V all around. Cut the end as a shallow square cone.

6. Make the base large enough to provide stability (Fig. 6-6C). Taper it to half thickness. Mark a flat 3-inch square at the center (Fig. 6-5D) and cut the mortise. Mark around the edges and

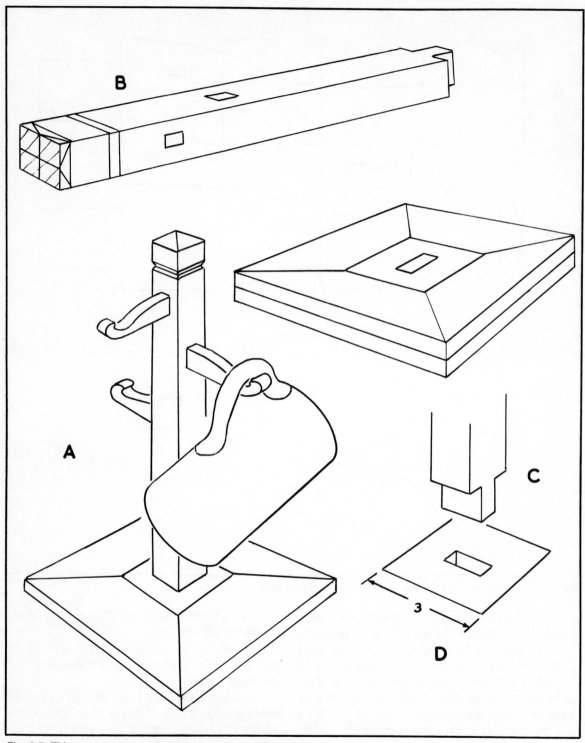

Fig. 6-5. *This square mug tree holds four mugs at different levels.*

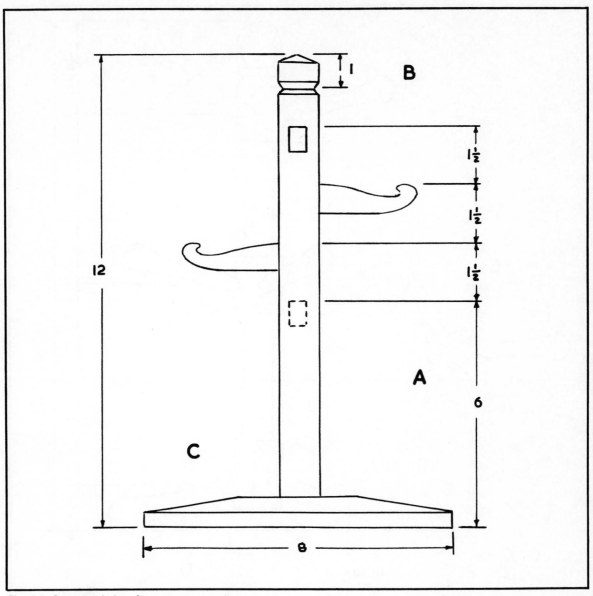

Fig. 6-6. Suggested sizes for a square mug tree.

plane the tapers.

7. Sand all parts before assembly. Take off any sharp edges.

8. Check the squareness of each joint as you make it because errors will be very obvious to viewers. Gluing the tenon in the base is sufficient, but it could also be wedged.

9. Finish with stain polish or use paint.

Materials List for Square Mug Tree

4 pegs	⅜ × ¾ × 4
1 pedestal	1 × 1 × 13
1 base	⅞ × 8 × 8

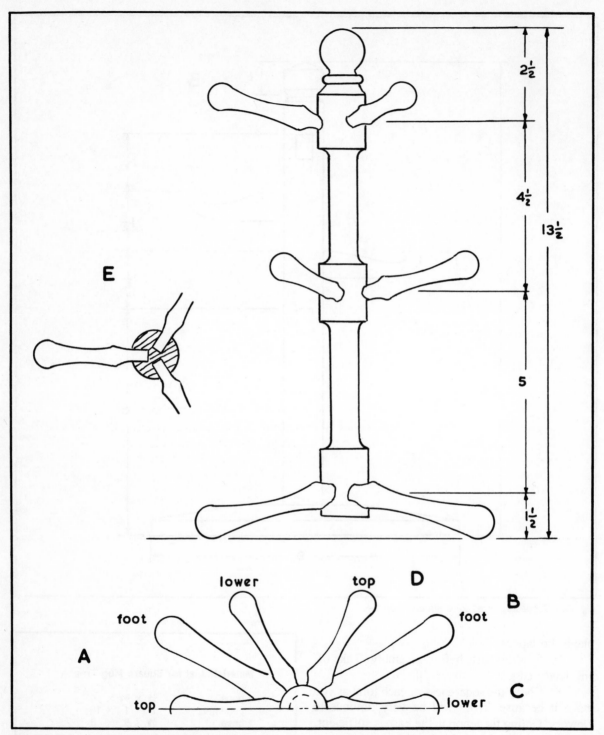

Fig. 6-7. Sizes and layout of the turned mug tree.

TURNED MUG TREE

A mug tree with all parts made on the lathe looks attractive and provides an interesting project for a woodworker with only the simplest lathe because all parts are of small diameter and are turned between centers. This turned mug tree is 13½ inches tall and has three feet covering about 8 inches. It is intended to hold six mugs.

The parts could be hardwood or softwood, but a moderate hardwood is easier to turn, with little risk of the grain breaking out. The sizes (Fig. 6-7) will suit most mugs, but if you have any unusual or bigger ones, the lower pegs could be lengthened.

The pegs are staggered in the circumference of the tree. At each layer they are evenly spaced, but the pegs on the top layer come midway between those on the lower layer when viewed from above, then the three feet come between both layer positions (Fig. 6-7A).

1. Start with the main spindle (Fig. 6-8A). Have the wood too long and turn it parallel to a 1¼-inch diameter. Mark where the thinner parts are to come and reduce them to a ¾-inch diameter (Fig. 6-8B).

2. Mark where the bottom will be cut off. Pencil around where the holes will be at the three positions. Turn the knob at the top (Fig. 6-8C). This is decorative, but it also serves as a handle for lifting.

3. Turn six pegs (Fig. 6-8D). Check that the knobs will pass through your mug handles. Drill a ⅜-inch hole in a thin piece of scrap wood and use it to test the parallel ends of each peg.

4. Turn three feet (Fig. 6-8E) to match the pegs but with the ends larger and 4½ inches long. The parallel part should fit a ⅜-inch hole.

5. To get the correct relative positions for the holes, divide the circumference of the spindle into 12. One way is to draw a circle the same size as the spindle and another, much bigger one around it (Fig. 6-8F). Divide the large circle into 12 and project lines inwards. Make the divisions by stepping off the radius around the circumference from the opposite ends of a diameter line. If you prefer to set out with a protractor, set the dividing lines at 30 degrees to each other.

6. Another way to divide the circumference is to wrap a strip of paper round the spindle and push a spike through the overlap. Open the paper flat and divide the distance between the spike holes into 12. Wrap the paper around the spindle again and mark through each of the twelve positions near the bottom end.

7. With the circumference divided into 12 at the bottom end, draw along every fourth position to mark the centers of the foot holes (Fig. 6-7B). Go around one-twelfth from those positions and project along the centers of the lower peg holes (Fig. 6-7C). G9o one-twelfth the other way from the feet positions and project along for the positions of the top pegs (Fig. 6-7D).

8. Mark the location of each hole position with a dent made with a spike or center punch.

9. Drill the holes until they almost meet (Fig. 6-7E). They are all at 15 degrees to horizontal (Fig. 6-8G). If possible, use a drill press with an angle setting or use the drill in a jig to maintain the correct angle. If you must drill freehand, use a hardboard template cut at a 75-degree angle as a sighting guide. Sand after drilling.

10. Assemble the feet to the spindle first and check that the spindle stands upright before final gluing. Fit the pegs in the same way.

11. Finish with stain and polish or paint the mug tree a bright color.

Materials List for Turned Mug Tree			
1 spindle	1⅜	× 1⅜	× 14
6 pegs	¾	× ¾	× 4
3 feet	1	× 1	× 5

LATTICE MUG RACK

Traditionally, crossing strips have been used for many types of racks. They can fold, but that makes bulky joints that could be a source of weakness. The mug rack in Fig. 6-9, which screws to a wall, has the crosspieces notched together so they cannot fold, but there is ample strength. The rack holds ten mugs, but it could be shortened to four or seven

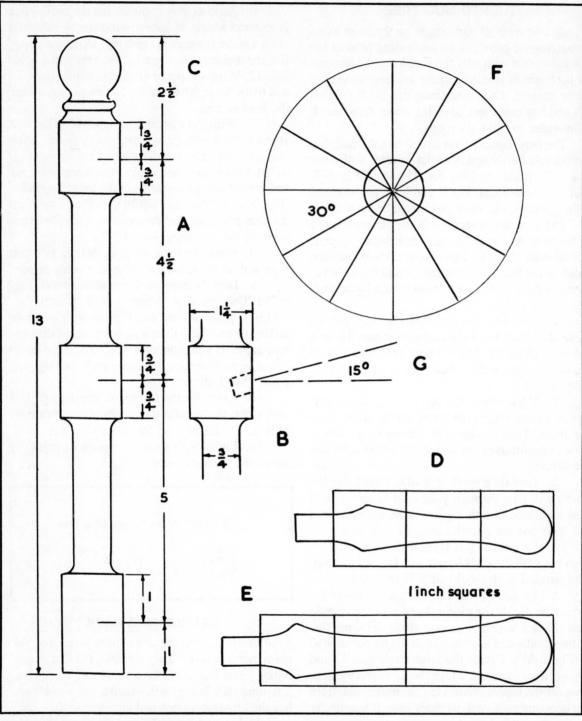

Fig. 6-8. Parts and angles for the mug tree.

Fig. 6-9. Halved strips and pegs make a rack for mugs and other things.

or lengthened to any number. If made with parts of the sizes shown, the finished rack is about 12 inches deep and 30 inches long. It is intended for pegs the same as those of the simple rack (Fig. 6-4B), but these or slightly larger Shaker pegs also would make the rack suitable for clothing or the cook's aprons and coveralls. The assembly is made of several strips halved together, then the dowel ends of the pegs go through the holes at the center of each joint (Fig. 6-10A).

1. Prepare sufficient strips of ⅝-inch × ¼-inch wood.

2. Mark out four pieces with three notches (Fig. 6-10B) and four pieces with two notches at the same spacing (Fig. 6-10C). Use the actual wood as a guide when marking the width of each joint. Cut the joints carefully to keep adjoining surfaces level.

3. Prepare the ten pegs, making the dowels long enough to go through the joints (Fig. 6-10D). If you turn your own, use a hole in scrap wood, made with the bit you use, to test the dowels as you turn them.

4. The ends of the strips are shown cut square. This is usual, but you could round or bevel them if you want your rack to have a custom appearance. In any case, finish the edges and ends smoothly.

5. Sand all parts before gluing the joints. Leave drilling the holes until the joints are made, the glue set, and any surplus glue removed.

6. Make sure the pegs fit squarely. Level any projecting dowel ends. Drill two ends strips for screws to the wall.

7. Finish the wood to match existing furniture.

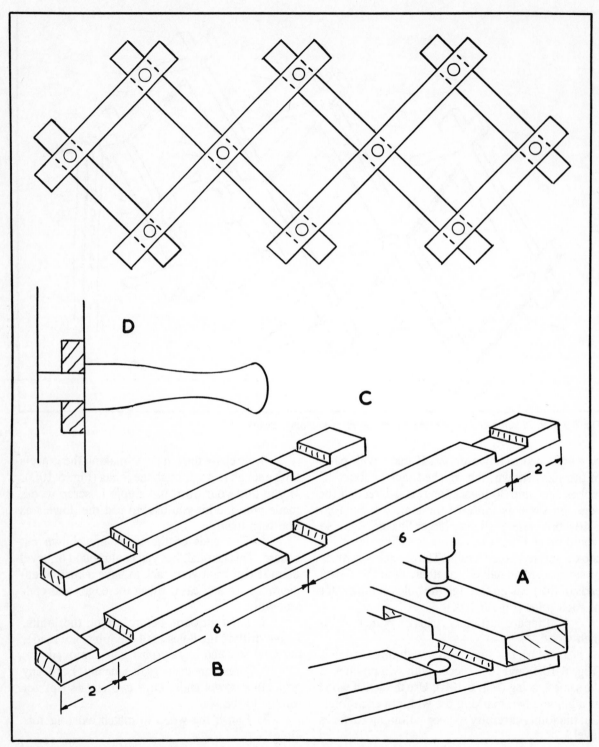

Fig. 6-10. Details of parts of the rack.

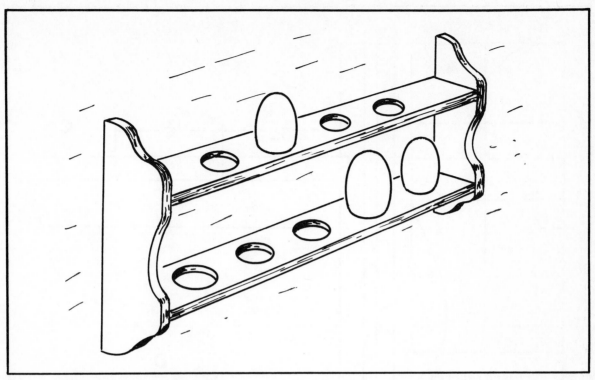

Fig. 6-11. This egg rack uses pierced shelves.

Materials List for Lattice Mug Rack

4 strips	⅝	× 1¼ × 17
4 strips	⅝	× 1¼ × 11
10 pegs	¾	× ¾ × 6

EGG SHELVES

Eggs are comparatively fragile and are best stored separately. Shelves with holes will protect eggs from damaging each other. Unless your hens lay unusual eggs, holes with a 1⅜-inch diameter can support eggs, and these could be in shelves 2 inches wide. Gaps between holes can be ¾ inch. These sizes settle the basic layout of egg racks.

The rack in Fig. 6-11 has two shelves supported between ends and is intended to screw to a wall, inside a cupboard door, or on any other vertical surface. There is ample clearance between the shelves, but the holes in one shelf come midway between those in the other shelf to reduce the risk of knocking an egg out of the top shelf when removing one from below.

The shelves could be made any length. With the spacing suggested (Fig. 6-12), a pair of shelves for five eggs on the top and six on the bottom would be about 13 inches long. Shelves fit into dadoes at the ends. Below the back of the top shelf is a strip that stiffens the assembly and can be drilled for fixing screws.

1. Prepare material 5⁄16 × 2 inches for ends and shelves.

2. Mark out the pair of ends (Fig. 6-12A). Use the 1-inch squares as a guide to shaping the outlines. For simpler shapes there could be bevels at top and bottom, with straight front edges.

3. Mark the dado widths to suit the shelves and cut them ⅛ inch deep (Fig. 6-12B).

4. Make the shelves the same length but mark the hole positions on them (Fig. 6-12C and D). Drill the holes. Be careful of grain breaking out. It might be advisable to drill partially from each side.

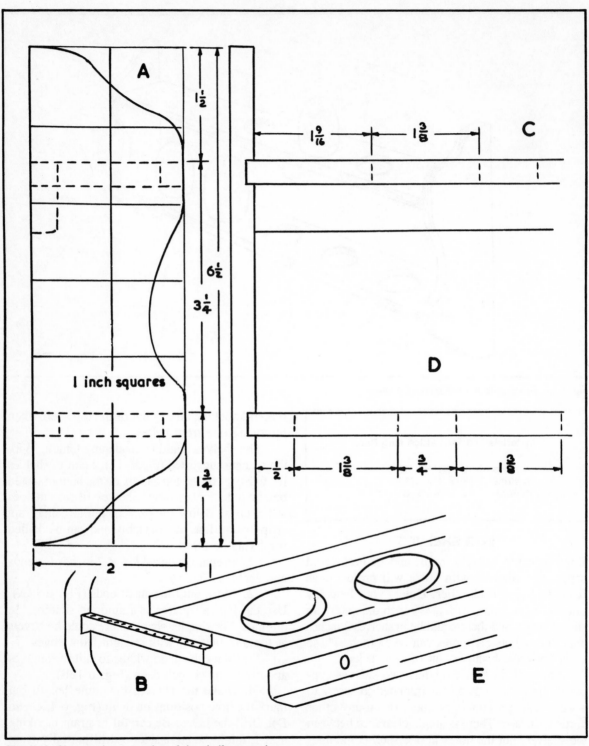

Fig. 6-12. Sizes and construction of the shelf egg rack.

5. Make the screw strip (Fig. 6-12E) to fit between the ends. Round its lower front edge. Drill it for a screw to the wall at each end.

6. Round the forward edges of the shelves and ends. Sand around the top edges of the egg holes.

7. Assemble the parts with glue and pins driven into the shelves through the ends and from the top shelf into the screw strip. Check the assembly for squareness and freedom from twist.

8. Finish with polish or paint.

Materials List for Egg Shelves

2 ends	5/16 × 2 × 7
2 shelves	5/16 × 2 × 14
1 screw strip	5/16 × 5/8 × 14

TAKE-DOWN EGG STAND

It is convenient to have eggs in a stand on a table or countertop. The stand in Fig. 6-13 holds twelve eggs, with four on a central top shelf and the others in two rows on a wider lower shelf. The ends are eggshaped and have finger holes so you can lift the stand.

The shelves fit to the ends with tenons, which are held with wedges. If the wedges are knocked out, the parts will pack flat. The shelves and ends could be made of ½-inch plywood or would look attractive if made butcher block fashion with several solid wood strips glued to make up the width. Softwood or hardwood could be used. Whatever is used for the shelves and ends, use hardwood for the wedges.

1. Mark out the two ends (Fig. 6-14A), but

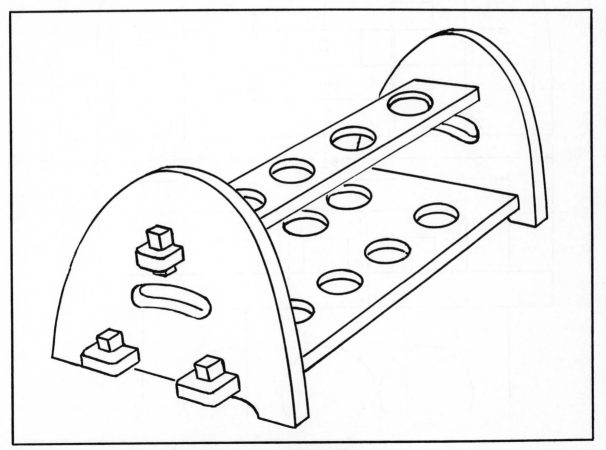

Fig. 6-13. This egg rack has wedged tenons and can be disassembled.

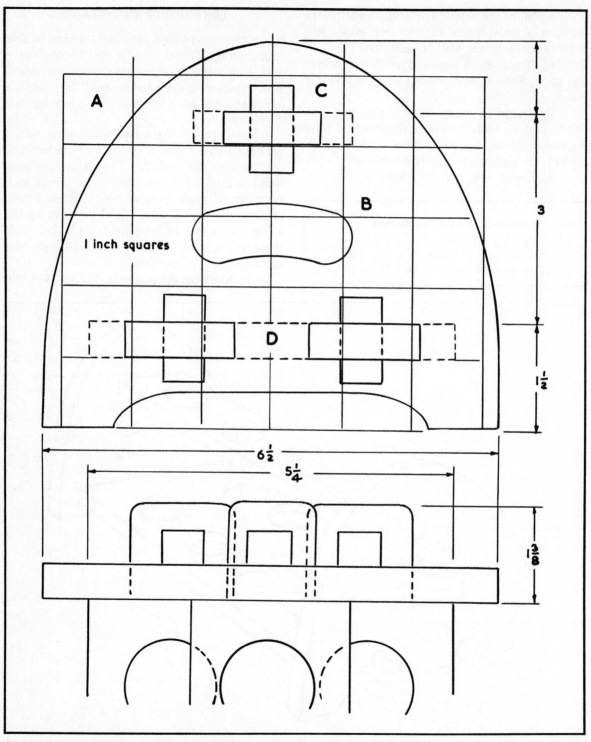

Fig. 6-14. Sizes and shape of the egg rack ends.

do not cut the outline until after the holes are made.

2. Make the finger holes by drilling two, ¾-inch holes and sawing away the waste between them (Fig. 6-14B). Smooth and round the edges.

3. The top shelf is 2¼ inches wide (Fig. 6-15A) and the bottom one is 5¼ inches wide (Fig. 6-15B). Both are 11¼ inches long, if the rack is to hold three rows of four eggs. Lengthening by 2 inches will allow three more eggs; you can arrange the rack to any reasonable length.

4. Mark a central tenon at each end of the top shelf (Fig. 6-15C) and mark the mortise to match on each end (Fig. 6-14C).

5. Mark the pair of tenons at each end of the bottom shelf (Fig. 6-15D) and mark the mortises to match on each end (Fig. 6-14D).

6. Cut the mortises and tenons, making them a push fit. Round the outer corners of the tenons. For the sake of appearance, let all tenons project the same amount and give them matching curves.

7. Mark and drill the 1⅜-inch egg holes.

8. Cut the outlines of the ends and round the upper edges.

9. Make six wedges from wood ⅝ inch thick; give them all the same taper (Fig. 6-15E). They could be slightly too long at first and trimmed later.

10. For the wedges to pull the tenons tight, the sockets for the wedges must be undercut (Fig. 6-125F). Then as a wedge is driven, its outer surface presses on the tenon and the inner surface bears on the surface of the egg stand end. Cut all the sockets to match the slopes and widths of the wedges.

11. Make a trial assembly. If necessary, trim the wedges to project the same amount above and below the tenon, then round all outer edges.

12. Separate the parts for sanding and finish with stain and polish or paint.

Materials List for Take-Down Egg Stand				
1 shelf	½	×	2¼	× 12
1 shelf	½	×	5¼	× 12
2 ends	½	×	6	× 7
6 wedges	½	×	⅝	× 1½

TURNED EGG STAND

A two-tier round egg stand to hold twelve eggs looks attractive in the kitchen and is an interesting project if you have the use of a lathe. All the parts of the stand in Fig. 6-16 can be made on a lathe.

Use hardwood. The two disks are ½ inch thick and well- seasoned to reduce the risk of warping. The two parts of the spindle are 1½ inches thick and could be made from a wood of a contrasting color. The knob at the top is both decorative and used as a lifting handle. The stand rests on three feet.

1. The two disks have similar arrangements of holes for eggs, but the upper disk has a 6-inch diameter and the lower one increased to a 6½-inch diameter for stability. Plane the wood to thickness and saw it slightly oversize. Mount a piece on a screw center and turn its arm with a slightly curved section (Fig. 6-17A).

2. Mark the egg holes in a circle of a 2-inch radius (Fig. 6-17B). Step off the radius around the circumference to get six equal spacings. Drill 1⅜-inch holes at these positions (Fig. 6-17C). Round the edges of the holes by sanding. Drill 1-inch holes at the centers for the spindle dowels.

3. On the underside of the bottom disk mark the positions of the centers of three feet (Fig. 6-17D), midway between alternate egg holes and 2⅝ inches from the disk center. Drill ⅜-inch holes halfway through at these positions.

4. Make the three feet with a ¾-inch diameter and a ½-inch depth with rounded edges similar to those of the disks. Turn dowels to fit the holes in the lower disk.

5. The spindles can be turned to any design you wish, but suitable shapes are shown (Fig. 6-17F and G). Thinning the center of the lower part makes it easier to grip an egg. The bottom of the spindle has a simple dowel in the lower disk. A similar dowel goes into the upper disk, but its center is drilled for a dowel from the top spindle (Fig. 6-17H).

6. Turn the lower spindle 3 inches between shoulders with a 1½-inch diameter. Turn dowels to fit holes at the centers of the disks. Make the

EAU CLAIRE DISTRICT LIBRARY

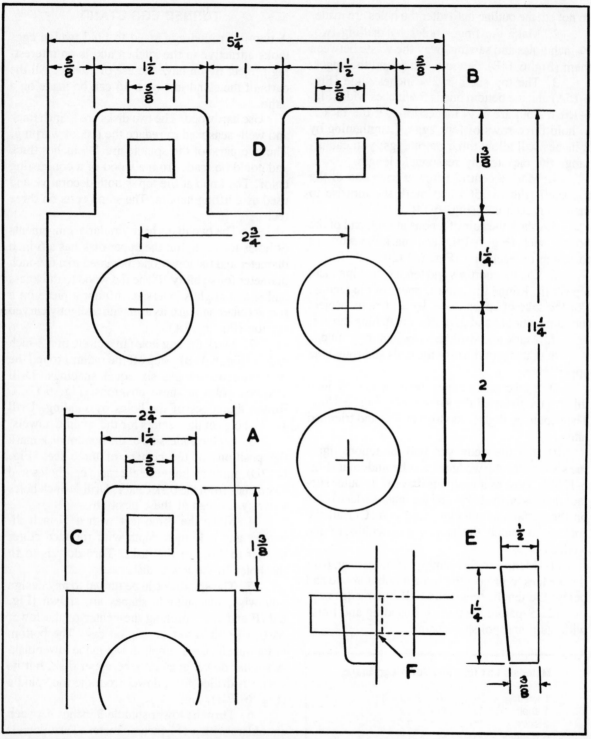

Fig. 6-15. Sizes of the egg rack shelves and wedge details.

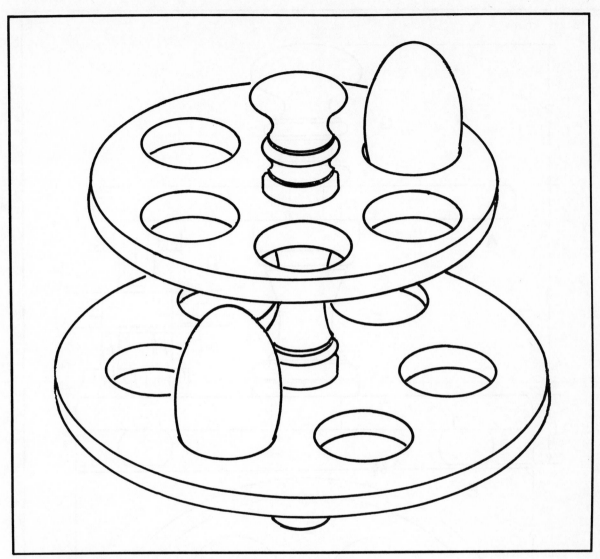

Fig. 6-16. The shelves of this egg rack are supported on a turned pillar.

pattern between the shoulders (Fig. 6-l7F).

7. Turn the top spindle (Fig. 6-17G). The knob has a 1½-inch diameter, but the shoulder can have a 1¼-inch diameter and the dowel a ½-inch diameter. Give the knob a good shape to grip. Drill the lower dowel to take the top dowel.

8. Glue the feet into the lower disk. When you join the disks with the spindles, arrange the upper egg holes so they come between the holes in the lower disk to give maximum clearance when removing eggs.

9. A clear, polished finish over an attractive wood will look good, or the stand could be painted.

Materials List for Turned Egg Stand

1 piece	½	×	7	×	7	
1 piece	½	×	6½	×	6½	
1 piece	1¾	×	1¾	×	6	
1 piece	1¾	×	1¾	×	3	

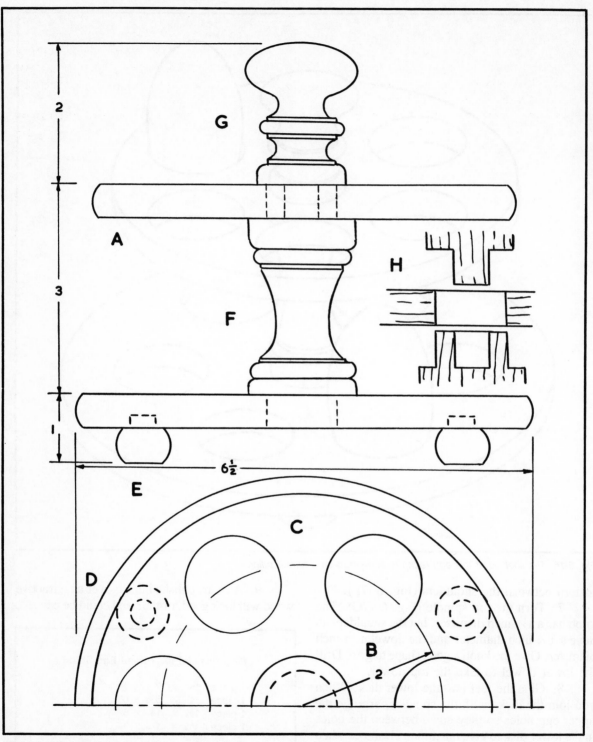

Fig. 6-17. Sizes and details of the round egg rack.

OCTAGONAL EGG STAND

You can make an egg stand similar in design to the turned egg stand without using a lathe by using octagonal outlines (Fig. 6-18). It is about the same overall size but holds eight eggs. By increasing the sizes of the trays, it could hold eight eggs on each layer, but it then would need to be about 10 inches across, with some waste space towards the center. As drawn in Fig. 6-19, the trays are ½ inch thick and the pedestal is octagonal.

The trays could be ½-inch plywood, but they will look better in solid wood, possibly several strips glued to make up the width. The pedestals are solid wood.

1. Plane the wood for the trays to thickness and mark them out square. To convert a square

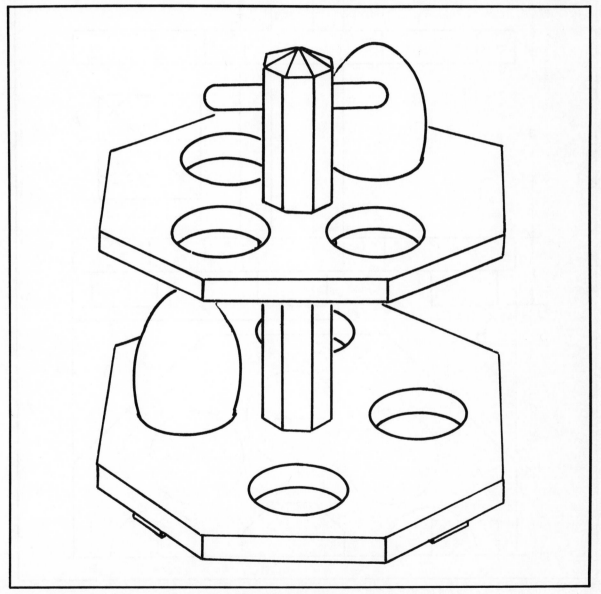

Fig. 6-18. This egg rack has octagonal shelves and matching pillar.

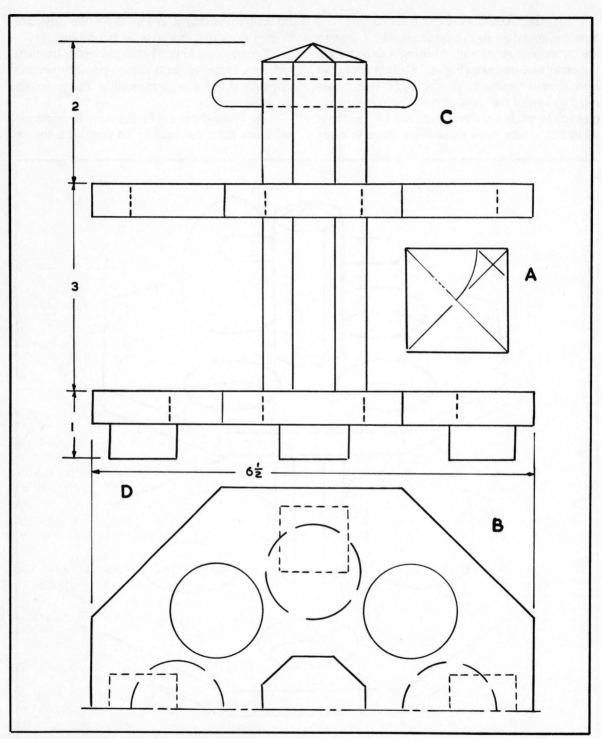

Fig. 6-19. Suggested sizes of the octagonal egg rack.

to a regular octagon, draw diagonals, then measure half a diagonal. Mark that distance from a corner along an edge (Fig. 6-19A). Do that in both directions from each corner and join the marks. If this has been done correctly, all eight sides should match. Before cutting the wood to size, mark the positions of the egg holes 2 inches from the tray center and opposite the centers of alternate sides (Fig. 6-19B). Drill 1⅜-inch holes and sand their edges.

2. When you cut the joints, arrange the assembly so the holes in the top tray will come between those in the bottom tray.

3. Prepare a piece of wood long enough for both parts of the pedestal. Make it 1½ inches square. At one end construct a regular octagon in the same way as described for the trays. Project the lines of the corners along to mark where the angles of the square have to be planed off, but you can leave planing the wood octagonal until the joints have been cut. These are mortises and tenons, but at the upper tray, the tenons fit into each other inside the mortise in the tray.

4. At the bottom of each piece, cut a tenon ½ inch wide and 1 inch across (Fig. 6-20A) centered on the wood and long enough to go through a tray.

5. At the top of the lower pedestal, cut a tenon 1 inch square, then remove the center to take the tenon on the upper part (Fig. 6-20 B and C). The tenons at the upper tray must not extend past its thickness, but it does not matter if the tenon at the lower tray was left too long and planed off later.

6. Cut a mortise at the center of the bottom tray to take the ½-×-1-inch tenon. Cut a mortise in the top tray to take the meeting tenons (Fig. 6-20D).

7. Make a lifting handle on the top pedestal with a piece of ⅜-inch dowel rod (Fig. 6-19C).

8. Round the top or shape it to a shallow cone (Fig. 6-20E). Round the ends of the dowel rod and glue it in a hole just below the top.

9. The feet can be pieces of ½-inch wood, 1 inch square (Fig. 6-19D). Make four and locate them under the bottom tray midway between the egg holes. Gluing might be sufficient or a screw could be driven upwards through each one.

10. When you assemble, see that the pedestal is square to the trays, which are parallel. Arrange the handle to cross between egg holes in the top tray and the holes in that tray over the spaces in the other tray.

11. Finish with stain and polish, although plywood would be better painted.

Materials List for Octagonal Egg Stand

2 pieces ½ × 7 × 7
1 piece 1½ × 1½ × 8

TOOL RACK

A cook can keep all her tools and implements in a drawer, in a box, or standing in a jar. She might appreciate having them separate in a rack standing on the table or countertop. The rack in Fig. 6-21 has two rows of holes to hold tool handles leaving working ends upward. There are two levels to allow for items of different lengths.

Suggestions are offered for sizes (Fig. 6-22), but you can assemble the spoons, spatulas, and other things you will put in the stand and arrange holes and slots to suit, allowing enough clearance but no excess length. As drawn, the central piece is ¾ inch thick and the other parts are ½ inch. Any wood can be used. Assembly is with glue and fine nails set below the surface and covered with stopping.

1. Decide on the layout and make the holes and slots large enough to allow an easy fit. The holes and their spacing will determine the length of the rack. For the instructions, this is assumed to be 12 inches.

2. Mark out the bottom (Fig. 6-22A).

3. Make the upright (Fig. 6-22B) the same length.

4. Allow for the thickness of the upright as you mark out the two upper parts. One fits at the side of the upright (Fig. 6-22C) and the other goes over it (Fig. 6-22D). Mark the holes and slots to

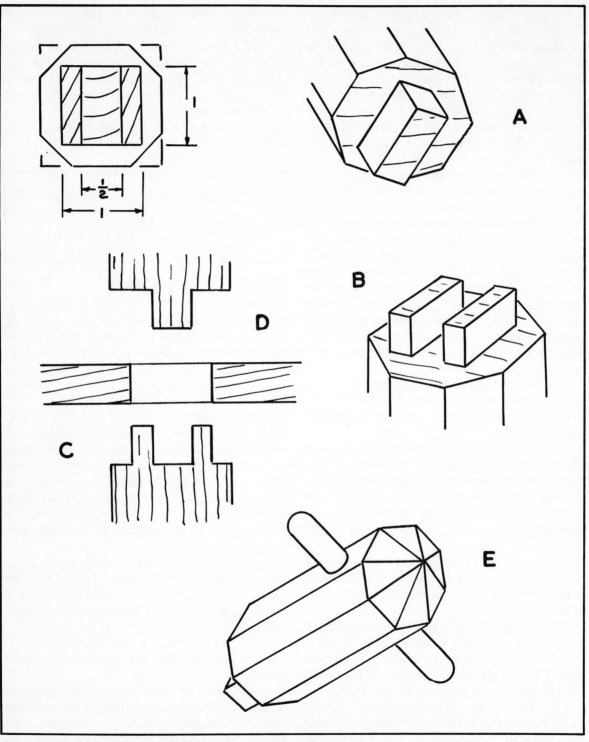

Fig. 6-20. Pillar joint for the octagonal egg rack.

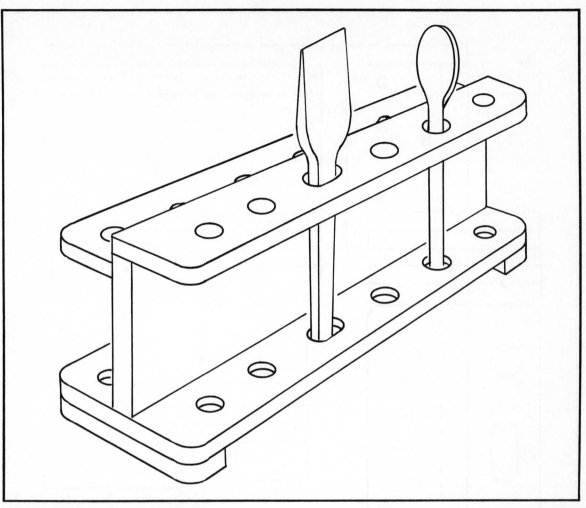

Fig. 6-21. A rack to take a variety of items.

match those on the bottom, so anything pushed through will stand upright.

5. Drill through the upper parts and round the edges of the holes by sanding.

6. The holes in the bottom should only go halfway through. They will look better if there is no mark from the central spur of the bit. Forstner bits make good holes because they do not have spurs (Fig. 6-22E). Alternatively, if you are not willing to accept the marks from the spurs of other bits, the bottom could be made of two pieces (Fig. 6-22F) with a drilled piece over a solid piece.

7. Feet across the ends (Fig. 6-22G) raise the rack and help it stand level.

8. Join the feet to the bottom, then round the outer corners of this and the top pieces.

9. Assemble with glue. The bottom can have screws upwards into the upright, but set and stopped nails will be neater elsewhere.

10. Finish the wood in any way you wish.

Materials List for Tool Rack			
1 bottom	½ ×	4¾ ×	13
1 upright	¾ ×	4½ ×	13
1 top	½ ×	2¾ ×	13
1 top	½ ×	2 ×	13
2 feet	½ ×	1 ×	5

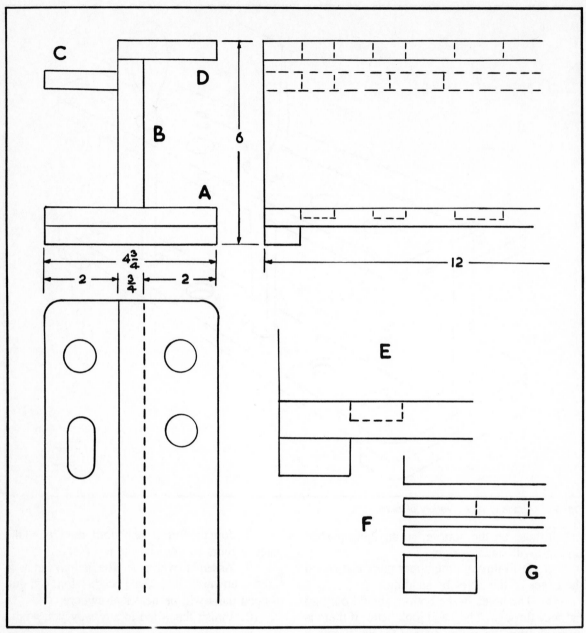

Fig. 6-22. Sizes and construction of the rack.

PAPER ROLL STAND

Paper kitchen rolls need to be readily available, yet it is unsatisfactory to leave them loose where they can roll off a table or unwind unintentionally. A vertical stand will hold a roll ready for use and can be lifted to wherever required. These paper roll stands could be made to suit plastic film or other rolled materials, as well as paper rolls, if the sizes are adapted. The sizes given (Fig. 6-23) suit most paper rolls, but measure the ones you use regularly and alter the sizes if necessary.

Two basically similar designs are suggested—

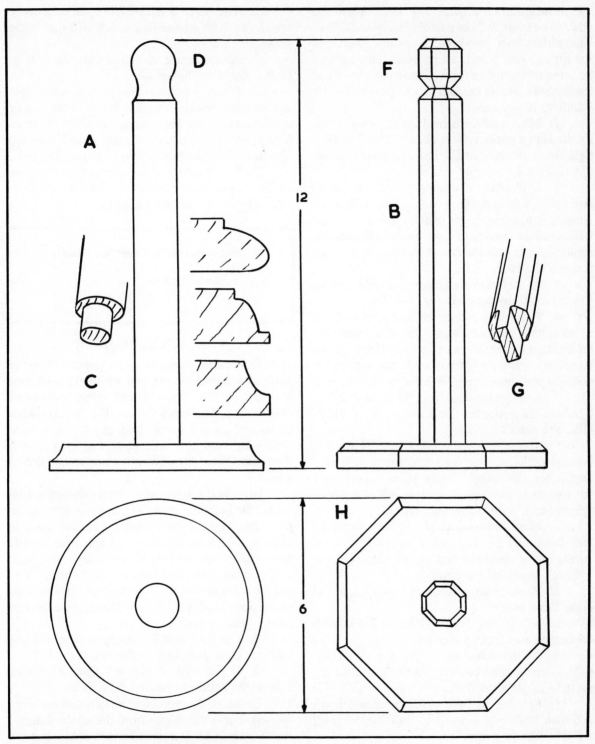

Fig. 6-23. Sizes for round and octagonal stands.

one to be made on a lathe (Fig. 6-23A) and the other to be made without a lathe (Fig. 6-23B). Both have pillars fitted into broad bases and knob tops for lifting. Any wood can be used. There might be some advantage in the weight to use hardwood for the base, but its breadth should provide ample stability, in any case.

1. Make sure the turned spindle passes easily through a paper roll. It does not have to be a tight fit—a 1⅛-inch or 1¼-inch diameter is suitable. Turn a cylinder of this size.

2. Drill a hole in a scrap of wood the same size as the hole in the base and use this as a gauge when you turn the dowel end (Fig. 6-23C). You will avoid the trouble of leveling the end after assembly if you turn the dowel just too short to go through the base.

3. At the top turn a knob to a shoulder about 1½ inches from the end (Fig. 6-23D).

4. Plane the wood for the base level and saw a disk slightly oversize. Mount this on a screw center and turn the rim and surface true. The edge can be turned to any design you wish. Some possible sections are shown (Fig. 6-23E).

5. Remove the base from the lathe and drill a hole at the center for the dowel on the spindle. Glue the parts together.

6. The parts of the other stand have octagonal outlines. Start by preparing a sufficient length for the spindle, truly square. Errors of squareness or differences in sizes will affect conversion to a good octagonal section.

7. Mark the wood for planing an octagon by measuring half the diagonal of an end from each corner on each face and marking it. Also mark the 1½-inch length of the knob.

8. Plane to an octagon and check that the eight faces match.

9. Shape the knob (Fig. 6-23F) with 45-degree cuts from each face.

10. At the other end mark a tenon (Fig. 6-23G) but do not cut until you mark and cut the mortise to get a good fit.

11. Prepare the base to thickness and mark a 6-inch square to convert to an octagon (Fig. 6-23H). Cut to shape.

12. The edges could be left square, but they are shown with a chamfer, which will match the knob.

13. At the center mark and cut a mortise to fit the tenon on the spindle.

14. If the spindle-to-base joint is not a tight fit, on either stand, make a saw cut in the end of the dowel or tenon for a wedge to be driven from below, otherwise use only glue. Check that the spindle is upright when viewed from any direction.

15. Finish with stain and polish or paint. Glue a disk of cloth on the underside of the base to prevent slipping or marking a surface.

Materials List for Paper Roll Stand

1 spindle	1¼	×	1¼ × 13
1 base	¾	×	6 × 7

PAPER ROLL HANGER

If it is more convenient to hang a paper roll on the wall, a suitable hanger can be made with two brackets and slots into which a rod can be dropped (Fig. 6-24). The sizes shown (Fig. 6-25) take a paper roll about 9 inches long and 4 inches wide with a hole through the center of at least 1-inch diameter. There are alternative turned and dowel rods.

Any wood can be used, but hardwood is better for the brackets; there will be some short grain here that might break in use if a fragile wood is chosen. Check the sizes of your usual paper rolls and modify the hanger, if necessary. The back could be cut square or given a shaped outline. The brackets are shown for a turned rod. If you wish to use dowel rod, you will need to increase the size of the hollow slightly.

1. Cut the wood for the back (Fig. 6-25A) and mark the positions of the brackets on it.

2. If you wish to give it a shaped outline, follow the squared drawing (Fig. 6-26).

3. Mark the wood for the two rackets (Fig. 6-25B). Draw the shapes from the squared drawing (Fig. 6-26B). If a turned rod is used, start the

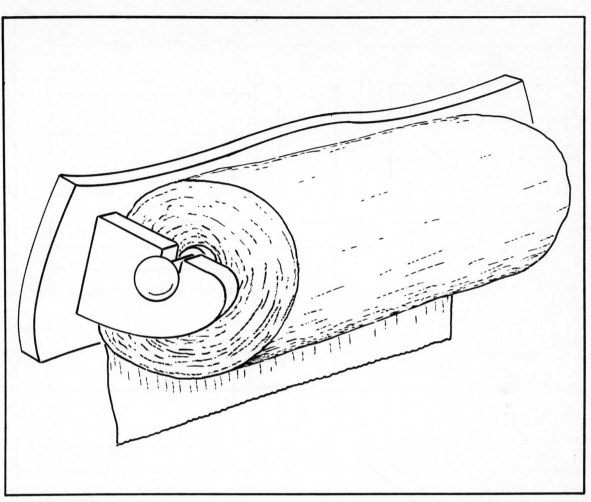

Fig. 6-24. Hanging rack for a paper roll.

slots with ⅝-inch holes to give easy clearance on the necks of the rod. If ¾-inch dowel rod is used, start with ⅞-inch holes.

4. Mark the tenons on the brackets and matching mortises on the back (Fig. 6-25C). It will be easier to hold the wood if you cut the joints before doing any shaping.

5. If the back is not being shaped, remove the corners (Fig. 6-25D) and bevel the front edges. If the back is shaped, round the front edges.

6. Shape the brackets and well-round all forward edges.

7. Join the brackets to the back. Check squareness.

8. Make a turned rod with a 1-inch diameter. Cut shoulders on the center part to make an easy fit between the brackets (Fig. 6-25E). Reduce those parts to ½ inch (Fig. 6-26C). Turn projecting ends into spheres, or make them elliptical or any other shape you wish, but keep the diameter about 1 inch. The completed turned rod should pass through the paper roll and drop into the bracket slots, where it will be retained without other restraint.

9. If you do not have a lathe, you can use ¼-inch dowel rod. Cut a piece to pass through the brackets and extend about ¼ inch. Round the ends if you wish. Drill across for two, ⅛-inch-diameter glued pegs (Fig. 6-25F) to stop the rod sliding side-

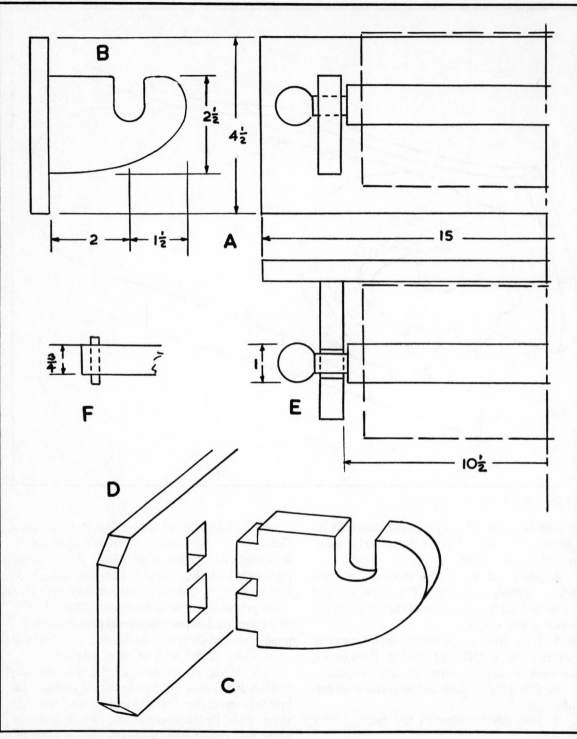

Fig. 6-25. Sizes and construction of the rack.

142

ways. Drill opposite ends at right angles to each other.

10. Finish in any way you wish to match other furniture. A dark stain or a bright paint will show up the light color of the paper roll.

Materials List for Paper Roll Hanger

1 back	½ ×	2½ × 5
2 brackets	⅝ ×	4½ × 16
1 rod	15 ×	1 diameter
or	15 ×	¾ diameter

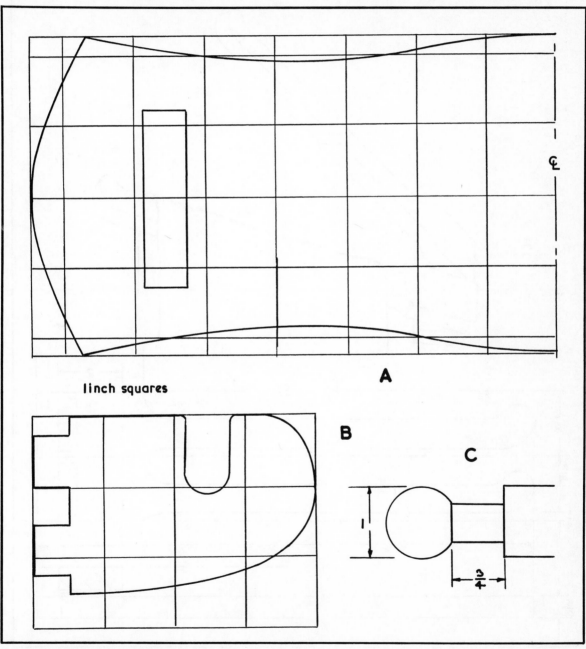

1 inch squares

A

B

C

Fig. 6-26. Shapes of the rack parts.

HINGED KITCHEN TOWEL RAILS

Kitchen towels and other cloths can be hung to dry or be accessible for use on rails that are hinged on the wall. One or more of them can be swung out for use, but any not needed can swing flat against the wall out of the way.

The block of rails in Fig. 6-27A is shown with two rails, but there could be any number. They

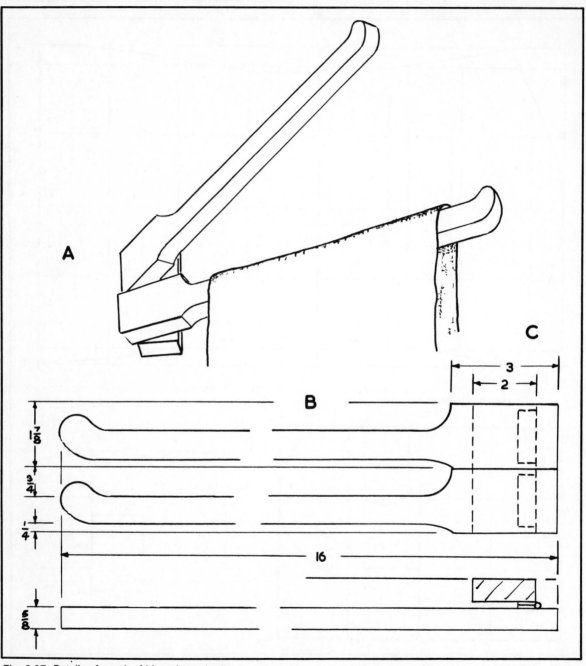

Fig. 6-27. Details of a pair of hinged towel rails.

are drawn 16 inches long, but the length can be arranged to suit your needs. Avoid too great a length because of the strain on the hinges and screws if the arms are pulled or knocked.

Any wood can be used but hardwood is better as it is stronger, particularly in the joints. The arms are arranged to open square to the wall or at a lesser angle. If you want them to swing farther, the ends can be cut back, but that brings screws closer to the end grain where breaking out under strain is a risk, particularly in softwood. All parts are cut from wood ⅝ inch thick.

1. Mark out the rails (Fig. 6-27B). Leave the inner ends parallel with square edges and ends. Leave the other parts with square edges or fully round the, particularly at the turned-ups ends.

2. Make the back (Fig. 6-27C) as long as the combined widths of the arms.

3. The hinges are 1½ inches long, preferably brass or plated for rust resistance.

4. Use screws as long as possible in the hinges for maximum grip.

5. Rivet the hinges instead of screwing them. Use soft rivets with their heads in the wood and their ends cut to rivet into the countersunk holes of the rivets. Copper, brass, or aluminum nails could be cut off and used as rivets.

6. Finish the block of rails in any way you wish. Drill for two screws through the back into the wall.

```
┌────────────────────────────────────────────┐
│ Materials List for Hinged Kitchen Towel Rails │
│                                              │
│ 2 arms   ⅝ × 1¾ × 17                        │
│ 1 back   ⅝   2  × 5                          │
└────────────────────────────────────────────┘
```

PIVOTED KITCHEN TOWEL RAILS

If the rails of a kitchen towel hanger pivot on a peg supported by arms projecting from a wall, the assembly is strong and attractive. Any reasonable number of rails can be included. Two are drawn in Fig. 6-28, but there could be three or four.

A close-grained hardwood is advisable. For one or two rails, the peg could be ¼-inch dowel rod, but for a greater number, it is better to use a metal rod. The rails are ⅝ inch thick, but the bracket parts can be ½ inch. The rails are arranged to pivot either way or at any angle to the wall. The rear overhang on the peg gives a good resistance to any unintentional strain on the arms.

1. Mark out the back of the bracket (Fig. 6-28A), allowing for the combined thicknesses of rails between the arm positions.

2. The arms (Fig. 6-28B) must be securely attached to the back. The simplest way is with screws (Fig. 6-28C). An alternative is to use dowels (Fig. 6-28D) in a similar arrangement. The strongest joints are with tenons (Fig. 6-28E).

3. Mark out the arms. Round the ends of the arms and drill them for the pivot rod. Round the ends of the back to match and drill for screws into the wall.

4. Make the two rails (Fig. 6-28F). Well-round all the shaped extending parts.

5. At the inner ends, mark the peg holes on opposite edges. With these centers mark the curve of the end of each rail (Fig. 6-28G). When the rail swings, its end will then be reasonably close to the back, for maximum strength, but its corners will not rub. Shape the ends and drill the peg holes from both edges to ensure them being as square as possible to the surfaces.

6. Join the arms to the back. Check that the rails make a tight fit between them.

7. You might need to use a temporary pin with a tapered point, or make the final peg too long and point it, so you can drive through all parts to get the holes into line. If the trial assembly is satisfactory, paint or varnish the parts before permanently assembling.

8. The peg, whether wood or metal, will probably hold by friction, but if it is slack, glue it in the arms. The peg ends can project and be rounded. If you ever need to take the assembly apart, you can then knock out the peg.

```
┌────────────────────────────────────────────────┐
│ Materials List for Pivoted Kitchen Towel Rails   │
│                                                  │
│ 1 back   ½ × 1½ × 8                             │
│ 2 arms   ½ × 1½ × 3                             │
│ 2 rails  ⅝ × 1½ × 19                            │
│ 1 peg    6 × ¼ diameter                          │
└────────────────────────────────────────────────┘
```

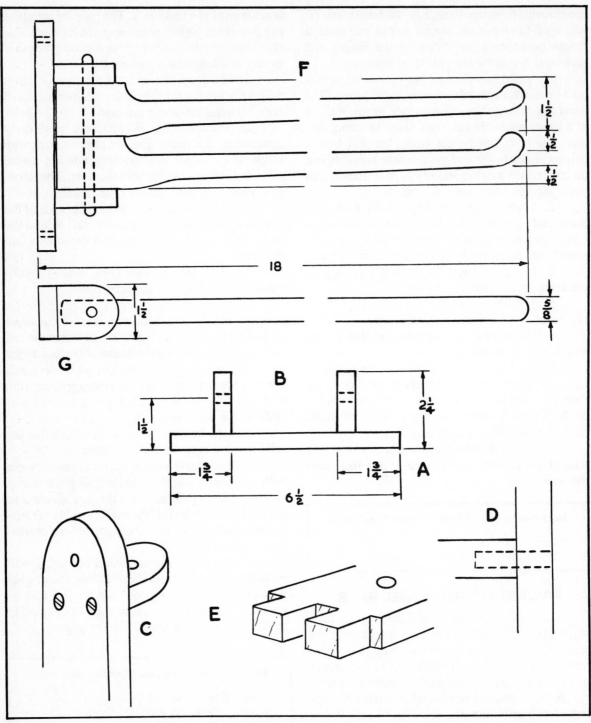

Fig. 6-28. Sizes of the towel rails.

DOUBLE-PIVOTED KITCHEN TOWEL RAILS

If you can conveniently use a large number of kitchen towel rails arranged in a vertical line, you can make a double version of the previous project. In this one there are two rails at each level; each can swing at any angle from flat against the wall to square to it. The previous design might be made with a wider bracket and the same rails, but this project is suggested with dowel-rod rails (Fig. 6-29). The same type of rail could be used for either of the previous two projects.

1. Make each arm with a solid hardwood block at the pivot and a length of ½-inch dowel rod glued into a hole in it (Fig. 6-29A). Make the dowel rod any length you wish.

2. The pivot end is not cut to a radius around the pivot hole, but the center used is ⅛ inch from it (Fig. 6-29B). This gives a little extra wood projecting for stiffness and resistance to loads that might lever downwards on the joints. There could be any number of pairs of rails, but a reasonable arrangement is four arms at each side.

3. Mark out the back (Fig. 6-29C). For four pairs of rails, space the gap between the arms 4½ inches to make a total length of 8½ inches.

4. Mark out the arms (Fig. 6-29D). The centers of the peg holes are 1¼ inches apart to give a ⅛-inch clearance between the curved rail ends when both sides are against the wall. Arranging the grain from front to back is a little stronger than having it across.

5. Join the arms to the back in any of the ways suggested for the previous project (Fig. 6-28C, D, E). Use similar pivot peg arrangements.

6. Apply finish to the wood before final assembly.

Materials List for Double-Pivoted Kitchen Towel Rails			
1 back	½	×	2¾ × 10
2 arms	½	×	2¾ × 3
8 rails	⅞	×	1⅛ × 3
8 rails	18	×	½ diameter
2 pegs	7	×	¼ diameter

PARALLEL KITCHEN TOWEL RAILS

The end of a cupboard, cabinet, or table is a good place to hang kitchen towels. A gap along a wall or behind a room door can be equally suitable. In such a position, double rails can usefully take two towels or other cloths.

The pair of kitchen towel rails in Fig. 6-30 consists of dowel rods in supporting brackets. They can be spaced to suit the towels or to position them over table legs or cabinet framing. The drawing shows 20 inches overall (Fig. 6-30A), but anything from 12 inches upward should suit kitchen towels. The rails are hardwood dowels. The brackets could be hardwood or softwood. Bracket parts are assembled by screwing from the back.

1. Make the bracket backs (Fig. 6-30B) 1½ inches wide with a centerline on each for the positions of screw holes. Bevel the front edges.

2. Make the supports using the squared drawing to get the shape (Fig. 6-30C). Round the outer edges.

3. Drill holes for the dowel rods. The joints will be stronger if the holes go through, but if you do not want the dowel ends to show, they could go part way.

4. Drill for screws, then glue and screw the brackets together.

5. When gluing in the rails, be careful of twist. Rest the backs flat on a surface while the glue sets.

6. A painted finish is probably the best treatment.

Materials List for Parallel Kitchen Towel Rails			
2 backs	½	×	1½ × 7
2 supports	½	×	4 × 5
2 rails	20	×	½ diameter

SPICE RACK

Spices and other powders and granules are kept in small jars. Usually there are so many that a special rack is justified. If it is possible to get suffi-

147

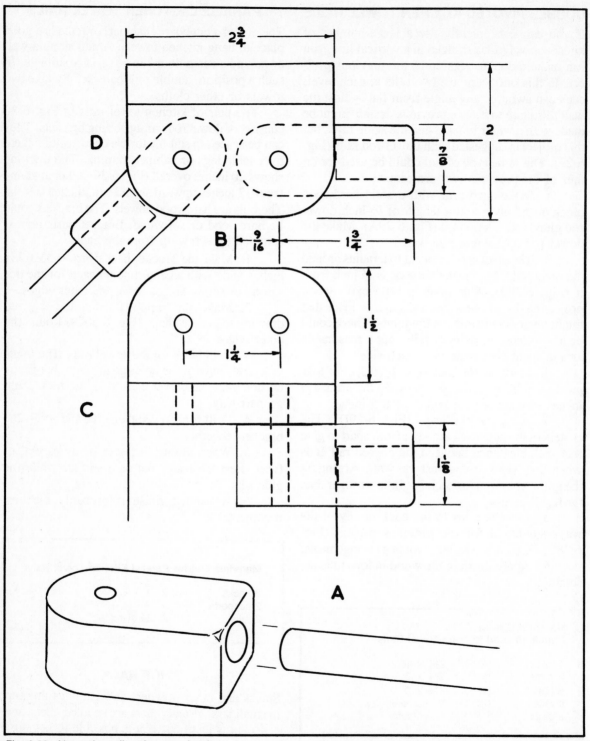

Fig. 6-29. Alternative rails using round rods.

148

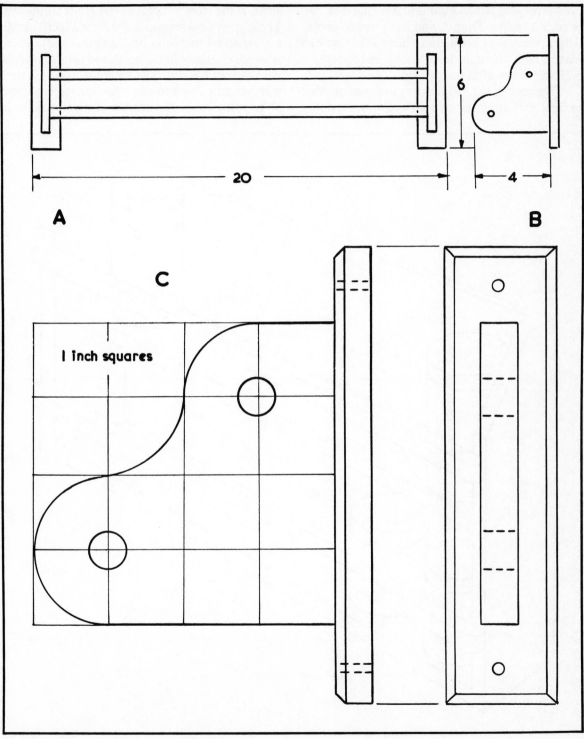

A

B

C

1 inch squares

20

6

4

Fig. 6-30. Sizes and shapes of the towel rack.

149

cient screw-top jars of a uniform size, the rack size is easy to settle. Even if you have to accommodate a variety of containers, however, you can make a rack to suit the largest sizes and the others will still make a reasonable fit.

The rack in Fig. 6-31 screws to a wall or other upright surface. It has two shelves with retaining strips at the front to prevent jars from falling out. The suggested sizes suit containers 2 inches in diameter and 4 inches in height (Fig. 6-32). There is ample clearance in the width and height. Lengthwise clearance is sufficient for ten jars on each shelf with an extra 1 inch to allow for moving jars about or gripping them. If sizes are altered, make sure

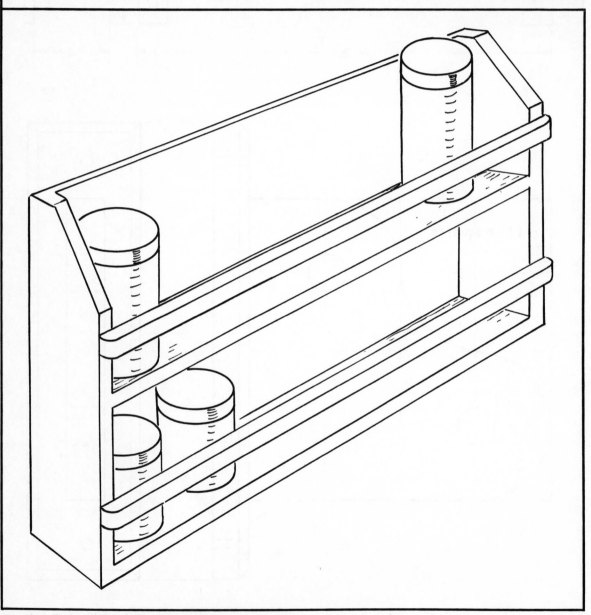

Fig. 6-31. These shelves hold small containers on two levels.

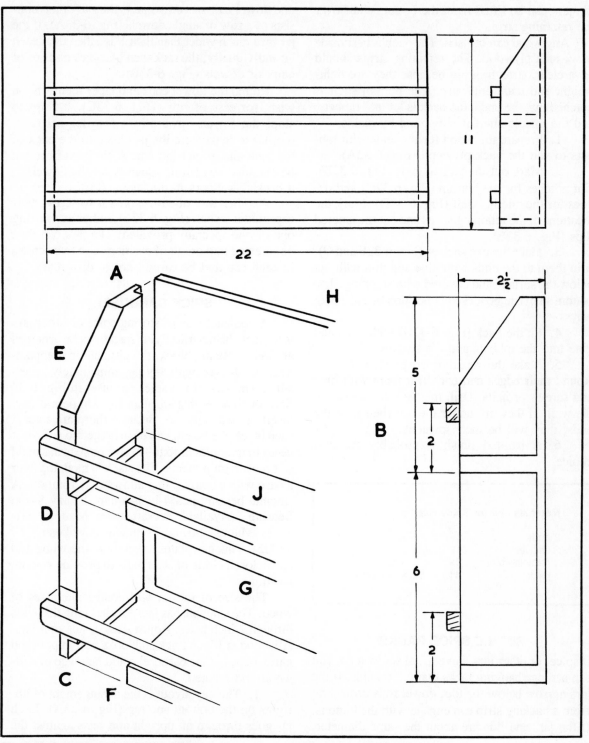

Fig. 6-32. Suggested sizes for the shelves.

the jars can be lifted from the bottom shelf over the retaining strip.

Any wood can be used. The back is best made of ¼-inch plywood. The retaining strips should have clear, straight grain because they are lightweight and must not warp. The bottom shelf is notched into the ends, the back is let into rabbets, and the middle shelf is supported by dadoes.

1. Prepare the wood for the ends with rabbets to suit the back plywood (Fig. 6-32A).

2. Mark out the pair of ends (Fig. 6-32B). Cut notches for the bottom (Fig. 6-32C) and dadoes for the middle shelf (Fig. 6-32D). Mark the locations of the retaining strips and cut the tapered tops (Fig. 6-32E).

3. Make the two shelves (Fig. 6-32F and G). Join them to the ends with glue and thin nails set below the surface and covered with stopping. The bottom shelf can be locked in position by nails both ways.

4. Fit the back (Fig. 6-32H) with nails and glue into the rabbets and the shelves.

5. Make the retaining strips (Fig. 6-32J). Round their edges and ends. Fit them with glue and screws or nails. Drill the back for screws to the wall. If they are under the top shelf near the ends, they will be inconspicuous.

6. A painted finish is probably the best choice.

```
┌─────────────────────────────────────────────┐
│  Materials List for Spice Rack                │
│                                               │
│  2 ends              ½  ×  2½   ×  12         │
│  2 shelves           ½  ×  2¼   ×  23         │
│  2 retaining strips  ⅜  ×  ½    ×  23         │
│  1 back              11 ×  22   × ¼  plywood  │
└─────────────────────────────────────────────┘
```

SIMPLE SPICE RACKS

If spice, or other jars, have metal screw tops, you can arrange hanging racks that use the lids. If the jars narrow below the top, dowel rods projecting from a backing strip can engage with the buttons. If the jars and lids are about the same diameter, one dowel can serve two jars; the rack then consists of a row of single dowels (Fig. 6-33A). If the jars are much wider than their lids , then treat each jar individually; the rack then becomes a series of pairs of dowels (Fig. 6-33B).

Round the dowel ends and taper them, if you wish, for ease of entry (Fig. 6-33C). It helps to slope the dowels upward by a few degrees (Fig. 6-33D) to make sure the jars keep to the back of the rack and do not fall out. A similar effect can be obtained by drilling squarely for the dowels in a back that tapers in thickness. (Fig. 6-33E).

Another way of storing jars is to screw their caps under a shelf (Fig. 6-33F), either an existing one or one specially provided. The jars can then be screwed into or out of position. Use two screws in each cap and be careful not to distort it.

SPICE CAROUSEL

A compact way of storing spice or other jars is to stack them vertically. If stacks can be arranged around a rotating block, the ultimate in compactness is achieved with any jar immediately accessible. The jars of the spice carousel in Fig. 6-34 fit through holes that are at an angle to permit easy insertion and removal. Because there are four at each level, the height can be arranged to suit your needs in multiples of four—twelve or sixteen should suit most requirements. The stack is mounted over a base with a bearing that allows easy rotation. A suitable bearing is a 4-inch-square "Lazy Susan Bearing" (Available at craft stores. Made by Triangle Manufacturing Company, Oshkosh, WI 54902). This has plates to screw to the wood and an enclosed circle of steel balls to provide smooth rotation.

The size of the jar will control the sizes of wood. The example has jars 4 inches long that slide through 2-inch holes. Adjust sizes to suit your jars. All wood is 1 inch thick and looks best in polished hardwood, but the carousel could be made of softwood and painted.

1. The key layout is the arrangement of uprights on the bottom and top (Fig. 6-35A). Each jar goes through an upright and rests against the

edge of the next upright. If you need to adjust sizes, this is where you do it.

2. Mark out the top and bottom as a pair, but do not cut to size until after matching dowel holes with the uprights.

3. Mark out the uprights to suit the number

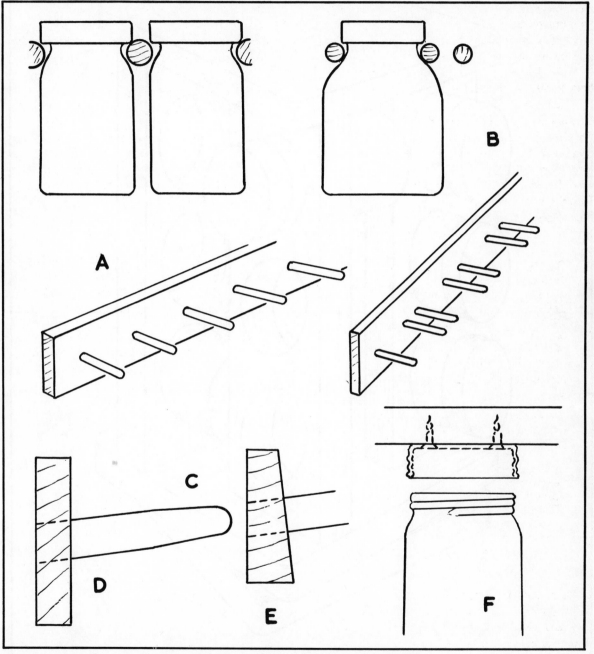

Fig. 6-33. A rack for spice jars can use dowels, or lids can be screwed under a shelf.

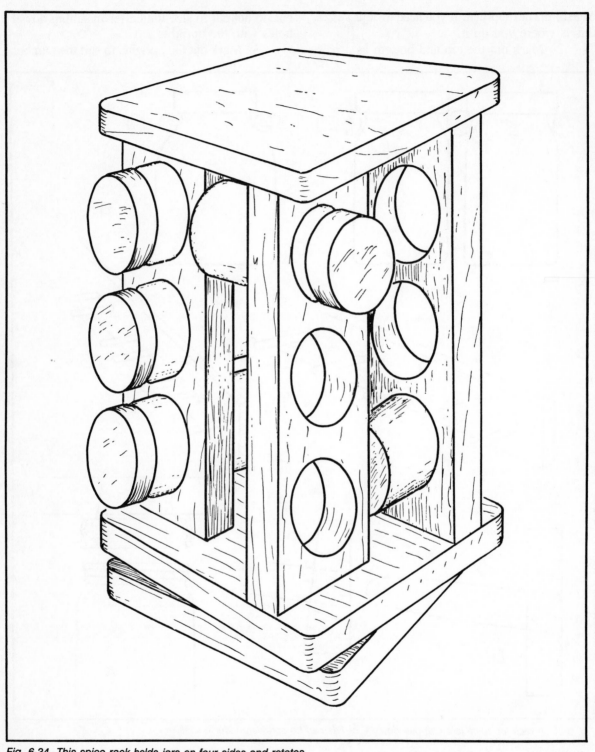

Fig. 6-34. This spice rack holds jars on four sides and rotates.

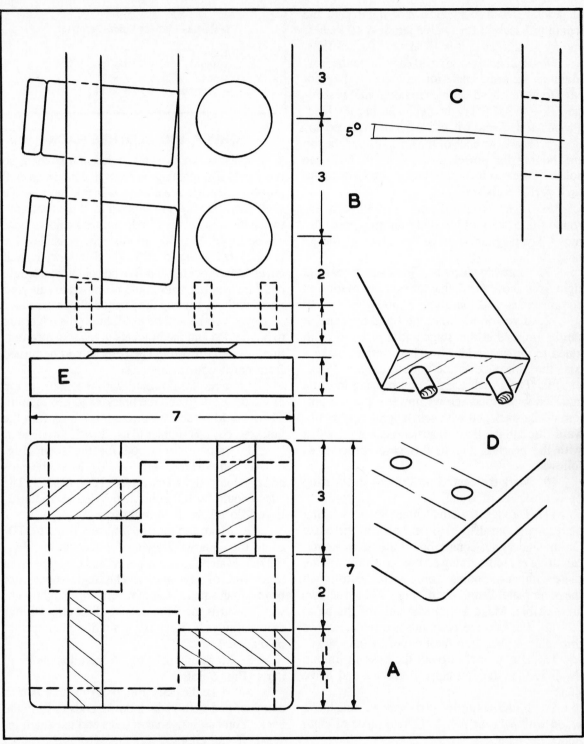

Fig. 6-35. Layout of the rotating spice rack.

155

of jars you wish to include. For eight jars, the length is 7 inches; for twelve jars it is 10 inches; and for sixteen jars, it is 13 inches (Fig. 6-35B).

4. Drill holes to give an easy fit on the jars. Maintain the same angle for all holes. It does not have to be much—5 degrees to horizontal is sufficient (Fig. 6-35C). Try the fit of a jar in a test hole. Too much slackness will cause the jar to tilt too far.

5. Mark the ends of the uprights and the top and bottom for dowels (Fig. 6-35D). Drill the holes. Dowels ⅜ inch or ½ inch taken ¾ inch into each part is satisfactory.

6. Lightly round the edges of all parts and round the corners of top and bottom pieces. Remove any raggedness from the edges of the jar holes.

7. Assemble the parts. Check squareness and sight from above to see that the outlines of top and bottom match and that there is no twist.

8. If you do not want the stand to rotate, it can be finished at this stage and a piece of cloth glued to the underside. If it is to rotate, make a base the same size as the bottom (Fig. 6-35E).

9. The 4-inch Lazy Susan bearing must be attached with wood screws upward into the bottom of the stack and with self-tapping screws upward through the base. Instructions are provided with the bearing, but in this case, proceed as follows.

10. Mark the central position of the bearing on both pieces of wood.

11. Through the small holes in the bearing plate, mark and drill ⁵⁄₃₂-inch holes in the base. On the underside, counterboard the holes so you can drive six self-tapping screws upwards into the plate without the points going so far as to touch the other plate. With 1-inch wood, ¾-inch screws are suitable. Make a trial assembly of the base.

12. Remove the base and use wood screws through the plate into the bottom of the stack.

13. Use an awl through the base to line up the holes for the self-tapping screws and drive them.

14. If the action is satisfactory, finish the wood with paint or polish. Glue a piece of cloth under the base.

Materials List for Spice Carousel	
1 top	1 × 7 × 7
1 bottom	1 × 7 × 7
1 base	1 × 7 × 7
4 uprights	1 × 3 × 14

SHELF AND CLOTHES RACK

Wall space is often overcrowded in a kitchen; so it is a help if something on the wall can have a dual purpose. Shelves are always wanted, but a single shelf needs brackets to support it. If the space between the brackets is filled, clothes hooks or pegs can be added. Several variations are possible. One is suggested in Fig. 6-36A. The 5-inch-wide shelf covers a backboard with five pegs in a total length of 27 inches, but sizes could be varied to suit your needs without altering the method of construction.

Any wood could be used, but if the edges are to be molded and the brackets given a shaped outline, use a hardwood. The pegs should be turned from hardwood, in any case.

The parts are doweled with the shelf on top of the back board and the brackets joined to both. There could be screws through the back into the brackets, but it is simpler to use dowels throughout.

1. Prepare the wood for the shelf (Fig. 6-37A) and the back (Fig. 6-37B). Mold the ends and one long edge of each piece (Fig. 6-37C). The edges could be left square, beveled or rounded, if you do not wish to mold them.

2. Make the pair of brackets (Fig. 6-37D) using the squared drawing for the outline (Fig. 6-37E). Match the two brackets and clean the front edges free of saw marks. The angle should not be less than square. Let the shelf slope slightly upward towards the front edge to discourage things from rolling off. Keep the grain direction upright or diagonal.

3. Mark and drill for ⅜-inch dowels in all parts (Fig. 6-36B).

4. Make the pegs (Fig. 6-37F) with a ⅞-inch diameter and with ½-inch dowel ends to fit in the back. You can buy Shaker pegs and use them instead, if you choose.

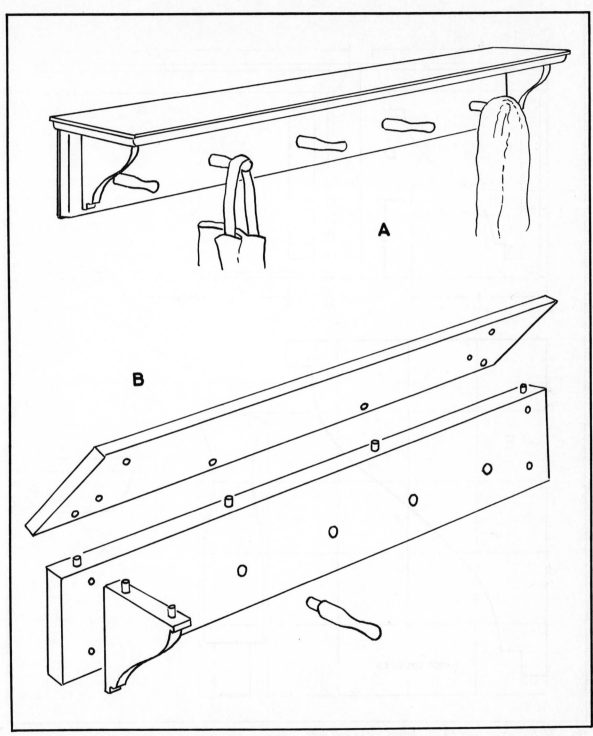

Fig. 6-36. This rack for clothing is combined with a shelf.

A

B

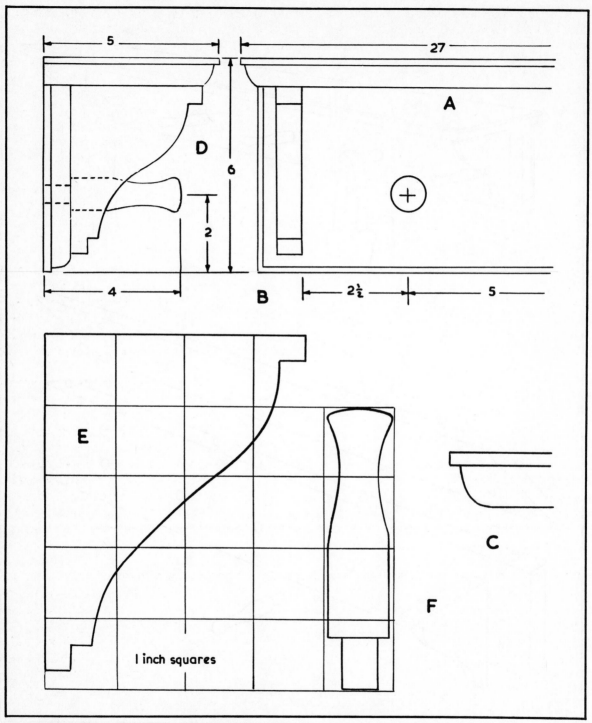

Fig. 6-37. Suggested sizes for the clothes hooks and shelf.

5. Join the brackets to the back but have the dowels ready to join to the shelf. Add the shelf and draw all joints tight. Glue in the pegs checking that they are all square to the back.

6. Drill through the back under the shelf for screws into the wall.

7. Finish to match other furniture.

Materials List for Shelf and Clothes Rack

1 shelf	¾	× 5	× 28
1 back	¾	× 5¼	× 28
2 brackets	¾	× 3¾	× 6
5 pegs	1	× 1	× 5

ROLL DISPENSER

Several materials in rolls are used in a kitchen, such as paper towels, plastic film, and aluminum foil. The wall unit in Fig. 6-38 will keep some of the rolls together, ready for use, as well as provide a space for string. The rolls are held by rods that drop into slots.

Dispenser sizes depend on sizes of rolls you wish to include and can be altered to suit. As shown (Fig. 6-39), space at the top for a paper roll is 9 inches long and up to 4 inches in diameter. Foil and film rolls are not as thick, but the sizes shown allow for up to 12 inches long. The space for string or other small items is about 3 inches wide. The top can serve as a shelf, but the bottom is open so the roll in that space can be unwound downward. The dispenser could have an open back, but it is better with hardboard or thin plywood against the wall.

In the simplest form, the dispenser might be nailed together. You can use screws or dowels, but the sockets for the rods have to be cut like dadoes by router or other means. It would be appropriate and neat to join all the parts with dadoes, preferably stopped so the joint details do not show at the front.

All the wood should finish ½×3½ inches. The dadoes and rod sockets should be cut halfway through (Fig. 6-39A). Any wood can be used, but it is easier to cut good joints in a mild hardwood than in the more fibrous softwoods.

1. Mark out a pair of ends (Fig. 6-39B). Allow for them to fit into a dado at the top (Fig. 6-39C). The shelf dadoes should stop ¼ inch from the front (Fig. 6-39D). The stopped holes that form the ends of the rod sockets are central in the lower two spaces (Fig. 6-39E) but further forward to allow for the thicker roll in the top (Fig. 6-39F). Mark the top hole in only one end as the other will come in the division (Fig. 6-39G).

2. Mark out the division to match the ends. Allow for it to fit into dadoes at its top and bottom.

3. Make the two shelves. Make them the same length and notch them to fit into the dadoes at the ends (Fig. 6-39H). The upper shelf (Fig. 6-39J) needs a dado to take the division, allowing plenty of end clearance for the paper towel roll.

4. If the small compartment is to be used for string, drill the shelf for a ½-inch piece of dowel rod on which the ball of string can rest (fig. 6-39K). An attractive use of this space is suggested in the next project.

5. The top (Fig. 6-39L and M) overlaps the ends. Use the top shelf as a a guide when making the top and its dadoes.

6. The rod sockets should slope up to the front and are shown at a 15-degree angle (Fig. 6-43N). The width should suit the rods and make a fairly close fit, while allowing them to be withdrawn. They are the same section for all positions. Clean any raggedness from the sockets.

7. Round the front corners of the top and the lower front corners of the ends. Take sharpness off all exposed edges.

8. Glue the parts together. There could also be fine nails driven through the ends into themselves, if you think they are necessary, but if a back is fitted, that will strengthen the joints.

9. A back can be a piece of hardboard nailed and glued on. For the neatest finish, the ends and top could have been prepared with rabbets to take it, but the hardboard edges are not very obvious in the finished dispenser.

10. The rods (Fig. 6-39P) are pieces of ¾-

inch dowel rod. Cut the ends squarely across so they fit snugly into the sloping sockets.

11. Any finish can be used. Good wood looks great polished or varnished, but the dispenser could be painted. A bright color can serve as a background to show how much is left on any roll.

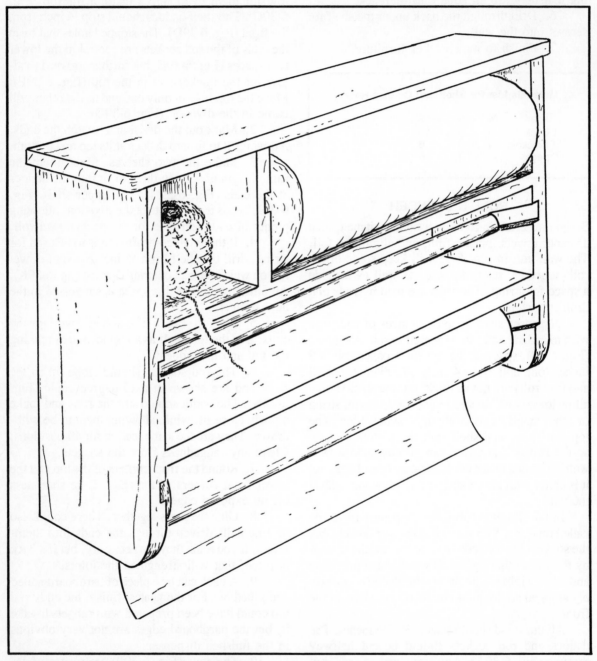

Fig. 6-38. This dispenser for rolls also holds string.

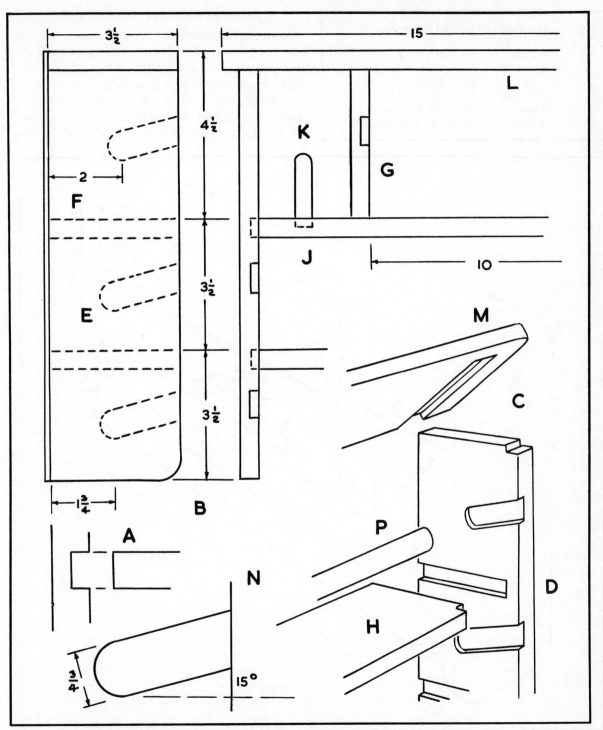

Fig. 6-39. Sizes of the dispenser.

COMPREHENSIVE DISPENSER

A wall dispenser can be made in the same way as the last project but with increased capacity. You can use your own ideas after measuring the rolls and other items you wish to include. The dispenser suggested (Fig. 6-40) holds a paper towel roll 9 inches long and up to 4 inches in diameter and aluminum foil and plastic film rolls up to 18 inches

Materials List for Roll Dispenser

2 ends	½ × 3½ × 12
2 shelves	½ × 3½ × 15
1 top	½ × 3½ × 16
1 division	½ × 3½ × 6
1 peg	3 × ½ diameter
3 rods	15 × ¾ diameter

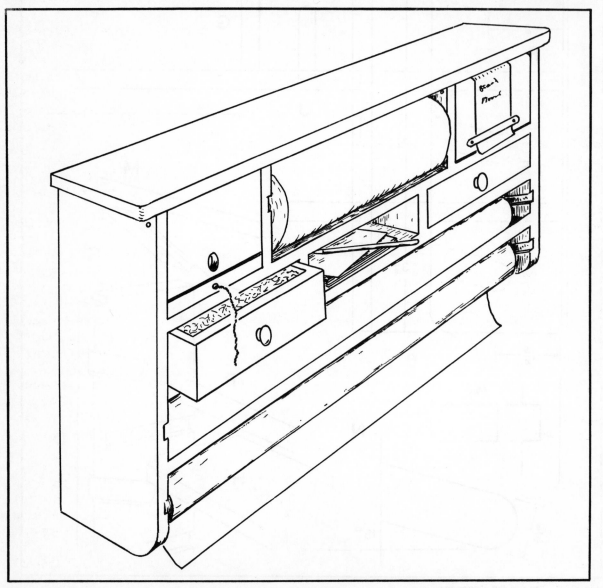

Fig. 6-40. This dispenser holds rolls and has drawers as well as string and paper containers.

long, in the same way as the other dispenser. The roll in the central section feeds over a cutting edge in front of it for tearing. The rack is open at the bottom so the roll there can be pulled downward.

Halfway down the dispenser is a 2-inch gap with a drawer at each end and storage space at the center. At each side of the paper towel roll at the top are compartments that could have several uses; one is shown for string storage, and the other holds a paper roll that leads through the front to make a tear-off notepad.

Any wood could be used, but a close-grained hardwood is advisable for the strip that provides a cutting edge for the center roll. Because the drawers are framed in fairly thin wood for neatness and adequate capacity, they would be better made of hardwood. Although the main structure could be softwood, a hardwood throughout would make this an attractive piece of furniture. The back and drawer bottoms can be hardboard.

Details of construction are generally similar to the previous project. Main parts could be nailed, screwed, or doweled, but dadoes are suggested for an assembly that can be regarded as good craftsmanship. Read the instructions for the simpler dispenser and follow the constructional details in Fig. 6-39 where they are appropriate.

1. Measure the rolls you wish to include. Allow very full clearance in lengths. The paper towel roll can extend a little forward, when new, but all other contents should fit within the thickness of the unit.

2. Mark out the pair of ends (Fig. 6-41A). Allow for them to fit into dadoes in the top. Locate the shelf positions and cut the dadoes stopped ¼ inch from the front edges. Mark the sockets for the rods but do not cut them until you are ready to cut the sockets in the divisions as well. Be particularly careful that the dadoes for the shelves are cut squarely; otherwise the drawers will not slide smoothly.

3. Two shelves are full width, but the bottom one is set back ¼ inch and fits into the dadoes without notching so the cutting piece can fit on its front edge (Fig. 6-41). It is plain throughout its length.

4. Mark the next shelf (Fig. 6-41C) for the drawer dividers. Mark the shelf above it (Fig. 6-41D) to match on its underside and for the compartment dividers on its surface.

5. Use that shelf as a guide when marking out the top (Fig. 6-41E), which overlaps at the ends.

6. Cut dadoes in the shelves and top in the same way as in the ends. Use the actual wood that is to fit to test sizes.

7. Make the drawer divisions (Fig. 6-41F) and compartment divisions (Fig. 6-41G) with their grain lines vertical and ends notched to fit the dadoes.

8. Mark the rod sockets in the compartment divisions. They are a little further forward than those in the sides to allow for the larger diameter roll of paper towels.

9. The rods are ¾-inch dowels. Check their size and cut the sockets to allow them to slide in and out without slackness. Slope up to the front about 15 degrees.

10. Round the front corners of the top and the front lower corners of the sides.

11. Assemble all the parts made so far. The back can be temporarily tacked on to hold the assembly in shape while the glue sets, but you might find it easier to do this later if it can be removed.

12. Make the cutting strip (Fig. 6-41B) ¼ inch thick to fit between the sides and with its top planed to about 45 degrees. Glue it to the front of its shelf.

13. In the string compartment, fit a ¾-inch-high strip across the front (Fig. 6-42A) and a thin strip standing ¼ inch above it (Fig. 6-42B) to act as a door stop. The door fits against this and has a rounded top to swing it up on two screws. (Fig. 6-42C).

14. Drill a ¾-inch hole in the door (Fig. 6-41H) so a finger can be used to pull the door open. In the strip below it, drill a hole for string to be pulled through (Fig. 6-41J). Countersink this on both sides—a ⁵⁄₃₂-inch-diameter hole should suit most string.

15. The notepad compartment holds a roll of paper of the type used in calculators and similar business machines. It will probably be about 2

inches wide, but it could be anything up to 4 inches.

16. At the bottom of that compartment put a door stop across (Fig. 6-42D) and make a door very similar to that on the string compartment. At its top it can pivot low enough for the paper to pass over it, or you can hinge it close up and allow just a gap to suit the width of the paper strip (Fig. 6-42E).

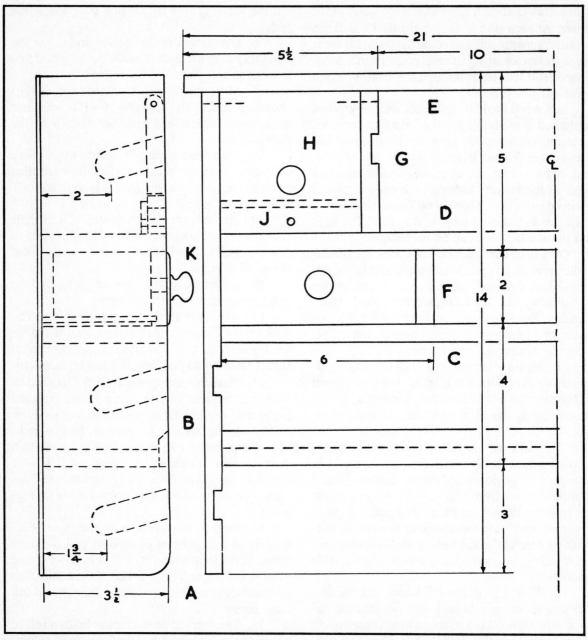

Fig. 6-41. Sizes of the larger dispenser.

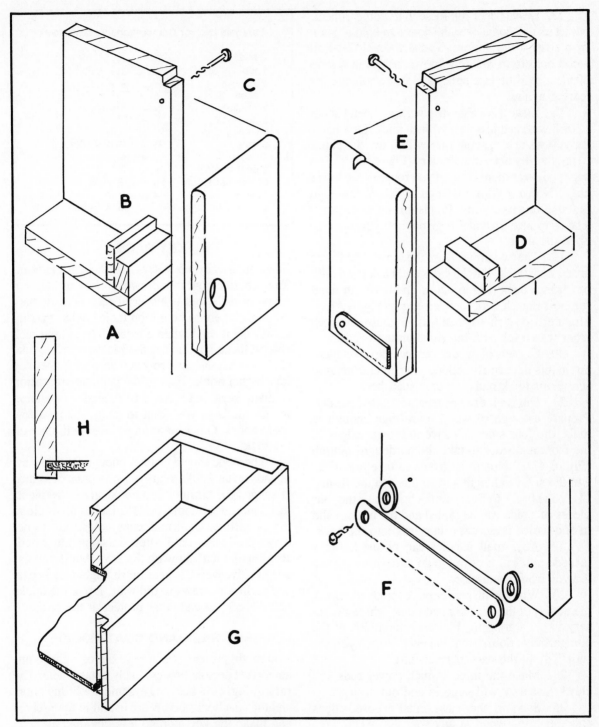

Fig. 6-42. Constructional details of parts of the dispenser.

17. Leave paper roll loose in its compartment, but let its end come over the door and hold it down by a strip at the bottom. The strip could be thin wood held from the door by washers, but a strip of metal will be less bulky and more suitable for tearing against.

18. Make a suitable strip with any metal about 3/8 inch wide and less than 1/16 inch thick. Drill holes for screws at a spacing that will allow the paper to pass easily between washers (Fig. 6-42F). The paper will tear more easily if you roughen the lower edge. Notch it with a triangular file so the edge is something like a saw. Precision is unnecessary. The strip also provides a grip when you want to open the door.

19. The two drawers are the same. The fronts are 1/2 inch thick, but the sides and back need only be 5/16 inch thick (Fig. 6-42G). The front can stand forward 1/8 inch with rounded edges (Fig. 6-41K). Slight errors of fit are then less obvious than if the front was level with the surrounding edges.

20. Corners of the drawers can be dovetailed, but in this light construction, you can glue and use screws or thick nails, as described here.

21. Cut each drawer front to fit its opening. Prepare a length of wood more than enough to make the four sides. Groove the lower edges of the front and sides to take the hardboard bottom (Fig. 6-42H). Notch the fronts to take the sides. Cut the sides to length and fit them to the fronts. Make the backs to fit above the bottom so the four pieces of a side can be joined and the bottom slid in and nailed or screwed upwards into the back.

22. Any small handles can be used, but a turned knob with a dowel to go into a hole in each drawer front is suitable.

23. With the dispenser back removed, check the action of the drawers and plane where necessary to get a good fit. Examine the action of the compartment doors from the back. When you are satisfied, fit the back permanently.

24. Make the three 3/4-inch dowel rods and check that they will slide in and out easily.

25. Sand off sharpness on all exposed edges and finish the wood in any way you wish.

Materials List for Comprehensive Dispenser		
2 ends	1/2 ×	3 1/2 × 15
1 top	1/2 ×	3 1/2 × 22
2 shelves	1/2 ×	3 1/2 × 21
1 shelf	1/2 ×	3 1/4 × 21
2 divisions	1/2 ×	3 1/2 × 6
2 divisions	1/2 ×	3 1/2 × 3 1/2
1 cutting strip	1/4 ×	1 × 21
3 rods	21 ×	3/4 diameter
2 doors	1/2 ×	4 × 5
2 door fronts	1/2 ×	2 × 6
drawer parts from	5/16 ×	2 × 26
1 back	14 ×	22 × 1/8 hardboard
2 drawer bottoms	3 1/2 ×	6 × 1/8 hardboard

KEY RACK

There are usually a few keys to be kept in a kitchen. They could be put in a drawer or box or hung on a row of nails, but if a special rack is made they are more likely to be put on their hooks, making them easy to find when needed. The simple rack shaped like a key in Fig. 6-43 is arranged to take six keys on hooks in a row and another longer key on a higher hook. The outline is in the proportion of many keys, but it could be extended or altered to suit the keys you want to hang. Allow a few spare hooks. Other items might find their place on the rack.

The wood should be thick enough for the screw threads on the hooks to grip—a minimum of 3/8 inch is suggested. Straight cup hooks are convenient.

The row of hooks are 1 1/2 inches apart along the centerline. Drill undersize holes, but do not drive the hooks until after finishing the wood. Bright paint will show up the keys, but if you use an attractive wood, a clear finish might look better.

Drill for screws to the wall. Drive the hooks and cut off the ends that project at the back.

KEY RACK AND COAT HOOKS

You might prefer to have keys out of sight so unauthorized persons are less likely to take them. The rack in Fig. 6-44 has the keys under a lifting door, and the coat hooks below are useful in themselves and make the key storage less obvious.

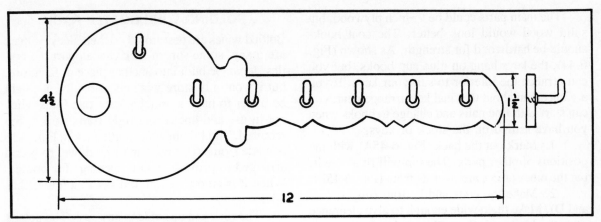

Fig. 6-43. A key rack cut in the shape of a key.

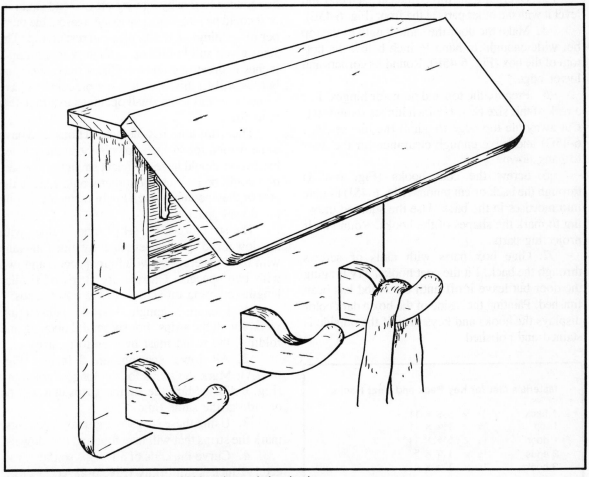

Fig. 6-44. The keys in this rack are hidden above clothes hooks.

The main parts could be ½-inch plywood, but solid wood would look better. The coat hooks should be hardwood for strength. As shown (Fig. 6-44), the keys hang on nine cup hooks, but you can arrange the interior to suit your keys. If you are uncertain about the final key arrangement, you can start with fine nails and change to hooks when you have settled on the stock of keys.

1. Mark out the back (Fig. 6-45A) with the positions of other parts. The top will fit above it, but the other pieces are over its front (Fig. 6-45B).

2. Make the ends and bottom (Fig. 6-45C and D). Make them wide enough to give clearance over the hooks; they are drawn 1¼ inches.

3. Overhang the top ¼ inch at each end and level it with the other parts at the front (Fig. 6-45E).

4. Make the door the same length as the top but wide enought to hang ½ inch below the bottom of the box (Fig. 6-45F). Round its corners and lower edge.

5. Prepare the top and door for hinges. For a rack of this size two, 1½-inch hinges should suit. Cut away the top edge to admit the hinges (Fig. 6-45G) and leave enough clearance for the door to hang down.

6. Screw the coat hooks (Fig. 6-45H) through the back or cut tenons (Fig. 6-45J) to glue into mortises in the back. Use the squared drawing to mark the shapes of the hooks. Round their projecting parts.

7. Glue box parts with nails or screws through the back. Fit the coat hooks. Try hinging the door but leave it off until the wood has been finished. Painting the inside of the box a dark color displays the hooks and keys even if the outside is stained and polished.

Materials List for Key Rack and Coat Hooks

1 back	½ × 8½ × 11
1 top	½ × 1¾ × 11
1 door	½ × 5½ × 11
2 ends	½ × 1¼ × 5
3 hooks	½ × 1½ × 4

FOLDING WINE BOTTLE RACK

Bottled wines are best stored on their sides. If there are many, some sort of rack can support the bottles. It can be built into another piece of furniture, but if you only store wine occasionally, it might be better to have a portable rack that folds when not in use and opens to a rigid framework when required. The folding wine bottle rack in Fig. 6-46 is made from strips held apart by dowel rods and arranged to provide square openings for bottles. When it is empty, it can fold flat to a few inches thick.

The rack can be made to any size. The details offered are for a rack for eight bottles. It could be reduced to five by leaving off two end squares, or it could be lengthened up to any reasonable number of openings. Extra bottles can rest on top. The sizes given suit bottles up to slightly more than 4 inches in greatest diameter. Check that your usual bottles will fit this size. It is not practical to have some large and some small openings in a rack that is to fold.

The strips are ½-×-¾-inch sections, and have to be drilled for ⅜-inch dowels. Straight-grained hardwood should have sufficient strength. The section could be increased but that would reduce the size of the openings which might mean increasing the dowel spacing.

The structure has a set of inner frames with the dowel rod spacers permanently glued in—one with five spacers, two with four spacers, and two with two spacers. Outside are strips of similar lengths pivoting on screws in the dowel ends.

1. Prepare enough ½-×-¾-inch-section wood for all the strips. For successful opening and folding, the wood must be a uniform size.

2. All dowel spacings are 5 inches (Fig. 6-47A). Mark the strips for the longest assembly (Fig. 6-47B). Mark the similar strips that will be outside at the same time.

3. Using these strips as a guide to spacings, mark the strips that will take four and two dowels.

4. Curve the ends of all strips so they project 1½ inches uniformly (Fig. 6-48A).

5. When all strips have been marked out,

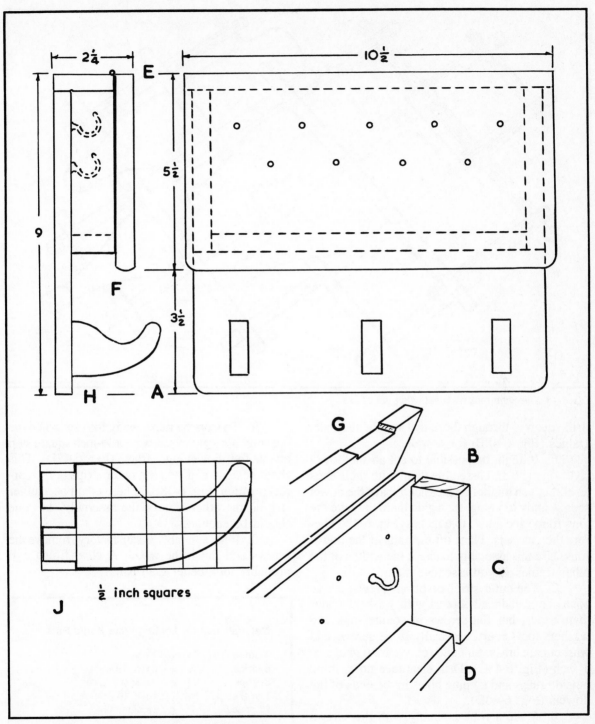

Fig. 6-45. Sizes and details of the key rack and hooks.

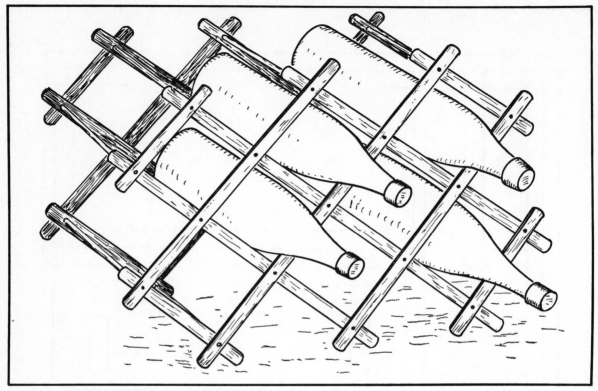

Fig. 6-46. This wine rack folds flat when out of use.

drill squarely through those that will be the inner frames (Fig. 6-48B) for dowels.

6. It might be possible to cut all the dowel rods to length and assemble them with their ends level, but you might find it easier to have the dowel rods slightly too long, then glue them to make the long frame and adjust to 6 inches (Fig. 6-47C) before the glue sets. Plane off the ends of the dowel rods. Use this assembly to check the widths of the other frames as you assemble them.

7. The outer strips pivot on screws. These could be roundhead screws with washers under their heads, but flat screws in countersunk cup washers look smart, especially if the screws and washers are brass. Suitable screws are 6 gauge × 1 inch (Fig. 6-48C). Drill clearance holes in all outside strips and tapping holes in the ends of the dowels (Fig. 6-48D).

8. Make a trial assembly with the screws only partly driven to test the opening and closing action.

9. To stop the rack, ready for use, when the openings are square, screw on a ½-inch square stop on one four-dowel inner frame (Fig. 6-47D). This should extend and stop the outer strips at the correct position (Fig. 6-48E). There could be another strip at the other side of the assembly, but one should be enough.

10. If the assembly is satisfactory, remove the screws and finish the wood. A clear finish will probably look better than paint.

Materials List for Folding Wine Bottle Rack

4 strips	½	×	¾ × 24
8 strips	½	×	¾ × 19
8 strips	½	×	¾ × 9
1 or 2 stops	½	×	½ × 10
18 spacers	7	×	⅜ diameter

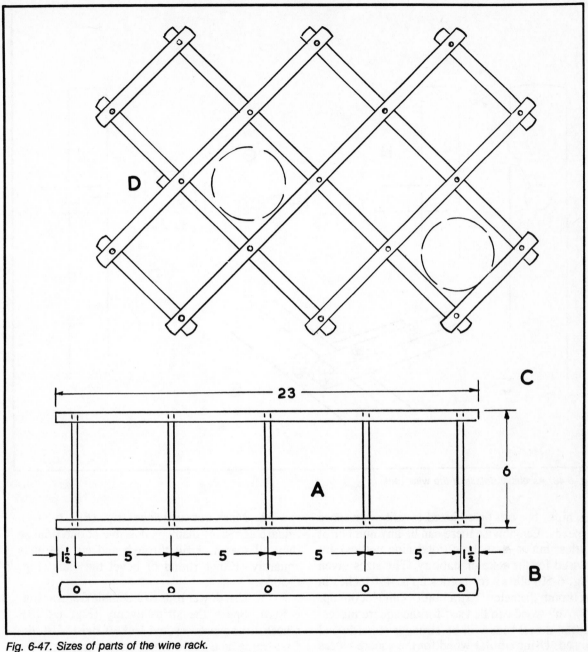

Fig. 6-47. Sizes of parts of the wine rack.

SECTIONAL WINE BOTTLE RACK

This is a more permanent wine rack that can be made to any size (Fig. 6-49). It is built up of units and assembled to the size you want. It can even be extended at some time in the future to accom-

modate a larger stock of bottles.

The rack consists of a number of 1-inch-square strips from back to front joined by dowel rods vertically and horizontally.

The vertical arrangement shown is three bot-

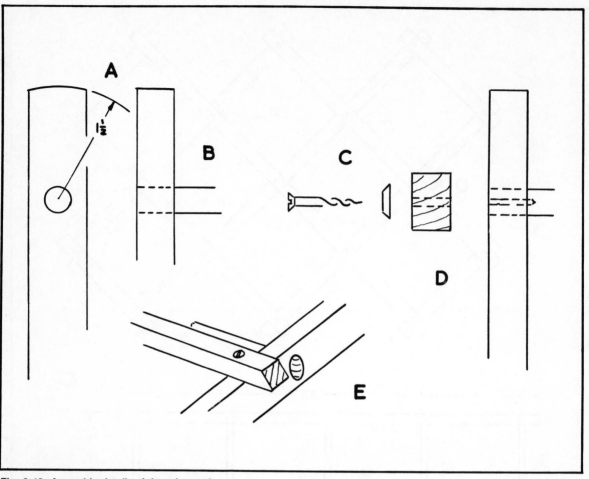

Fig. 6-48. Assembly details of the wine rack.

tles high, but can be adjusted to suit your space or needs. Lengthwise there can be any number of bottles, but at least three (total nine bottles) are advised for the sake of stability. The sizes given (Fig. 6-50) allows for bottles up to 4¼ inches in maximum diameter. Extra bottles can rest on top.

Any wood can be used for the square pieces, but the dowel rods will be stronger if hardwood is used. Using similar wood for the square pieces gives a uniform appearance if the rack is given a clear finish.

1. The dowel rods can be ⅜, ⁷⁄₁₆, or ½ inch in diameter. Choose a drill that will make a close fit on a dowel. Prepare enough 1-inch-square strips so all parts are the same.

2. Mark out sufficient strips (Fig. 6-51A). Square across as many as possible at one time so they all match. Drill through and cut the ends squarely. Either round or bevel the ends (Fig. 6-50A).

3. Use dowel rods to assemble frames (Fig. 6-51B). Space the strips evenly (Fig. 6-50B). Check for squareness and lack of twist. Use the first frame as a guide when assembling the other frames. Four frames are needed for a nine-bottle rack, then one more for each additional three bottles.

4. In the other direction, use dowel rods to go through all the frames in one length or make joints within the thickness of the square strips. Ar-

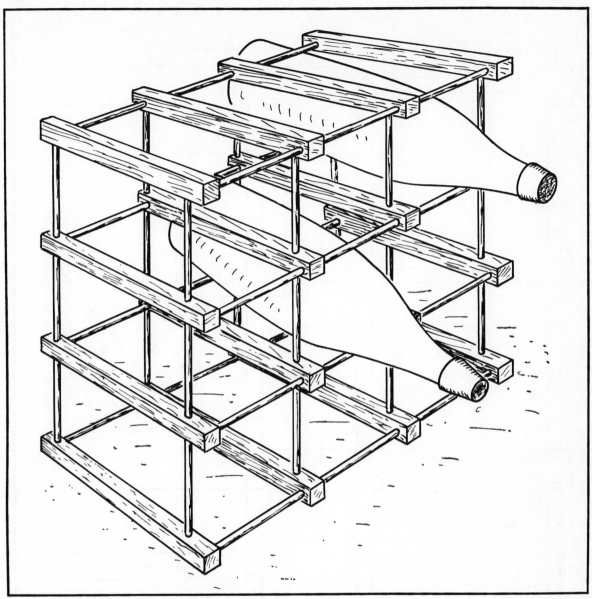

Fig. 6-49. A wine rack made of square pieces and dowels.

range spacing of the frames so the sizes are the same as vertically and the openings are square (Fig. 6-50C).

5. The dowel rods can go through the outside frames, but if you expect to extend later, stop the rods halfway (Fig. 6-50D). More dowels can then be glued in later to join on one or more additional frames.

Materials List for Sectional Wine Bottle Rack (nine bottles)

16 pieces   1 × 1 × 11
16 rods   17 × ⅜, ⁷⁄₁₆, or ½ diameter

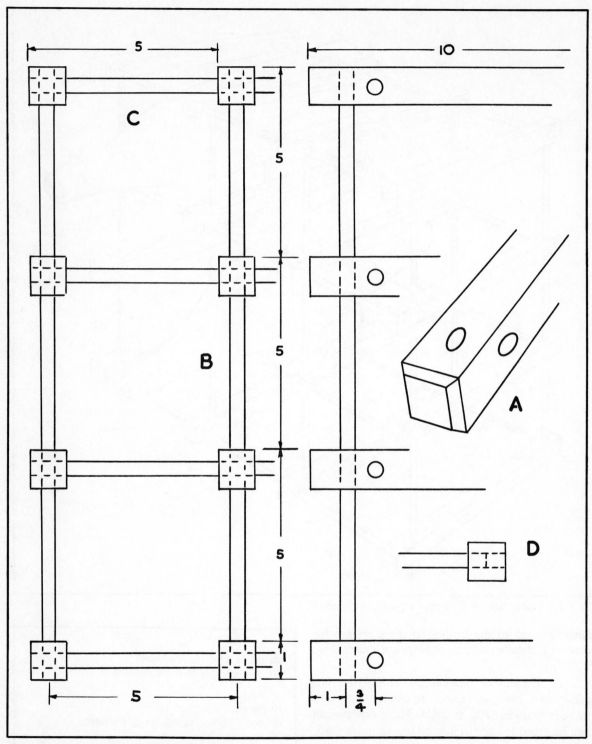

Fig. 6-50. Sizes and details of the wine rack.

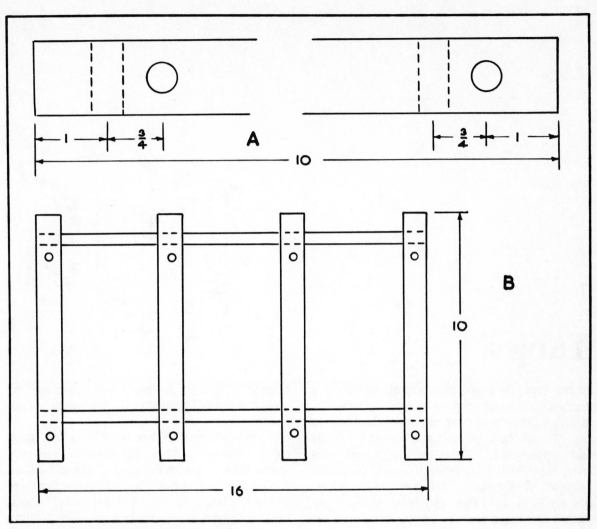

Fig. 6-51. Details of a section of the wine rack.

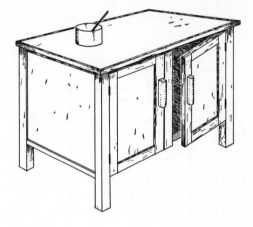

7

Tables

At one time, the center of nearly all activity in a kitchen was a table standing away from the walls, at which the cook and her helpers could work. In many homes the same table also served for meals and maybe laundry. Today much of a cook's activity has moved to countertops around the walls, but there is still a place in most kitchens for at least one table. A table can accommodate the many kitchen activities that are better performed on a surface accessible from all sides, and it is probably bigger and stronger than any available countertop.

The size and type of table will vary according to space and needs, but usually the kitchen table is more of a workbench than an attractive piece of furniture, such as might be found in other rooms. Even then, there is no reason why it should not be good looking. Fitness for purpose brings a certain beauty, and proportions can be attractive.

A kitchen table should be rigid. A shaking working surface is no use to a cook. Therefore, the table needs strong, well-braced legs. The top also must be substantial to hold up to hammering and chopping and have no tendency to flex or

bounce. The table is free-standing and can be moved about and pushed out of the way when not needed.

The traditional kitchen table has a bare wood top so it can be scrubbed occasionally. Your cook might prefer one with Formica or a plastic-coated top similar to other built-in countertops, but there is an advantage in having a top that cannot be seriously damaged, no matter how rough the cutting and chopping on it might be. A thick wood top can be sanded, scraped, or planed to renew its smooth appearance.

A table for use with a normal chair should be 28 inches to 30 inches high. If you expect to stand to work at it, make it 4 inches higher. If your kitchen seating is made to suit a breakfast bar or other high countertop, make a high table. Much depends on intended use. If children will have meals at the table, it might be better at the lower sitting height, but otherwise a cook might find a few inches more worth having.

A kitchen table often has one or more drawers, and they can be useful, but there is a limit to their depth if chairs are to be used. Rails are needed under the tabletop to provide stiffness. To clear the knees of anyone sitting, the lower edge of a rail should not be more than about 7 inches below the surface of the table. When the thickness of the top and framing around the drawer has been allowed for, the actual depth capacity of the drawer within a rail cannot be much. It can still be quite a large area to provide space for such things as knives, books, and the many smaller items used in a kitchen.

If chairs will not be used at the table, and work will be done while standing or sitting on a high stool, all of the space below the tabletop can be made into storage. The table can develop into an island, although it might cease to be movable and must remain in one place all the time.

Any wood can be used for kitchen tables. For strength and rigidity, softwoods would have to be a larger section than most hardwoods. Avoid open-grained woods that might splinter in use or if knocked. Several coats of a clear finish will seal most woods and reduce the risk of splintering or grain breaking. There is a fashion for pine and other softwoods with knots, but for a working top that is to be scrubbed, they would be unsatisfactory since the harder knots will finish higher than the surrounding wood after several vigorous washes. This problem can be corrected by planing, however. A table with a light-colored top looks hygienic, and it could have legs and rails in a darker harder wood.

The emphasis should be on providing ample strength. Size is also important. Some traditional kitchen tables were enormous. There would not be space in a modern kitchen for them, but a table as large as can be conveniently fitted in will be more use than a small, unsteady table of insufficient area for some work. Consider appearance, but utility is what you are providing when you make a kitchen table.

PLAIN KITCHEN TABLE

The sizes of the table in Figs. 7-1 and 7-2 are suggestions and can be altered to suit your needs. The method of construction is typical of that used in a variety of tables made from solid wood. Strength comes from the joints between the rails under the top and the legs. This leaves all the lower part free from more rails and stretchers so stools, boxes, etc., can be stored underneath while still allowing you to move the table without affecting these items.

Because wood expands and contracts in its width, do not attach the broad tabletop too tightly. It might vary in width ¼ inch or more from time to time. With rigid fixing, joints might be broken or cracks might develop in the top as the wood moves. Attaching with buttons allows for movement. The legs are 3 inches square. All other parts are 1 inch thick. Joints between rails and legs can be mortises and tenons or dowels. Tenons would provide maximum strength, but dowels should be strong enough.

1. Prepare the material for the legs. Mark them to length and with the positions of the rails together so they match.

2. Mark out the opposite pairs of rails together. If dowels are to be used, mark the lengths for cutting inside the legs. If tenons are to be used, they will be the shoulders and the tenons extend a further 1 inch.

3. Cut grooves inside the top edges of all rails (Fig. 7-3A). Make them ⅜ inch wide and deep ½ inch from the edge, though slight adjustments to suit your equipment will not matter.

4. If dowels are used, they should have a ½-inch diameter and penetrate the legs and rails at least 1 inch (Fig. 7-3B). Mark their positions centrally using five dowels in each joint with one close to the groove (Fig. 7-3C).

5. If tenons are to be cut, make them ½ inch thick. Because the depth of a rail is too great for single tenons, divide it into two with a haunch at the top (Fig. 7-3D). Let the tenons penetrate each leg about 1 inch.

6. Cut the legs to length. At the top, leave a little length for trimming level with the rails after assembly. At the bottom, round or bevel each surface to reduce the risk of grain breaking out if the table is dragged and to reduce marking the floor covering.

7. You can leave the legs square, but they

Fig. 7-1. A substantial kitchen table of basic design.

will look better if you round the outer corners (Fig. 7-3E).

8. Assemble the long rails to their legs on a flat surface to avoid twist. Check squareness by measuring diagonals. Sight across the legs to see they are not twisted in relation to each other. Assemble the second side over the first so they match.

9. Let the glue set before joining these assemblies with the short rails. Again, check squareness by measuring diagonals. Stand the table on a flat surface and sight across to check for twist.

10. Make the top by gluing sufficient boards to make up the width. Level the surfaces, square the ends, and round the outer corners. The amount of overhang allowed should be sufficient for any clamp-on equipment the cook wishes to use.

11. Make the buttons from a ⅞-×-1½-inch strip. Three across each end and five along each side, making sixteen altogether, should hold the top securely. Cut a button (Fig. 7-3F) to slide in the groove, then when the screw is tightened, it pulls the top tight onto the rails.

12. Invert the top and the framework on it. Mark the positions of the parts to center them.

13. Position buttons about 1 inch from each leg and the others evenly spaced between them. Fit a button into a groove so there is a gap (Fig. 7-3G) to allow for movement. Locate all the but-

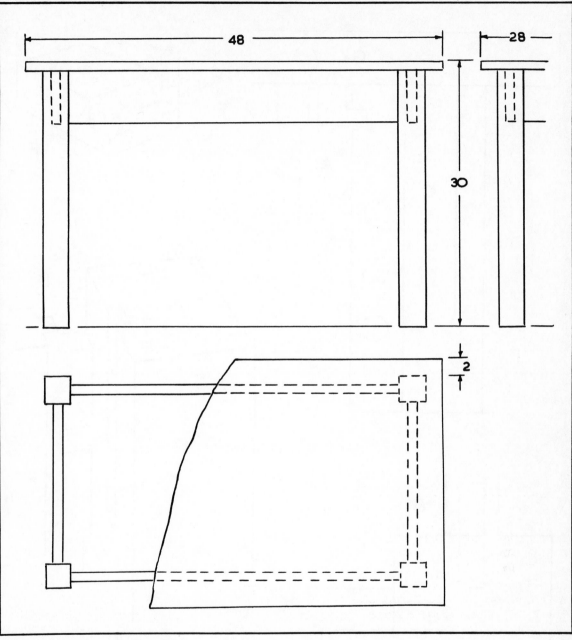

Fig. 7-2. Suggested sizes of the table.

tons before tightening the screws. Do not use glue under the buttons. When the table has been in use some time, turn it over and examine the buttons. If the wood in the top came from a very different environment, it might have shrunk or expanded so much in the kitchen that you might have to reposition some buttons.

14. Even if the top is to be left untreated, the other parts can be stained and polished or varnished.

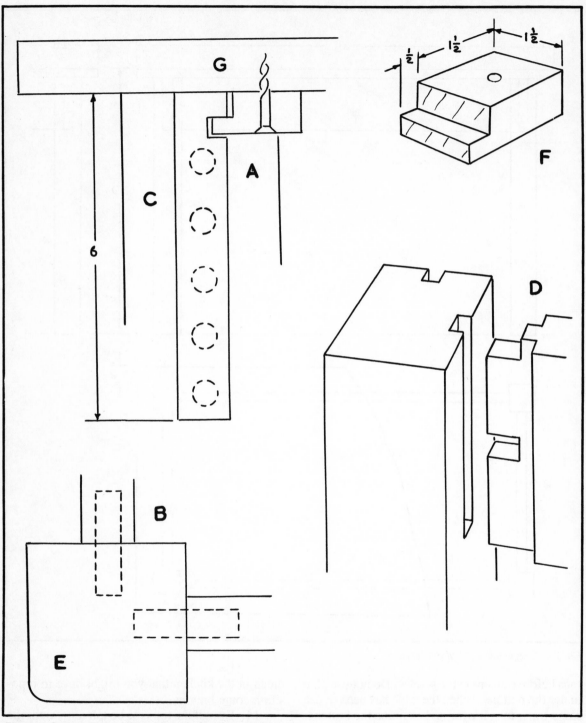

Fig. 7-3. Construction of the table with dowels or tenons.

TABLE WITH SIDE DRAWER

A drawer fitted into the rails under a table is a logical way of using the space. Whether the drawer comes at a side or an end depends on the use of the table. For tables that are pushed against a wall with a long side outwards, a side drawer is accessible even when the table is out of use. The table in Fig. 7-4 has a drawer centered in one side al-

Materials List for Plain Kitchen Table

4 legs	3	×	3	×	30	
2 rails	1	×	6	×	42	
2 rails	1	×	6	×	22	
16 buttons	⅞	×	1	×	3	

Fig. 7-4. A table with a drawer and shaped legs.

most the full depth of available space. This makes the outside measurements of the drawer 4 inches deep, 18 inches wide, and 21 inches back to front.

The table is made in a similar way to the first project (Figs 7-1 to 7-3), so be sure to read the instructions for that table. Typical sizes are shown (Fig. 7-5), but you can vary them to suit your needs and space.

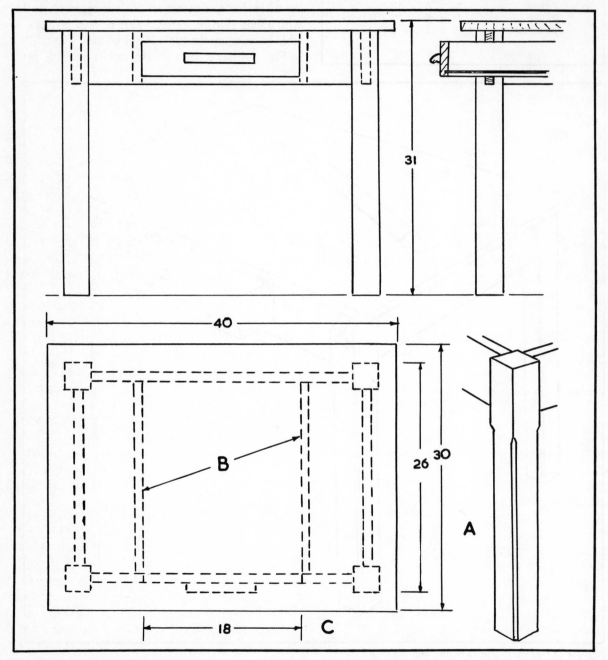

Fig. 7-5. Sizes of the table with drawer.

A solid wood top is specified. Most parts are 1 inch thick, and the legs are 3 inches square. The front can be a solid piece with a hole cut for the drawer front, or it could be built up of top and bottom strips with spacers between.

1. Mark out all legs together, with the positions of the rails marked on two surfaces. You can leave the legs square, round them on the outer corners as suggested for the first project, or cut stopped chamfers on one or four corners of each leg (Fig. 7-5A).

2. Mark the two pairs of rails. They could be doweled or joined to the legs with mortise-and-tenon joints (Fig. 7-3C and D).

3. If the front rail is to be solid, mark and cut a central hole for the drawer 4 inches deep (Fig. 7-6A) and 18 inches wide (Fig. 7-5B). If the front rail is to be built up, cut two pieces 1 inch square the full length and 4-inch pieces to fit between them and leave an 18-inch gap at the center. Glue these parts together. See that the overall sizes of the front rail match those of the back.

4. Cut two pieces of 1-×-6-inch section to act as drawer guides across the table (Fig. 7-5C). Mark them for dowels into the rails and add 1-inch-square strips to act as runners and kickers (Fig. 7-6B). See that these assemblies match the ends of the openings and mark for similar dowels in the back rail so the drawer guides will be parallel.

5. Cut grooves for buttons (Fig. 7-3A) in the end and back rails.

6. Assemble the front and back rails to their legs. Check squareness by measuring diagonals and sight across to check freedom from twist. See that the front and back assemblies match.

7. When you add the end rails, include the drawer guides. Check squareness by measuring diagonals across the tops of the legs. Squareness is important because the drawer needs a parallel square space if it is to fit properly and slide smoothly.

8. A good fit for the drawer is easier to achieve if you make it before adding the top. This drawer has its front level with the rail and is traditionally constructed using dovetail joints. You could make it with its front overlapping the rail and with other joints, if you wish.

9. Cut the drawer front (Fig. 7-7A) to fit the opening with only minimum clearance all around. Cut the wood for the sides (Fig. 7-7B) to slide easily between the runners and kickers and slightly too long.

10. Groove these pieces for the drawer bottom. You could use ⅛-inch hardboard, but for a drawer of this size, ¼-inch plywood is better.

11. Mark and cut stopped dovetails between the sides and the front (Fig. 7-7C).

12. Mark the lengths of the drawer sides. The back of the drawer must clear the buttons holding the top. A gap of 2 inches is ample. When you fit the drawer, put blocks on the drawer runners to stop the drawer when its front is level with the rail.

13. Make the drawer back (Fig. 7-7D) to fit above the grooves in the sides. Its top could be ⅛ inch below the top edges of the sides. Cut through dovetails. Let the tails extend slightly—you can plane them off after assembly—so they hit the stops or back rail when the drawer front is level with the front rail.

14. Assemble the four parts of the drawer. When the glue has set, plane off any excess wood at the joints and try the drawer in position. If necessary, plane the sides and edges to make a good fit.

15. Slide the bottom in from the back. If the fit of the drawer is still satisfactory, screw the bottom upwards into the back.

16. A long handle is advisable because you can reach and grasp it from any position. It can be plastic or metal, but one that can be made is suggested. It is most easily shaped on the edge of a board (Fig. 7-6C), then cut off. Attach it with glue and screws from inside the front.

17. Make up the top by joining sufficient boards. Level the surfaces and square the ends.

18. Make enough buttons (Fig. 7-3F). There could be three or four at the ends and four or five at the back rail. They are not used at the front rail.

19. Because the front rail has to be attached securely to the top, allow for any expansion or contraction towards the back with buttons. Glue between the front rail and the top and supplement by screwing upwards. In the drawer opening, drive

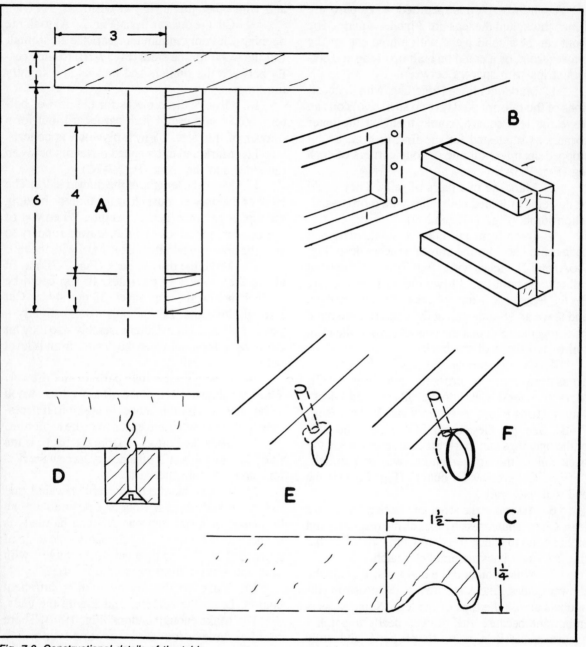

Fig. 7-6. Constructional details of the table.

three screws (Fig. 7-6D). Countersink so the screw heads are below the surface and cannot interfere with the drawer. Toward each front leg, drive pocket screws from inside. One way is to cut a pocket with a gouge so a hole goes diagonally and the screw head comes within the pocket (Fig. 7-6E). A similar effect is obtained by using a large drill to make a sloping recess (Fig. 7-6F).

20. Finish the table in any of the ways suggested for the first table.

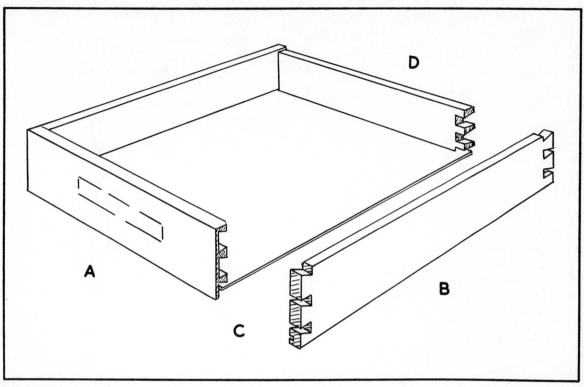

Fig. 7-7. Drawer details.

Materials List for Table with Side Drawer				
4 legs	3	× 3	× 31	
2 rails	1	× 6	× 23	
2 rails	1	× 6	× 35	
2 drawer guides	1	× 6	× 23	
4 drawer guides	1	× 1	× 23	
1 drawer front	1	× 4	× 19	
2 drawer sides	¾	× 4	× 22	
1 drawer back	¾	× 3½	× 19	
1 drawer bottom	18	× 22	× ¼	plywood
1 top	1	× 30	× 41	

FORMICA-TOPPED TWO-DRAWER TABLE

For the greatest drawer capacity within the rail level of a table, there needs to be a drawer at each end, taken in until they almost meet in the middle. The top could be solid, as in previous tables, but this example has a plywood top covered with Formica. Such a top is not able to take such heavy hitting as a thick solid top, but it is strong enough for most purposes in a kitchen. The plastic surface is easy to clean and hygienic for rolling out pastry and similar purposes.

The table could be any size, but suitable measurements are suggested. Having drawers as wide as possible in each end means that some of the benefits of end rails for stiffening are lost; there are lower rails also shown across the ends (Fig. 7-8). Things can still be pushed under the table from either side, and chairs can be used for seating at the sides. At the sizes shown, this could be a breakfast table for up to four people.

The legs are shown square, but they might be rounded or chamfered as suggested for previous tables. The top has a 2-inch overlap on the legs, making the end drawers 20 inches wide and about 15 inches deep. The side rails are 6 inches deep, but at the end there are rails 1 inch deep above and below 4-inch drawers. Any wood can be used.

1. Mark out two pairs of legs (Fig. 7-10A) with the positions of rails. Leave cutting to length until after joints have been prepared.

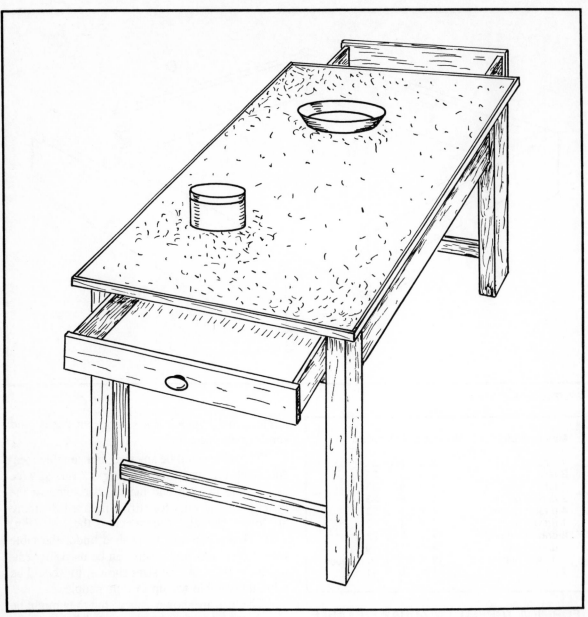

Fig. 7-8. A table with end drawers and lower rails.

2. The side rails are 1-×-6-inch section arranged centrally on the legs (Fig. 7-9A). Parts can be assembled with dowels or mortise-and-tenon joints. For dowels, cut the side rails to length between the legs (Fig. 7-10B). For tenons, allow a further 1 inch for ½-inch wide tenons at each end (Fig. 7-10C). Cut the tenons with a haunch at the top. If dowels are used, allow for five at each end.

3. The end rails are 1-×-3-inch sections horizontal above and below the drawers (Fig. 7-10D). The underside of the lower ones should be level with the bottom edges of the side rails. All four rails are the same. There could be dowels, but you might prefer mortises and tenons (Fig.

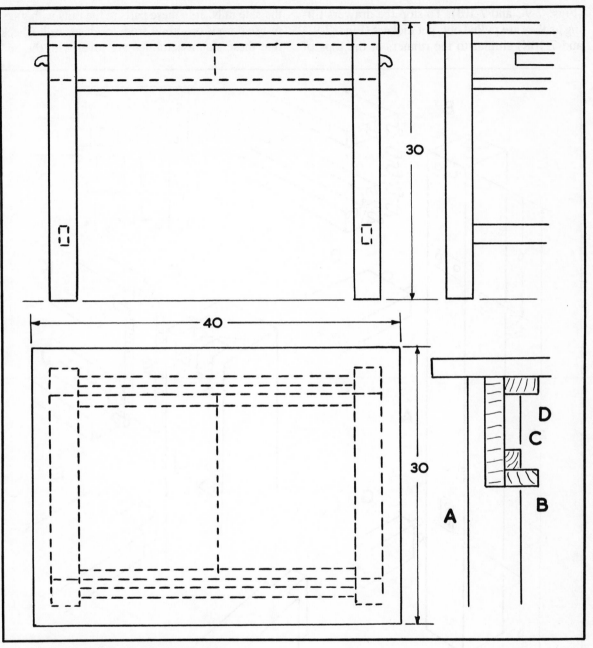

Fig. 7-9. Sizes of the table with end drawers.

7-10E and F). Take the dowels or tenons 1 inch into the legs.

4. Make the bottom end rails the same length as the drawer rails and arrange dowels (Fig. 7-10G) or tenon joints (Fig. 7-10H).

5. The drawers fit between the legs; they have to be guided between the side rails. Make 1-×-2-inch runners to carry the drawers (Fig. 7-9B). To keep the drawers in line, put guides on these to keep their inner surfaces level with the legs

(Figs. 7-9C and 7-10J). To stop the drawers tilting as they are pulled out, put kickers (Figs. 7-9D and 7-10K) similar to the runners at the tops of the side rails. Join these parts to the rails with glue, or use dowels or screws from inside as well. Check that these side assemblies are level with the end

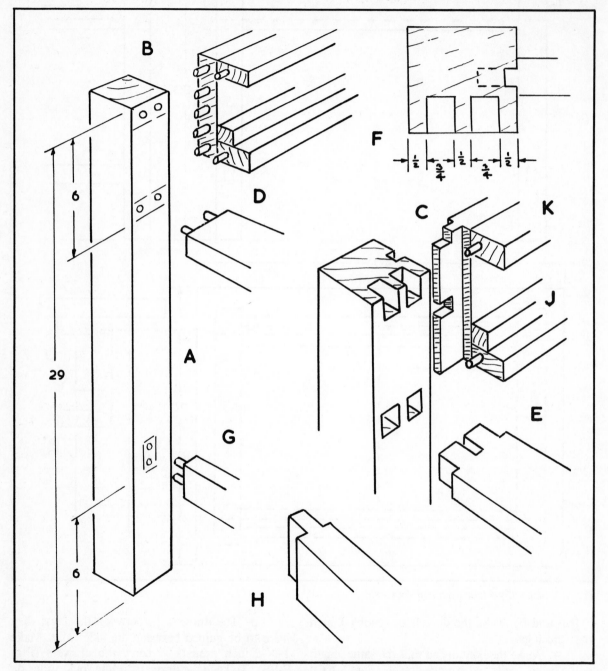

Fig. 7-10. Constructional details of the table with end drawers, using dowels or tenons.

188

rail arrangements on the legs. Prepare the ends of the runners and kickers for dowels into the legs.

6. Assemble the pair of ends first, with their three rails into the legs. Check squareness and lack of twist.

7. Add the lengthwise rails and square the assembly while it stands on a level surface.

8. Mark the centers of the drawer rails and allow for the drawers coming to within about ½ inch of that. This will give you the length of the drawer sides. The two drawers do not have to be the same length. One could be longer than the other if there is an awkward size to be fitted in. You will put stop blocks on the runners later, but do not fit them until after you have made and fitted the drawers.

9. Make the drawers the same way as in the last project (Fig. 7-7) with dovetails and the front level with the legs.

10. Alternative drawers could be made with the drawer fronts overlapping the rails and legs and with dowels at the corners instead of dovetails.

11. Overlap the front of each drawer (Fig. 7-11A) over the legs and the top rails by ⅜ inch. Round or chamfer the front edges. Mark on its inner surface the size of the opening.

12. Cut pieces for the drawer sides slightly too long. Groove them for the bottoms (Fig. 7-11B), which could be hardboard or thin plywood.

13. Mark the sides and front for dowels. Because a groove across the front would show at the ends, put a strip across there to support the bottom (Fig. 7-11C).

14. Mark the lengths of the sides and allow for the back coming above the bottom and a short distance in from their ends (Fig. 7-11D).

15. Check the sizes of parts in the table framework. Assemble the drawers. Fit handles.

16. If dovetailed fronts that fit between the legs are used, arrange central stops on the guides so the fronts come level. If overlapping fronts are used, they can act as stops to prevent the drawers going in too far, but to avoid straining their joints, also put stops on the runners.

17. Cut the plywood top to size. Cover it with Formica. Edges can be covered with plain strips

of wood mitered at the corners (Fig. 7-11E). It might be better to take the strips under as well (Fig. 7-11F). Plastic molding could be glued on.

18. As plywood does not expand or contract, the top can be firmly glued and screwed on. Drill screw holes through the top end rails and the side kickers. If the joints fit closely and are glued, screws at 12-inch intervals should be adequate.

19. Finish the wood in any way you wish.

Materials List for
Formica-Topped Two-Drawer Table

4 legs	3 ×	3	× 30
2 side rails	1 ×	6	× 34
4 end rails	1 ×	3	× 24
2 bottom rails	1 ×	2	× 24
2 drawer runners	1 ×	2	× 34
2 drawer kickers	1 ×	2	× 34
2 drawer guides	1 ×	1	× ¾
2 drawer fronts	¾ ×	4½	× 21
4 drawer sides	⅝ ×	4	× 19
2 drawer backs	⅝ ×	3½	× 21
2 drawer bottoms	19 ×	21	× ⅛ hardboard
			or ¼ plywood
1 top	30 ×	40	× ¾ plywood

CHEF'S TABLE

A professional chef or cook likes to have a substantial table with deep drawers and racks for pots. There might be hooks for tools at the ends and knife slots in the top. As the table will only be used while the user is standing, it can be higher than normal. There is no need for sitting knee space underneath. The table in Fig. 7-12 is designed as a work place for a serious cook. It is intended to have a thicker top and 1¼ or 1½ inches is suggested. As the shelves underneath also stiffen the legs, a reduced section of 2 × 3 inches is drawn (Fig. 7-13A).

For constant professional use, the top and framing should be a light-colored hardwood. For normal home kitchen use, however, you might select a lighter softwood, which would be an advantage if the table has to be moved much.

Because the drawers open at the front, use any clamp-on equipment at an end where the overlap is greater. The shelves are made up of slats screwed on, but you could use solid wood or plywood, if

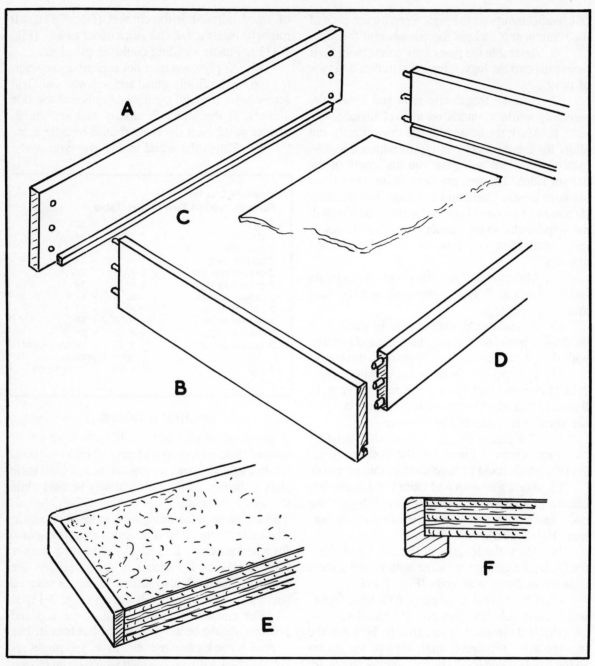

Fig 7-11. A doweled drawer and a plywood top.

you wish. Check the sizes of pots or other items you wish to store and adjust the shelf heights if necessary.

1. Prepare the wood to size and mark out

the two pairs of legs with the positions of the parts that will be attached to them (Fig. 7-14A). Details of the main joints are not shown, but they could be dowels or mortise and tenons, as described in

Fig. 7-12. This table with drawers and shelves is intended for use when standing.

the previous project. Allow for the chosen joints when marking out the legs and other parts. Round or chamfer the outer corners of the legs, if you wish.

2. Prepare the wood for the top end and rear rails, 1-×-8-inch section. Groove the rear rail only for buttons (Fig. 7-3A and F).

3. At the front there are rails 1-×-2-inch sec-

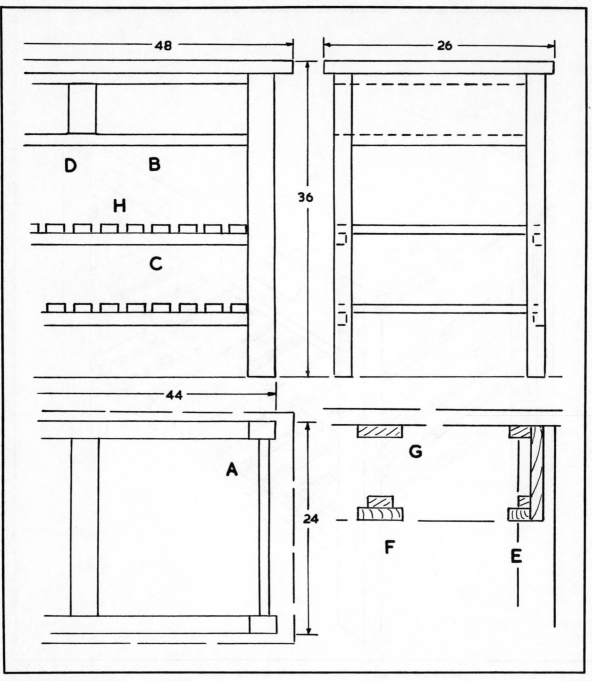

Fig. 7-13. Sizes and layout of the table.

tion above and below the drawer fronts (Figs. 7-13B and 14B). Prepare them to match the length of the rear rail.

4. Cut the mortise-and-tenon joints or drill for dowels between all rails and legs.

5. Make the shelf rails (Figs. 7-13C and

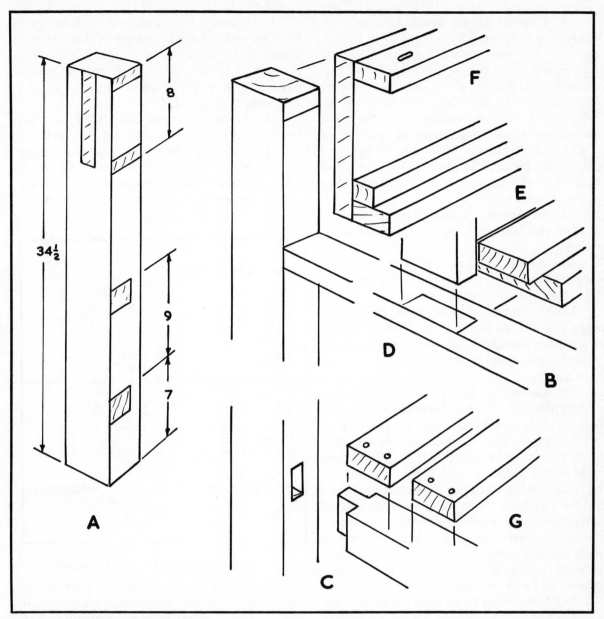

Fig. 7-14. Assembly details of the table.

14C) with tenons or dowels. Arrange them so the front surfaces of rails and legs are level.

    6. Make a division to fit between the drawer rails (Figs. 7-13D and 14D) with its front surface level with the rails.

    7. The arrangement of drawer guides, runners, and kickers at the legs is similar to the last project (Fig. 7-13E). At the center behind the division, there has to be a 5-inch-wide strip to act as runner for both drawers, with a 3-inch piece on it to guide the drawers (Figs. 7-13F and 14E). Another 5-inch piece acts as a kicker above (Fig. 7-13G). Arrange both 5-inch pieces to dowel or tenon into the front and back rails.

8. When the tabletop is added, screw it upwards through the top drawer rail at about 12-inch intervals. This means that if it expands or contracts, any movement will be towards the back. The buttons at the rear rail will allow for this movement. At the ends, make slot holes in the kickers (Fig. 7-14F) so the screws can slide when the wood moves. Slots ½ inch long and two or three screws at each end is adequate. Make sure the slots are countersunk enough underneath to keep the screw heads clear of the drawer edges. Put similar slots in the central kicker.

9. Join the outer runners, guides, and kickers to their end rails. Join the central guide to its runner.

10. Make the long assemblies first, with all long rails into the legs, and check that back and front match and are without twist.

11. Fit the central pieces between the rails when you join the legs with the short rails. See that the table stands upright and the legs are the same distance apart, back to front, at the bottom as at the top.

12. The slats are 1-×-2-inch section, spaced 1 inch apart (Fig. 7-13H) and screwed to their rails (Fig. 7-14G). Round their ends and upper edges.

13. Drawers can be made in any way you wish. They could be dovetailed (Fig. 7-7) with the front level with the rail. The drawer backs could come against the rear rails, for maximum capacity, but the drawer fronts are easier to adjust level if the drawers are made shorter and stops put on the runners when the fronts are correct. The drawer parts could be doweled, with the fronts overlapping the openings (Fig. 7-11). Make wooden handles or fit knobs or metal handles.

14. Make the top by gluing boards. Level the surfaces and square the ends. Round the corners and take sharpness off the edges.

15. Invert the framework on the underside of the top. Locate it and first drive the screws at the front. Drive screws through the kickers at the midpoints of the slots. Fit the buttons with enough clearance to allow movement.

16. Leave the top untreated, but stain and polish or varnish the rest of the table.

17. Hooks in one or both end rails are useful. They could be metal screw hooks (Fig. 7-15A). You could use thin dowels at an angle (Fig. 7-15B). If you want to retain a particular piece of equipment, it might be better with a slotted block and a turnbutton (Fig. 7-15C).

18. At one end arrange knife slots through the top (Fig. 7-15D) just outside the rail. Several fairly short slots are better than a few long ones to hang the knives near upright. Drill most of the waste from a slot and clean it through with a chisel. To protect you and the blades, put a piece of plywood across the legs (Fig. 7-15E).

Materials List for Chef's Table

4 legs	2 ×	3	× 36
1 rail	1 ×	8	× 43
2 rails	1 ×	8	× 23
2 rails	1 ×	2	× 43
1 division	1 ×	3	× 8
4 rails	1½ ×	1½	× 43
26 slats	1 ×	2	× 25
2 drawer runners	1 ×	2	× 23
2 drawer guides	1 ×	1	× 23
2 drawer kickers	1 ×	2	× 23
1 drawer runner	1 ×	5	× 23
1 drawer guide	1 ×	3	× 23
1 drawer kicker	1 ×	5	× 23
2 drawer fronts	¾ ×	6½	× 19
4 drawer sides	⅝ ×	6	× 23
2 drawer backs	⅝ ×	5½	× 19
2 drawer bottoms	19 ×	23	× ⅛ hardboard or ¼ plywood
1 top	1½ ×	26	× 49

BREAKFAST TABLE AND BENCHES

A table that can be worked on in the kitchen as well as used for meals has obvious advantages. It might not be as strong and the height will be less than a table intended for standing, however. The table in Fig. 7-16 could be used with chairs, but benches are included. They stow under the table and can have other uses in the kitchen, on a deck or patio, or elsewhere in the home.

A table gets its greatest stability from having a leg at each corner. Because this table has substantial pedestals and a good spread to its feet (Fig.

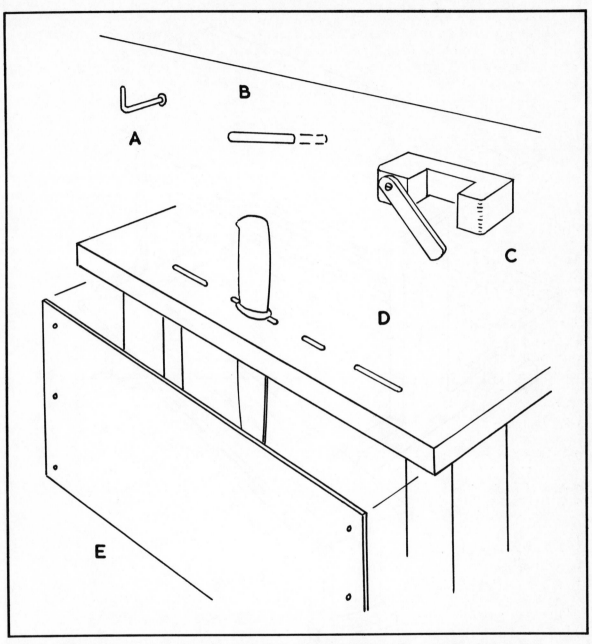

Fig. 7-15. Things can be hung at the end of a table (A-C). Knives fit into slots with a protective sheet (D, E).

7-17), it should stand up to most tabletop work done by a cook.

Any wood could be used. The top is shown as solid wood, but it could be thick plywood covered with Formica. The joints are mortises and tenons. You could use dowels, but they should be thick (⅞-inch or 1-inch diameter is suitable) and fairly close together to give enough glue area for strength. Arrange holes in the pedestal tops so those from the stretcher are kept clear of those in the legs.

Fig. 7-16. This pedestal table has matching bench seats.

1. Mark out the legs (Fig. 7-17A). Allow for the thickness of the tabletop and the pads under the feet as well as the thicknesses of the pieces across when settling on the leg length between shoulders. Mark the position of the lower stretcher (Fig. 7-18A) to make it the same height as the stretchers under the benches for a neat appearance.

2. The leg tenons can be ¾ inch thick and

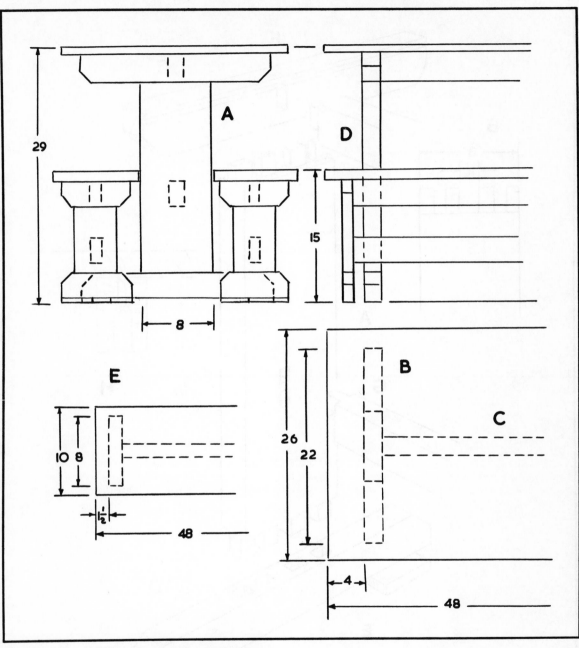

Fig. 7-17. Sizes and layout of the table with benches.

1 inch, or slightly more, long. Mark out with a gap at the center (Fig. 7-18B) to clear the tenon from the top stretcher. Mark the bottom the same, although there is no stretcher at that level.

3. Mark out the pedestal tops (Figs. 7-17B and 18C) and feet (Fig. 7-18D) together, with mortises to match the legs. Bevel the ends.

4. Groove the inner surfaces of the top pieces for buttons.

5. Make pads 4 inches long (Fig. 7-18E) and

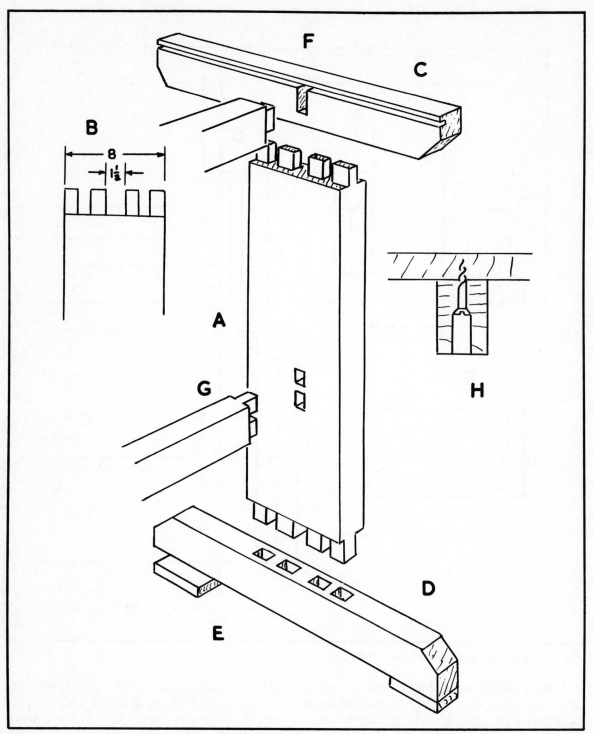

Fig. 7-18. Constructional details of the table.

glue them under the ends of the feet.

6. Make the two stretchers (Fig. 7-17C), allowing the lengths to overhang the tabletop 4 inches at each end. The tenons can be ¾ inch thick and 1 inch long. At the top stringer, cut down the tenon to below the groove and the same amount up from the lower edge (Fig. 7-18F). At the lower stringer, cut the tenon to the edge and divide it (Fig. 7-18G).

7. The lower stringer needs no further work, but drill the top stringer for screws upward into the tabletop. Five screws in the length of the stringer should be sufficient. To avoid very long screws, counterbore the holes (Fig. 7-18H). As they will be out of sight in the finished table, there will be no need to plug them.

8. Assemble the two pedestals. Check that they match. Let the glue set.

9. Join them with the stretchers. Check that the ends are vertical and the assembly is square when viewed from above. Measure and compare diagonals in all directions while the table is standing on a level surface.

10. Make the top by joining boards, level the surfaces, and square the ends.

11. Invert the top and the framework on it. Screw through the counterbored holes in the top stringer. Make and fit buttons to engage with the slots in the pedestal tops. Allow for a total of eight—two each side of each leg. As any expansion or contraction will be in a direction along the grooves, fix the buttons close to the pedestal tops.

12. The two benches are identical and made in a very similar way to the table; they look like miniature versions of it. They have the same overall length as the table, but the legs come outside the table legs (Fig. 7-17D) and are not so far from the bench ends (Fig. 7-17E). Check bench sizes against your table.

13. Make both benches at the same time, with parts for each marked out together so they match. Make the four pedestals (Fig. 7-19). Adjust the heights to make the tops 15 inches from the floor.

14. On the legs, leave a gap between tenons to clear the mortises and tenons of the top stretcher, with single tenons each side (Fig. 7-19A).

15. When you mark out the pedestal tops, allow space for counterbored screws upward into the top (Fig. 7-19B). With this width bench top, there is no need to allow for expansion and contraction.

16. Make the stretchers the same lengths between shoulders. At the top there can be a single cut-down tenon (Fig. 7-19C), but at the bottom divide the tenons to the full depth. All tenons can go through and be wedged, or you could make them about ¾ inch long. Drill counterbored holes in the top stretcher (Fig. 7-18H).

17. Assemble the bench ends. Check that they match. Let the glue set.

18. Join them with the stretchers. Check squareness and be sure the benches fit into the table.

19. Make the bench tops. Round their corners and take sharpness off the edges.

20. Invert each framework on its top. Screw upwards through the stringer, then up through the pedestal tops.

21. Finish in any way you wish. A clear finish has a light, clean look, but lower parts might be stained first to emphasize the lighter tops.

Materials List for Breakfast Table and Benches

Table

2 legs	2 ×	8	× 25
2 pedestal tops	2 ×	3	× 23
2 pedestal feet	2 ×	3	× 23
4 pedestal pads	½ ×	2	× 5
2 stretchers	2 ×	3	× 40
1 top	1 ×	26	× 49

Two benches

4 legs	1¼ ×	5·	× 12
4 pedestal tops	1¼ ×	3	× 9
4 pedestal feet	1¼ ×	3	× 9
8 pedestal pads	½ ×	1¼	× 4
4 stretchers	1¼ ×	3	× 45
2 tops	1 ×	10	× 49

TABLE WITH CHILDPROOF DRAWERS

If you wish to arrange drawers in a kitchen table so a child cannot pull them out, yet you do not wish to fit locks, you can arrange drawers that must be lifted to open them. They push in normally, but before you can pull them out, you must lift them

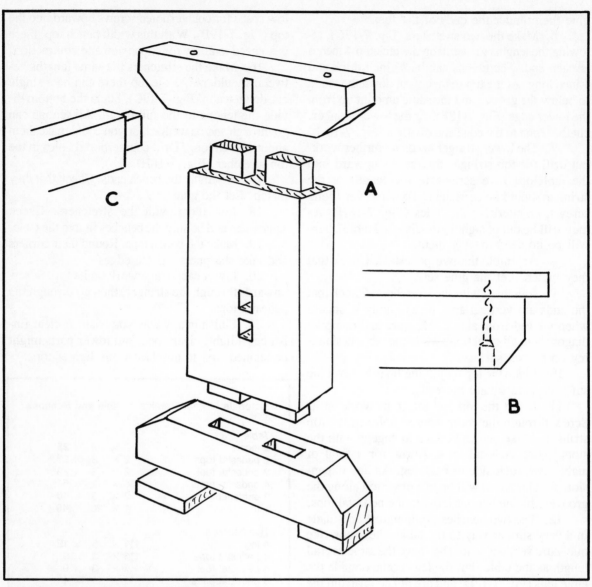

Fig. 7-19. Constructional details of the benches.

about ½ inch. The weight of a full drawer might be more than a small child can lift, even if he discovers what action is needed.

The principle can be used for the drawers in many tables, but the example in Fig. 7-20 is a table of average size with a drawer at each end. The top could be solid wood or thick plywood covered with Formica, as suggested for earlier tables. The rails are slightly deeper than usual, for rigidity,

but they are cut away to give leg room when sitting on a normal chair.

Since there has to be clearance in each opening to allow a drawer to be lifted, the drawer is given a false front to cover the gap. The fronts are as wide a the space between legs, but they extend ¾ inch above and below the drawer depth. The fronts also serve as stops when the drawers are pushed in. The drawers are shown dovetailed, but

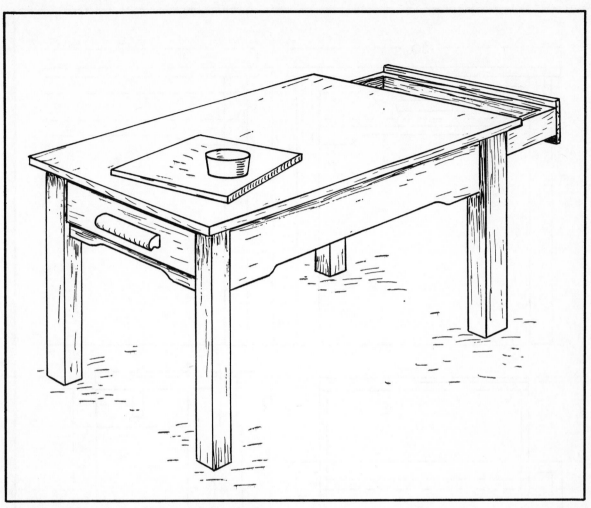

Fig. 7-20. A table with end drawers and shaped rails.

any of the other drawer corner joints could be used. Mortises and tenons are shown for rail-to-leg joints, but they could be doweled.

Any wood might be used. Drawer parts will be more durable if made of hardwood. Their bottoms can be thin plywood or hardboard.

1. Make the four legs and mark the positions of rails (Figs. 7-21A and 7-22A) but leave a little extra at the tops until joints have been cut. There is a gap of 3½ inches between the end rails (Fig. 7-23A), and the bottom edges of rails are level all around.

2. Make the side rails (Fig. 7-21B). Allow 1 inch at each end for tenons and reduce the bot-

tom edge by 1 inch with a curve 5 inches from each shoulder (Fig. 7-21C).

3. Make the top end rails, which are parallel strips 1 inch deep (Figs. 7-22B and 7-23B).

4. Make the bottom end rails (Fig. 7-22C) with the depth reduced to match the shaping on the side rails (Fig. 7-21C).

5. Mark the tenons ½ inch thick (Fig. 7-21D). Cut separate haunched tenons on the deeper rails (Fig. 7-22D). Mark and cut the mortises to match.

6. Fit the drawer runners (Figs. 7-22E and 7-23C) to the side rails at this stage or leave them until after the framework has been assembled and

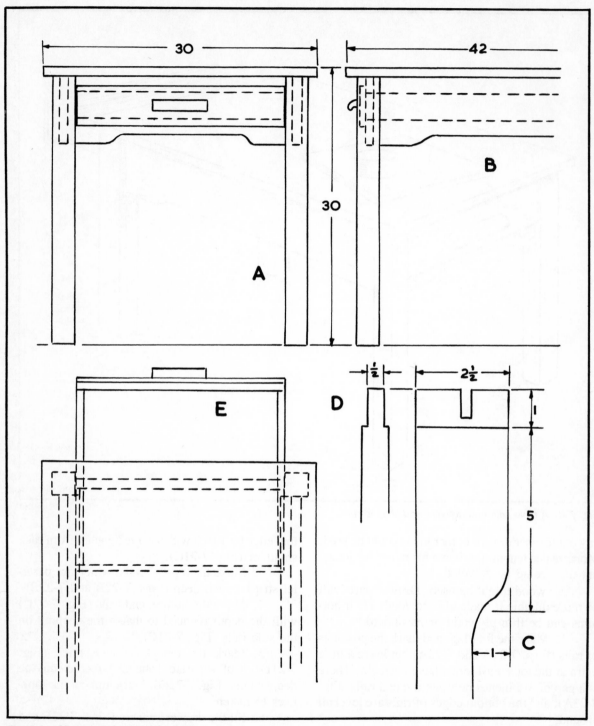

Fig. 7-21. Sizes and details of the table.

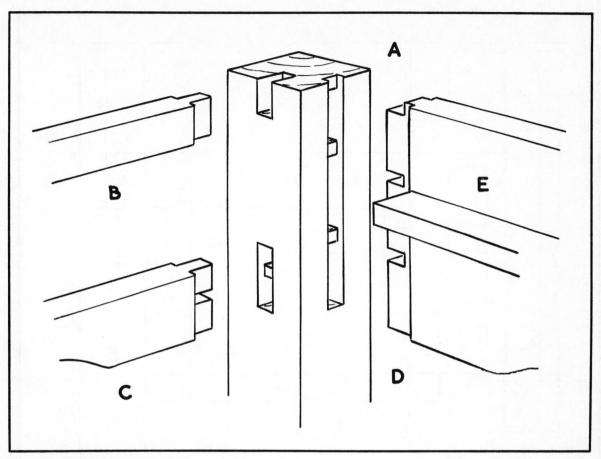

Fig. 7-22. Details of rail joints to legs.

the drawers are being fitted. Glue the runners to the side rails and from inside, counterboring the screw heads.

7. To fit a solid top, groove inside the top edges of the rails to take buttons. To fit a plywood top, drill screw holes through the shallow end rails and make pockets for screws inside the top edges of the deep rails.

8. Assemble the end rails to their legs and check squareness, then add the side rails. Check for squareness cornerwise as well as vertically.

9. Make the drawers so they almost meet at the center of the table or less than that if you wish. Check the height of each drawer opening. It should be 3½ inches (Fig. 7-23A). Whatever the depth, make the drawers ½ inch less.

10. Make the main front of each drawer (Figs. 7-21E and 7-23D) long enough to fit easily between the legs.

11. Cut the drawer sides to the same depth. Groove these parts for the bottom (Fig. 7-23E). Make the drawer back and cut the corner joints.

12. Groove the drawer sides (Fig. 7-23F) to fit on drawer runners. Stop the groove level with the leg edge or slightly forward of that. Make the grooves as deep as the runners plus ½ inch (Fig. 7-23G) to allow for lifting.

13. Assemble the drawer parts and check their action in the framework.

14. Make and fit blocks under the drawer sides, as wide as a side, but ⅜ inch deep (Fig. 7-23H). A length of 3 inches is suitable. Taper the

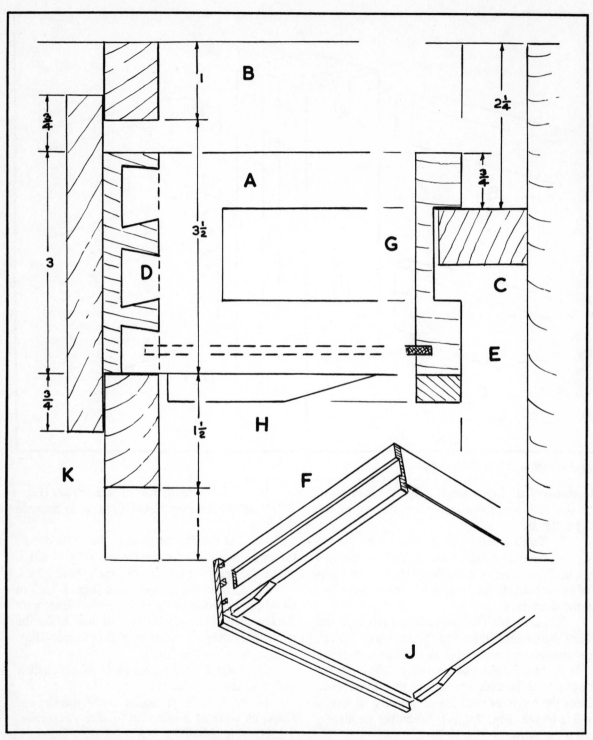

Fig. 7-23. Drawer details showing method of preventing a child pulling it open.

rear edges (Fig. 7-23J). Position each block to give its forward edge about a ⅛-inch clearance against the lower end rail. A depth of ⅜ inch allows a ⅛-inch clearance at the top when the drawer is lifted.

15. Make the false drawer fronts (Fig. 7-23K) the same length as the main fronts but extending ¾ inch above and below. Round or mold the front edges.

16. Make or buy handles. Attach the false fronts with screws from inside. Some of these can also hold the handles. Test the action of the drawers. Rub wax on the sliding surfaces. See that each drawer lifts and releases easily and that it drops to the secured position when it is pushed in.

17. Make and fit the top.

18. Finish the wood in any way you wish.

Materials List for Table with Childproof Drawers

4 legs	2½	×	2½	×	30	
2 rails	¾	×	7	×	38	
2 rails	¾	×	1	×	26	
2 rails	¾	×	2½	×	26	
1 top	1	×	30	×	42	
2 drawer fronts	¾	×	3	×	24	
2 drawer fronts	½	×	4½	×	24	
4 drawer sides	⅝	×	3	×	20	
2 drawer backs	⅝	×	3	×	24	
2 drawer bottoms	20	×	24	×	⅛	plywood or hardboard
2 drawer runners	¾	×	1¼	×	40	
2 drawer handles	1	×	1¼	×	7	
4 drawer stops	⅜	×	⅝	×	4	

CUPBOARD TABLE

If a table is framed and enclosed, the structure has considerable strength because there are no long, unbraced legs. It is then possible to make parts of lighter wood. Enclosing the space below provides useful storage, but the table is no longer suitable for sitting with knees underneath. An enclosed table can be higher, since it normally will be used while standing. If placed against a wall, it could have shelves or another unit built onto it or attached to the wall.

The cupboard table in Fig. 7-24 is enclosed to within 9 inches of the floor, to allow easy cleaning below. It has a pair of doors and no internal fitting. There could be shelves or other compartments.

Nearly all parts are either 2 inches square or 1-×-2-inch section, with plywood panels. For a painted finish, softwood could be used. The top is plywood with a veneer or Formica surface and solid wood edging. The parts can be tenoned (Fig. 7-25), but dowels could be used in the main construction. The strongest doors are tenoned.

1. Sizes need not be as shown (Fig. 7-26), but if the table is made much bigger, leg sections should be increased.

2. Mark out the four legs. The two back legs are the same in both directions (Fig. 7-26A). The front legs are a pair with markings the same in one direction, but the other way, the legs are mortises for the lower rail behind the doors (Fig. 7-26B). Fit ½-inch plywood bottom of the cupboard in a rabbet in the front bottom rail. Arrange the other rails so the plywood rests on them (Fig. 7-27A).

3. Plow grooves in the legs to suit the plywood panels. If possible, stop the grooves at the mortise positions. This can be done with a router. If you have to use a plow plane and follow through below the lower mortises, the grooves will not be very obvious below the cupboard when the table is finished. A depth of ⅜ inch in all parts is adequate (Fig. 7-27B).

4. On the flat rails, make all tenons ¾ inch wide and long with miters where the corners meet (Fig. 7-27C). Continue the grooves for plywood then into the tenons (Fig. 7-27D). If dowels are used, cut the rails to the shoulder lengths and put dowels in each side of the groove (Fig. 7-27E).

5. The four end rails (Fig. 7-25A) are the same. If the table top is to be 24 inches across and overhang 1 inch, the rails are 18 inches between shoulders (or ends if doweled).

6. The top and bottom rear long rails (Fig. 7-25B) are similar but 30 inches between shoulders. The front top rail is the same but without a groove.

7. Make the front bottom rail (Fig. 7-25C) the same length between shoulders, but cut a rabbet in it to take the plywood cupboard bottom (Fig.

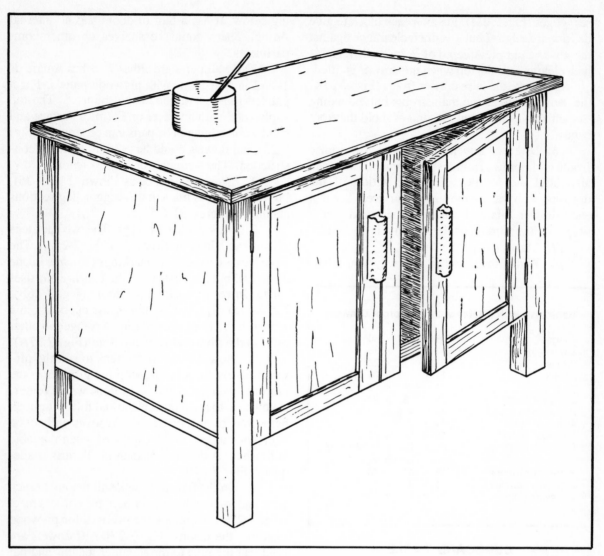

Fig. 7-24. This table has enclosed storage below.

7-27F) and cut back the ends to form tenons (Fig. 7-27G).

8. At the front there is a vertical dividing strip between the doors (Figs. 7-25D and 7-26C). It overlaps at the bottom and can be drilled for two dowels into the rail. At the top, mark and cut a mortise-and-tenon joint.

9. Cut and fit all joints. Make sure the mortises are deep enough for the tenoned parts to pull close against the shoulders.

10. Cut the two end plywood panels squarely but make them slightly undersize. This stops them from pressing in the bottoms of grooves and preventing the frame joints pulling tight.

11. Assemble the two end frames. Fully glue the frame joints, but there is no need for glue all around the plywood edges. Check that the assemblies match and are square and without twist. If necessary, use a nail or screw downward in each top joint to supplement the glue.

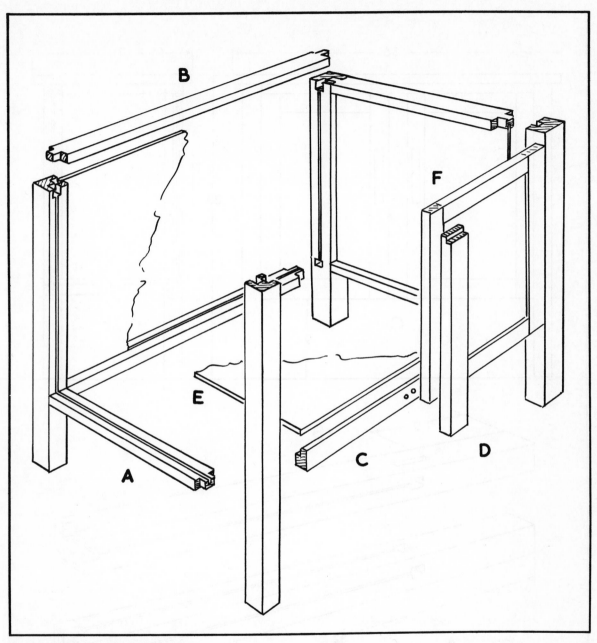

Fig. 7-25. Details of the table framing.

12. When the glue in the ends has set, prepare the back plywood panel and assemble it and the lengthwise rails to the end assemblies. Have the table on a flat surface. Although the plywood will hold the back square, check that the front is true and there is no twist.

13. Cut the bottom plywood. At the ends and back it should rest on the rails (Fig. 7-27H). At

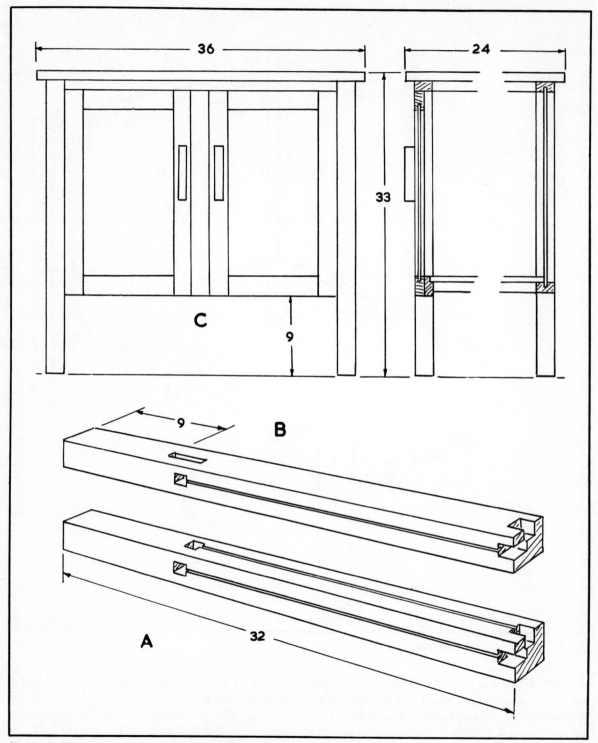

Fig. 7-26. Suggested sizes for the table and leg details.

208

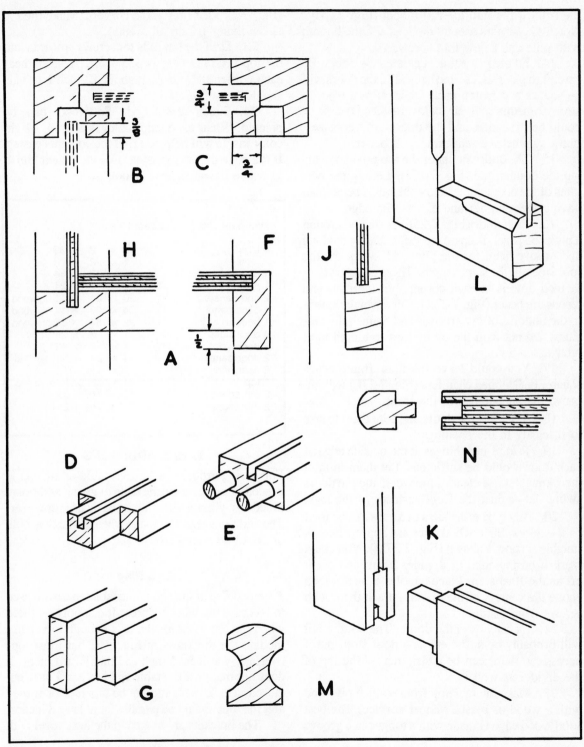

Fig. 7-27. How parts of the table are made.

the front it fits into the rail rabbet (Fig. 7-27F). Notch the corners around the legs. Fit the bottom with glue and a few thin screws.

14. Fit the piece that separates the doors. Be careful to get it square and central so the doors will be square and match each other. If you want to store something of an awkward size, the piece could be off center and the doors different sizes, but a symmetrical appearance is better.

15. The doors fit under the top rail and overlap the bottom one (Fig. 7-27J). Letting the bottoms of the doors come below the rail is better than having them higher and expose the edge.

16. Each door (Fig. 7-25F) is framed around a plywood panel. Prepare the strips slightly too long and groove them for the plywood. Mark out the four sides all the same length. There could be two, $\frac{3}{8}$-inch dowels at each corner, but mortises and tenons are better (Fig. 7-27K). Cut down the tenons to the bottoms of the grooves and haunch the outsides. Do not trim the door sides to length until after assembly.

17. You could leave the door frame edges square, but stopped chamfers (Fig. 7-27L) will improve the appearance of the front.

18. Assemble the doors and trim them to size to fit easily in the openings.

19. Two, 2-inch hinges at the outside edge of each door should be sufficient. Let them in until their knuckles are clear of the wood and the doors swing flat against the front surfaces of the legs.

20. Any type of handles or knobs can be used on the doors. Strip wood ones are appropriate. A suitable section is shown (Fig. 7-27M). You could work it on the edge of a wider board and cut it off as the final step. Place handles 6 inches long above the centers of the doors. Attach them with screws from inside.

21. Fit catches to the doors. The bottom rail will probably be sufficient as a door stop, but if necessary, there can be a strip across the top of the divider as well.

22. Make the tabletop from ¾-inch plywood with a wood or plastic veneer surface. The best solid wood edge is made with a tongue in a groove

(Fig. 7-27N). Miter at the corners. Make the top to overhang 1 inch all around.

23. Drill the top rails for screws upwards into the top inside the plywood panels. A screw near each corner and others at about 12-inch intervals should be sufficient.

24. Finish the wood. Softwood can be painted. Whatever outside color is chosen, a light color inside will help you find the contents easier. If the edge on the top is hardwood, a clear finish to frame the surface will look good.

Materials List for Cupboard Table				
4 legs	2 ×	2	× 33	
2 rails	1 ×	2	× 22	
4 rails	1 ×	2	× 34	
1 divider	1 ×	2	× 24	
2 end panels	20 ×	24	× ¼	plywood
1 back panel	24 ×	28	× ¼	plywood
1 bottom	22 ×	34	× ½	plywood
4 door sides	1 ×	2	× 25	
4 door rails	1 ×	2	× 15	
2 door panels	14 ×	24	× ¼	plywood
2 door handles	1 ×	1½	× 7	
1 top	24 ×	36	× ¾	plywood
2 top edges	⅞ ×	1½	× 37	
2 top edges	⅞ ×	1½	× 25	

TABLE ADDITIONS

For most purposes, a kitchen table is all that is needed. You can alter the table to give it additional functions without affecting its basic use, however. The additions could be made when the table is built or could be added later.

End Flap

A hinged flap at the end of the tabletop can be used to increase the working area. It can only be fitted when the top overlaps the legs enough to accommodate the thickness of brackets, but most tops overlap by at least 1 inch and that is sufficient. It does not matter if the table end has a rail or is enclosed. The legs should not be tapered, or if they are, the tops should be parallel for at least 8 inches.

The brackets are hinged to the legs, level with

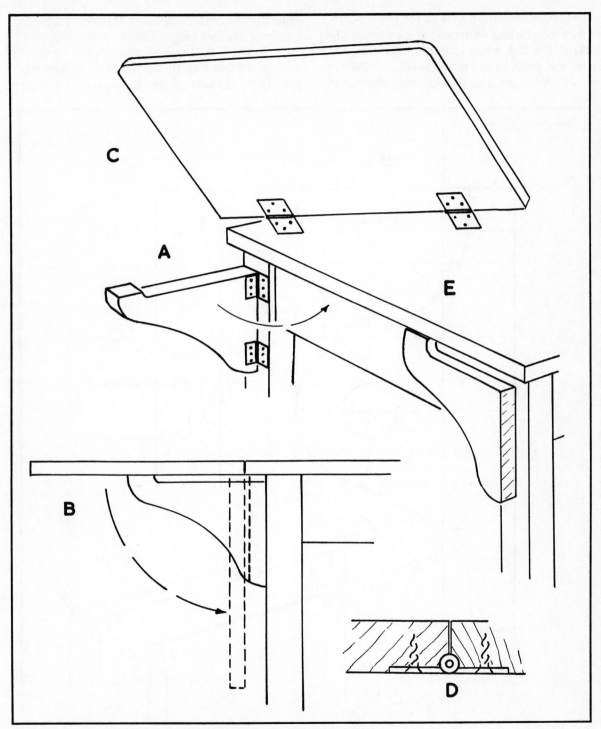

Fig. 7-28. A hinged flap at the end of a table increases the working area.

their outsides when a flap is raised (Fig. 7-28A), so they must be kept short enough not to meet when closed. The flap width should not be more than twice the reach of the brackets (Fig. 7-28B).

1. With the sizes settled, make the flap the same thickness as the tabletop and constructed in the same manner (Fig. 7-28C).

2. Make the brackets thinner than the overhang of the tabletop; for most tables 1 inch is ample. Allow the vertical part to be slightly shorter

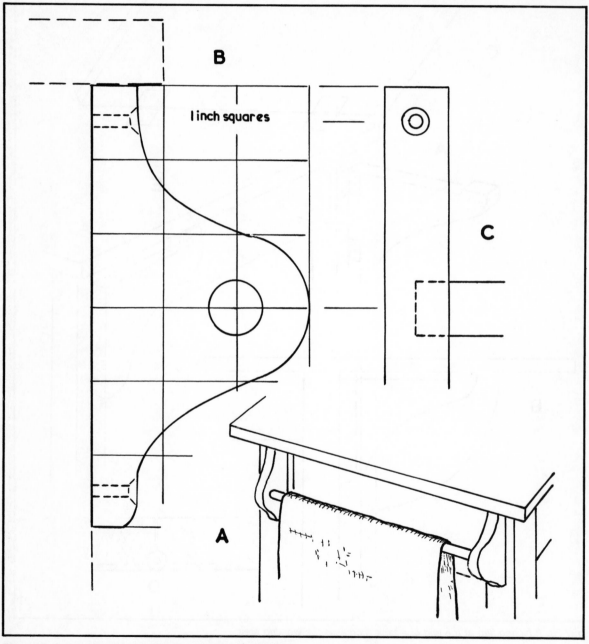

Fig. 7-29. A towel rail can be added to the end of a table.

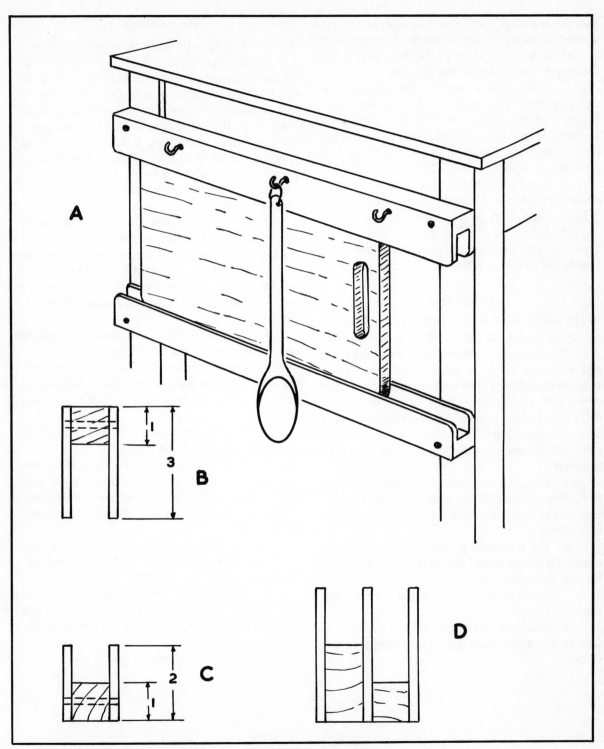

Fig. 7-30. One or more boards can slide into a guide at the end of a table.

than the horizontal part. For a 10-inch extension, the height could be 8 inches. Cut down the top edge so only a short pad touches the flap. Shape and round the outer edge of the brackets.

3. Use ordinary hinges on the brackets. Install them under the flap, but for a neater and closer fit, use back-flap hinges. Because they swing back further and are countersunk for screws on the opposite side, they have to be let into the wood with the knuckle upwards. (Fig. 7-28D).

4. Locate the brackets so that their pads come against the tabletop when closed (Fig. 7-28E). Glue cloth on the pads if you wish.

5. Screw on the flap and test the action. There should be no need for stop blocks under the flap as the brackets will lock square to the legs.

Towel Rail

A rail under one end of a table can hold towels or drying cloths. A single rail is shown in Fig. 7-29, but a rail at the other end or more than one rail at one end could be added. The sizes shown will suit most tables. The rails are made of ¾-inch dowel rod and the supports of ¾-inch or ⅞-inch solid wood. The supports are shown close under an overhanging top (Fig. 7-29A), but you can position them lower down the legs and with their tops rounded.

1. Use the 1-inch squares to outline the supports (Fig. 7-29B). If you alter sizes, allow sufficient flat at the ends to take the screws. Round the shaped edge.

2. The rail could go through, but it will be neater if it is only taken halfway (Fig. 7-29C). Drill for the fixing screws.

3. Cut the dowel rod to length to center the supports on the legs.

4. When you are satisfied that the assembly will fit, finish the wood before mounting it in position.

Board Rack

One or more pastry or chopping boards can fit vertically into a rack at one end of a table to be ready for use. It might be worthwhile to make a set of matching boards when you make a table and its rack or make different sizes for each end of the table. With the usual open table, you can put a board rack inside the legs. It is then possible to have an end flap or a towel rail outside an end and a board rack inside. If a board rack is fitted outside, drive screw hooks into it at one or both levels for hanging other equipment.

The rack in Fig. 7-30A is built up with 1-inch-square strips and ¼-inch plywood. The vertical spacing of the two parts is arranged to make an easy fit on the board. A board is kept in the lower part by gravity, but the top part is given deeper cheeks to keep boards of different widths from falling over.

1. Cut the 1-inch-square strips to length to suit the spacing of the table legs.

2. Make cheeks of plywood the same length and 3 inches wide for the top (Fig. 7-30B) and 2 inches wide for the bottom (Fig. 7-30C). Round the corners.

3. Join the parts with glue and pins. Drill the screws into the table legs.

4. Do not make the total thickness more than the overhang of the tabletop. Fit the upper part closely if you wish. Space the two parts with plenty of clearance inside to insert or pull out a board easily.

5. The parts could be made to take two boards. If they are different widths, arrange the spacers to suit (Fig. 7-30D).

6. The parts could be left open to let a board slide in from either side. If you only want to use one side, fit stop blocks between the cheeks at one side.

7. Add screw hooks, if you wish.

8

Chairs and Stools

Much work in the kitchen is done while standing, but apart from any desire to rest, you could have better control of some operations when seated, either at chair height or in a higher position that brings your hands to the same level as they would be if standing. From a seated position, it is easier to do delicate work than if you are pivoting on your feet.

Kitchen seating is not intended for relaxation, at least not for long periods. It must stand up to rougher usage than chairs and stools elsewhere in the home. Seats might be stood on for instance; consequently, the prime consideration is utility. There should be no fear of a chair or stool collapsing or even becoming shaky. It must resist tipping even when the use is unusual. There can be some concession to comfort, but flat unpadded seats and backs are acceptable, while chairs used elsewhere should have shaping or padding.

Kitchen seating must be soundly constructed with wood of ample sections. Use mortise-and-tenon or doweled joints where appropriate. Avoid nailed or screwed construction for most parts; if it is, use glue as well. Any finish applied will reduce absorption of water, but apply one that does not make a surface slippery, especially if you will be standing on the seat.

DUAL-HEIGHT STOOL

For things just out of reach, the cook needs something to stand on to get at a high shelf or cupboard. A child also might need to stand on something to see what is happening at a table or countertop.

The stool in Fig. 8-1 offers two heights, depending on which way it is turned. The sizes suggested (Fig. 8-2) are 7 inches one way and 10 inches the other with a top 16 inches long. If you alter sizes, make sure treads are wide enough—6 inches is about the minimum advisable for reasonable stability.

The two tops can be ½-inch plywood, although slightly thicker solid wood could be used. The legs and rails are solid wood. For most purposes softwood will be satisfactory.

Fig. 8-1. A two-way stool gives a choice of heights.

1. Make the two ends (Fig. 8-2A). Cut back the two edges that will meet the floor 2 inches from the corners to form feet. Mark the position of the rail.

2. The rail could be joined to the ends with three or four, ½-inch dowels at each end (Fig. 8-2B), or you can cut mortise and tenon joints (Fig. 8-2C). In both cases, take the joints right through the ends for maximum strength or stop them if you prefer not to mark the outsides.

3. Join the rail to the ends and see that the assembly stands square and level.

4. The two tops overlap each end by ½ inch. Make the wide top 1 inch narrower than the length of the ends (Fig. 8-2D). To make a hand hole in it (Fig. 8-2E), drill two, 1-inch holes with their

216

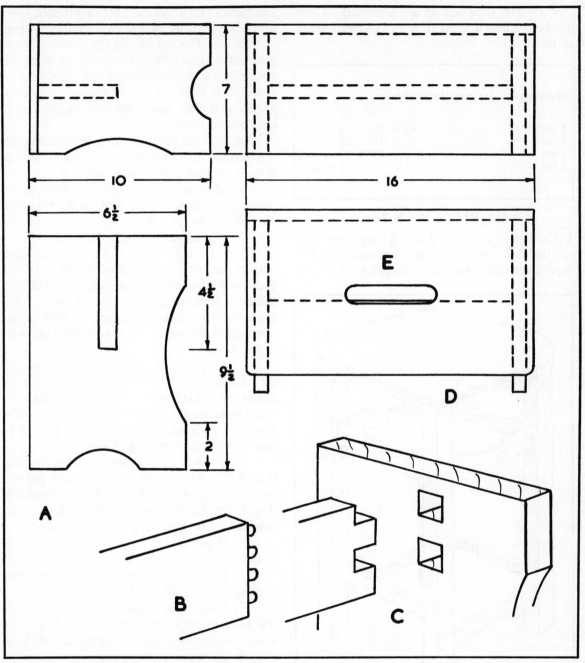

Fig. 8-2. Sizes and alternative construction of the stool.

centers 4 inches apart, then cut away the waste and round the edges. Round the two exposed corners. Join the top to the ends with glue and screws.

5. Add the other top the full width in the same way. Glue and screw into the rail as well as the end.

6. The stool can be left untreated. If you paint or varnish it, sand off any gloss on the tread surfaces.

```
Materials List for Dual-Height Stool

2 ends                    ¾  ×  6½ × 10
1 rail                    ¾  ×  4½ × 16
1 top                     8½ ×  17  × ½ plywood
1 top                      7 ×  17  × ½ plywood
```

TALL STOOL WITH TRAY

The tall stool in Fig. 8-3 is at a height that will suit the cook working at a table or countertop, but experiment before settling on the height of the one

Fig. 8-3. This tall stool has an upholstered seat and a storage tray.

you make. The lower rails are at different levels to suit legs of different lengths when they are used as footrests. The top can be left as a flat board, but simple upholstery is suggested. A short distance down is a tray with scooped edges for easy access. It is large enough for cleaning materials, gloves, and other things the cook might want to keep within reach.

The legs are parallel. All joints are straightforward and can be dowel or mortises and tenons. Straight-grained hardwood is advised.

1. Mark out the four legs (Fig. 8-4A) as two pairs. Leave some excess wood at the tops until after the joints have been cut.

2. If you use dowels, cut the rails to length to fit between the legs. If you use tenons, those lengths are between shoulders. Allow ¾ inch at each end for tenons. Mark as many of the rails together as possible to ensure them matching. Because the stool is shown square, all rails are the same length, but you could make it wider one way, if you wish.

3. At the top, the four rails come level with the outsides of the legs (Fig. 8-4B). If you use tenons, cut them to one side (Fig. 8-4C). The lower rails have central tenons (Fig. 8-4D). If you use dowels in both positions, make two, ⅜-inch diameters at each joint (Fig. 8-4E).

4. The tray sides come central on the legs (Fig. 8-4F). The tenons are to one side and half thickness (Fig. 8-5A), the full depth of each side (Fig. 8-5B). Cut hollows in each side for easy access and round those edges.

5. If you dowel the tray sides, use three, ¼-inch dowels (Fig. 8-4G).

6. Prepare the tenons and their matching mortises or drill all the dowel holes.

7. Make ½-inch-square strips to fit inside the tray sides to support its bottom (Fig. 8-5C). Attach them to the tray sides with glue and fine nails.

8. Assemble two opposite sides, then join them with the other rails, checking that all angles are square and the stool stands level.

9. Make a plywood or hardboard bottom for the tray. Notch it around the legs. Glue it in position.

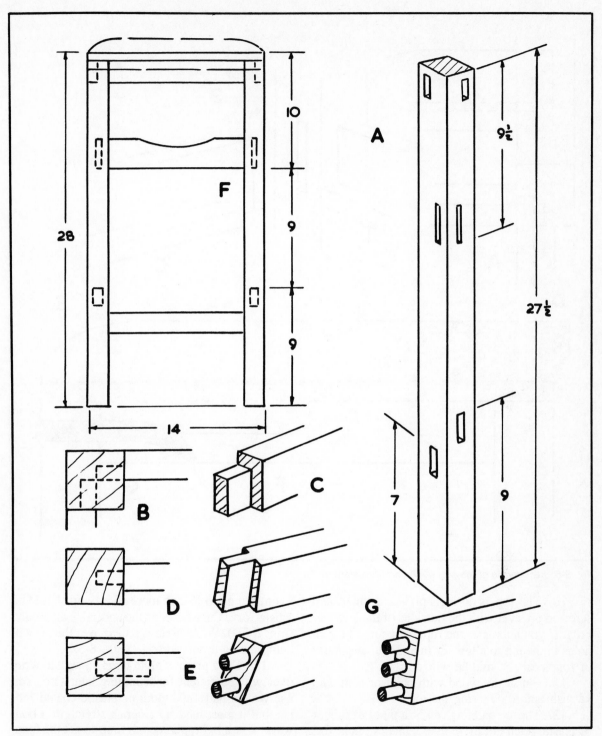

Fig. 8-4. Sizes and joint details of the tall stool.

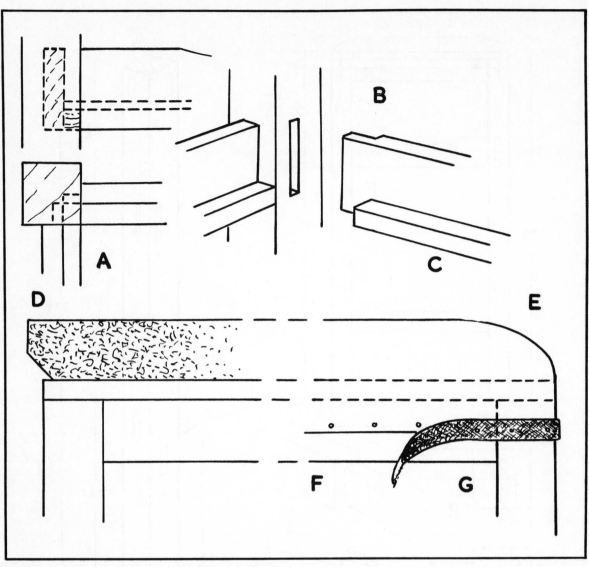

Fig. 8-5. Joint details of the tray (A-C) and upholstery (D-G).

10. The top is ½-inch plywood glued and screwed on level with the outsides of the legs and rails. If you upholster the top, drill some ½-inch holes in the top to allow air in and out. A pattern of four near the middle will do.

11. Finish the wood with paint or stain and varnish before covering the top.

12. The top padding can be a piece of rubber or plastic foam not more than 2 inches thick. Cut it oversize. How much to allow depends on the foam, but up to ½ inch more all around should be satisfactory. Cut a bevel on the underside all around (Fig. 8-5D). When cloth is pulled over this, it will compress to a curved edge (Fig. 8-5E).

13. Cut a piece of cloth large enough to wrap over with sufficient for trimming later. You can use woven patterned cloth or plastic-coated fabric, but it must have a moderate stretch in it both ways. Use a light, plain cloth first, to get the foam to shape, then cover with the outer cloth. Much

depends on the choice of cloth and foam, and you might have to experiment.

14. Use tacks and start by pulling the cloth over and centering it on each side. Work outwards from that at about 1-inch intervals, keeping the tacks in a straight line (Fig. 8-5F). At the corners, pull diagonally and fold the vertical parts of the cloth.

15. Trim the cloth in a straight line below the tacks.

16. For neatness, cover the tacks and edge with tape or *gimp* (Fig. 8-5G), which is a patterned upholstery tape that is fixed with inconspicuous, fine black nails.

Materials List for Tall Stool with Tray			
4 legs	1½ ×	1½ ×	28
8 rails	¾ ×	1½ ×	14
4 tray rails	½ ×	2 ×	14
4 tray strips	½ ×	½ ×	12
1 tray bottom	13 ×	13 ×	¼ plywood
1 top	15 ×	15 ×	½ plywood

KITCHEN CHAIR

Quite often a chair no longer needed elsewhere in the home is brought into the kitchen, but it might be weak and have loose joints. If it is upholstered, it will be unsuitable for standing on. The chair in Fig. 8-6 has a basic shape with a flat wooden seat that is parallel to the floor to make a safe platform to stand on or to put pots on without them tilting. The legs are upright, and there is a simple backrest, which will provide some comfort although not for long periods.

The seat and back are ½-inch plywood. Other parts are hardwood. Softwoods do not have as much strength in the joints to stand up to the probable hard use of the chair. Joints could be doweled, but the instructions that follow call for tenons. If dowels are chosen, cut off the rails at shoulder level.

The rear legs are closer together than the front legs, and therefore the side rails are not square. Except for these angles, all rail joints are the same.

Fig. 8-6. A robust kitchen chair.

1. Main sizes are shown in Fig. 8-7A. To get the angles of the sides and the lengths of the sloping rails, set out the plan view (Fig. 8-7B) either half or complete. Set an adjustable bevel to the angle and use that instead of a square when marking the side rail shoulders.

2. Mark out the pair of rear legs (Figs. 8-7C and 8-8A). Because all joints will have barefaced tenons, the outside edges are level (Fig. 8-7D), except the rear rail under the seat which can be at the forward edges of the legs. At the top of each leg, bevel from half thickness to 4 inches down to take the back. Round the rear corners.

3. Mark out the pair of front legs from the rear legs to make the joints the same height. The top joints are open, but they will be covered and strengthened by the seat. Cut all mortises to half the thickness of the rails.

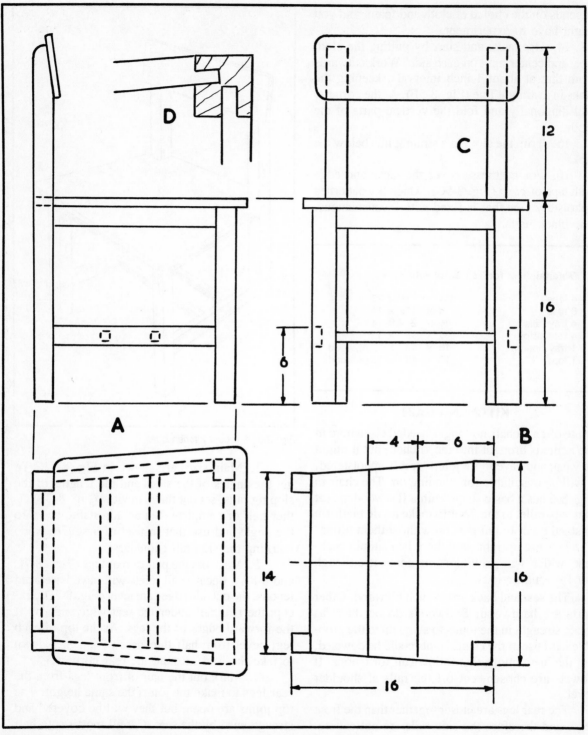

Fig. 8-7. Main sizes of the kitchen chair.

4. Make the rear seat rail (Fig. 8-8B) and the back (Fig. 8-8C), which overlaps 1 inch at sides and top.

5. Assemble these parts to the legs. Use screws through the back. Check that these parts are square and the legs parallel. Allow the glue to set.

6. Join the front rail to the front legs. Put

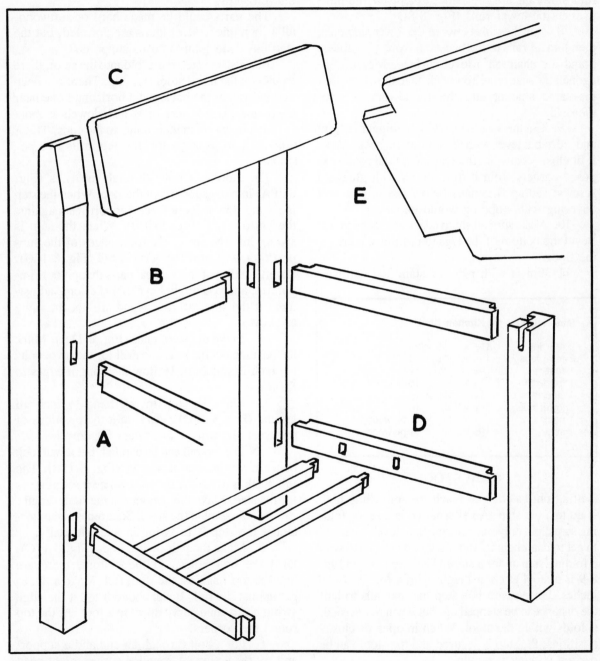

Fig. 8-8. Chair joints and the arrangement of rails.

a temporary strip across the bottoms of the legs to hold the assembly square.

7. From your setting out, get the lengths of the side rails and the two, ¾-inch-square rails. The four side rails are the same, except for the mortises in the lower rails (Fig. 8-8D).

8. Join the rails between the lower side rails, then join all rails to the back and front assemblies. Stand the chair on a level surface. Measure diagonals at seat level to check that the sides flair the same amount and the framework is symmetrical.

9. Cut the seat to be a ½ inch bigger at front and sides but level with the legs at the back. Make it fit closely between the rear legs, then round exposed corners. Join it to the rails with glue and screws; setting fine nails below the surface and covering with stopping would be neater.

10. Make sure all sharp edges are rounded off. Bevel the bottom of the legs to minimize marking the floor.

11. Finish with paint or stain and varnish.

```
┌─────────────────────────────────────────┐
│                                           │
│  Materials List for Kitchen Chair        │
│                                           │
│  2 rear legs    1½ × 1½ × 29              │
│  2 front legs   1½ × 1½ × 16              │
│  1 rear rail    ¾ × 1½ × 14               │
│  1 front rail   ¾ × 1½ × 16               │
│  4 side rails   ¾ × 1½ × 16               │
│  2 lower rails  ¾ × ¾  × 16               │
│  1 back         5 × 17 × ½ plywood        │
│  1 seat         16 × 17 × ½ plywood       │
│                                           │
└─────────────────────────────────────────┘
```

STEP STOOL

Getting onto a chair to reach for something high is quite a big step. An alternative is a set of folding steps; but only one intermediate level is needed to get to chair height, and that can be arranged with a folding step under a stool. The step stool in Fig. 8-9 is a stool at chair height with a top 10 × 16 inches. Underneath is a step that extends to half the distance to be stepped up, but when not needed, it folds within the stool. When in open or closed positions, the step is secured and the stool can be carried without it moving.

As drawn (Figs. 8-10 and 8-11) the step stool is 8 inches from floor to step and step to top. If you alter sizes, arrange these distances the same so anyone using the stool is not disconcerted by uneven steps.

The parts could be made hard or softwood, all 1 inch thick. Most joints are doweled, but the step has dado joints into its supports.

Because the step must fold into the stool, there cannot be the usual stool framing. There is a deep vertical rail at the back and a horizontal one near the bottom. Use ½-inch or ⅝-inch dowels at about 1¼-inch intervals in their joints to the ends. These rails also act as stops for the step in its two positions.

The stool has bolts through the ends (Fig. 8-10A) into the supports of the step. When the step is swung down, its notched support rests against the bottom rail (Fig. 8-10B). When the step is swung into the stool, the front edges of the supports come against the vertical rail (Fig. 8-10C). Careful fitting of the vertical parts that pivot is important, and you might have to make some adjustment if the sizes of your wood are not the same as shown.

1. Make the stool ends (Fig. 8-11A). Mark the positions of the rails and drill for the pivot bolts (¼ inch is suitable). Hollow the bottom edges to form feet.

2. Make the top to overhang ½ inch all around (Fig. 8-10D). Mark on it the positions of the ends and rail, with centers for dowels.

3. The top rail can be parallel, but it will look better if you reduce its center (Fig. 8-11B). The full depth is needed at the ends where it forms stops for the step. Make the bottom rail the same length.

4. Assemble the stool. Squareness is important if the step is to swing in and out easily.

5. Make the pair of step ends (Fig. 8-11C). Drill the bolt holes. At the bottom, there are notches to fit against the stool rail. Make a flat to go against the rail. Bevel above it to let the edge swing clear, then curve down to a foot. At the top round the corners.

6. Put a bolt through an end and a support and try the action. A rounded corner might need

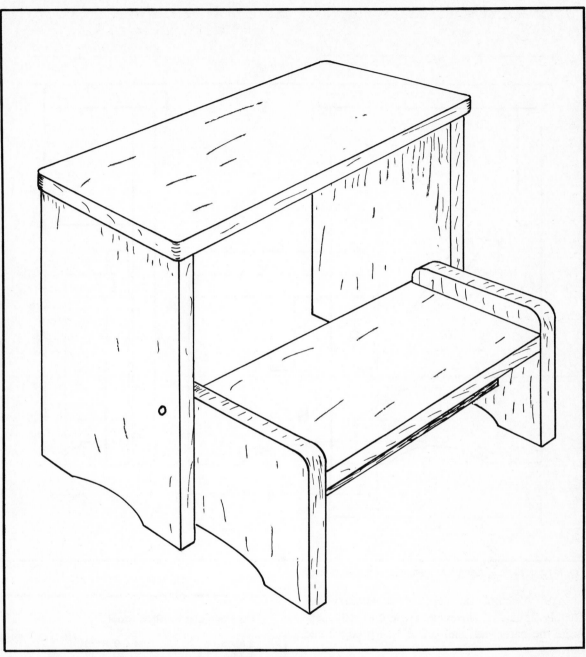

Fig. 8-9. This stool converts to steps with a pivoting section.

adjusting to clear the bottom rail as the step closes (Fig. 8-10E).

7. Cut dado grooves for the step and mark for dowels in the rail (Fig. 8-11D).

8. The step need not be a very close fit in the stool. Make its lengthwise parts so the finished assembly is about ¼ inch less overall than the inside of the stool.

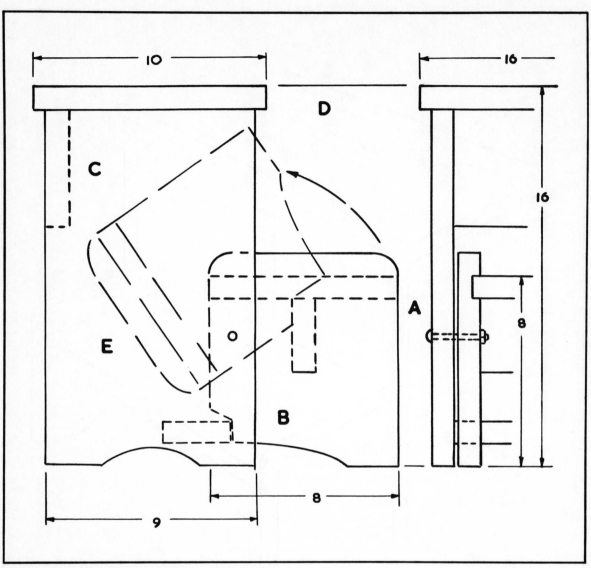

Fig. 8-10. Sizes and tilting arrangements of the step stool.

9. Assemble the step, then make a trial assembly. If the step closes and opens correctly, separate the parts and sand off all sharp edges and corners.

10. Finish with paint or stain and varnish. In the final assembly, put washers between the stool ends and step supports and have a washer under each nut, which should be a locking type if possible.

Materials List for Step Stool

2 ends	1 ×	9 × 16
1 top	1 ×	10 × 17
1 rail	1 ×	5 × 14
1 rail	1 ×	3 × 14
2 step supports	1 ×	8 × 10
1 step	1 ×	8 × 13
1 step rail	1 ×	3 × 13

226

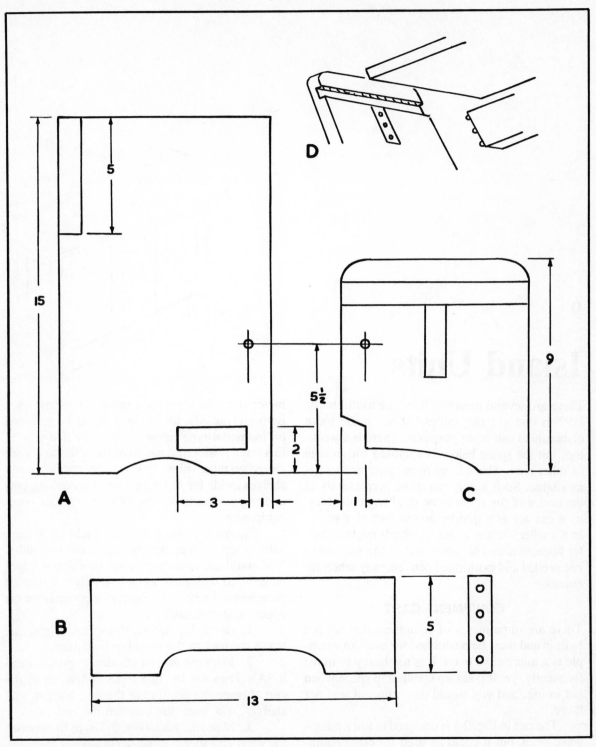

Fig. 8-11. Sizes of stool parts.

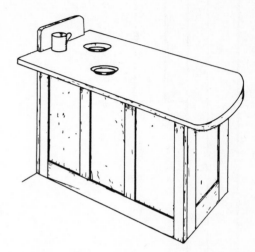

9

Island Units

There are several pieces of furniture useful in the kitchen that are like tables but are made more elaborate to suit other purposes. There is a worktop, but the space below is enclosed for storage or other uses. There is no open space as there is in a table. Such a unit can stand permanently at the center of the room to be used from all sides, or it can act as a divider across part of a room. In a smaller kitchen, a unit on wheels might be better because it can be stored out of the way when not needed and positioned conveniently when required.

EQUIPMENT CART

There are some pieces of equipment that are not built in and must be positioned for use. An example is a microwave oven. It is too heavy to move frequently, yet it takes up countertop space when not in use, and you would then rather it was not there.

The cart in Fig. 9-1 is designed to suit a microwave oven, but it could be used for other equipment; it might serve as a mobile worktop for a barbecue outside, for instance. It can be mounted on industrial-type rubber casters, or if it will be in a fixed position, it can have feet. The top is enclosed on three sides. There is a pair of doors and shelves inside for storing microwave cooking pots and trays. Check the size of your oven or other equipment.

The main parts of the cart could be ¾-inch solid wood, with pieces glued to make up widths. You could use ¾-inch plywood with lipped edges or finished with paint to hide the plys. Veneered particleboard with self-adhesive strip veneer on cut edges is also suitable.

1. Obtain the casters, check their height, and make the cart to the height you require.

2. Mark out the pair of sides (Figs. 9-2A and 9-3A). They are the full depth and width of the cart. Locate the position of the top, bottom, and shelves. The back fits between the ends.

3. Make the back (Fig. 9-3B) to fit between the ends and to the same depth.

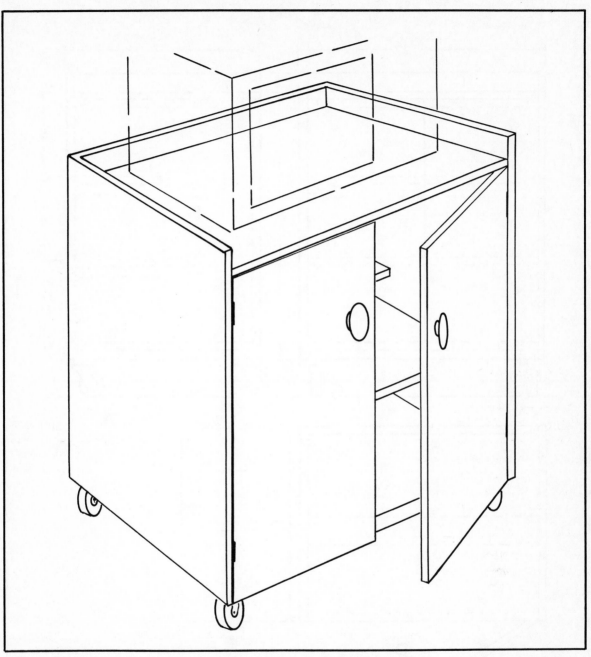

Fig. 9-1. This stand with storage can be used for a microwave oven or other equipment.

4. Make the top and bottom (Fig. 9-3C and D). The top extends to the front edges of the sides, but the bottom is set back by the thickness of the doors.

5. Frame the top around with 1-inch-square strips underneath, but set back the front strip by the thickness of the doors (Fig. 9-3E).

6. Frame the bottom underneath with

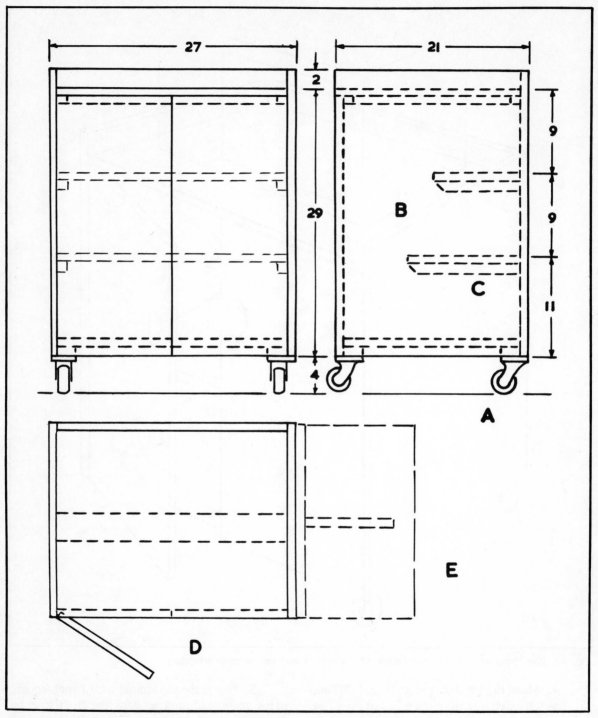

Fig. 9-2. Sizes of the mobile stand.

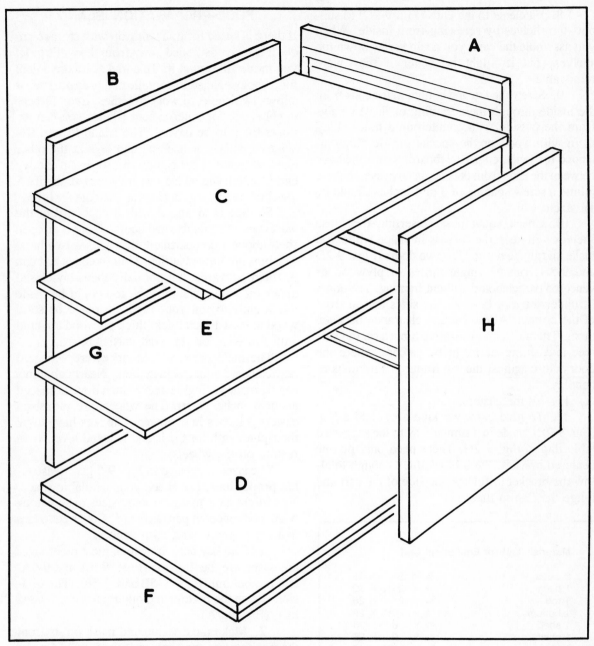

Fig. 9-3. Arrangement of the parts of the microwave stand.

1-×-2-inch strips level with the edges. The increased width provides bearing for the casters at the corners.

    7. Make the shelves (Figs. 9-2B and 9-3G).

They are shown 6 and 9 inches wide, but make them to suit your needs. Do not make them too wide, or they will block your view of articles underneath.

8. Fit cleats to the ends (Fig. 9-2C) to support the shelves by screwing from inside. When you assemble the cart, you could screw down the shelves, but it might be better if they were removable.

9. Screw the top and bottom to the ends from the inside through their framing or drive screws from the outside with counterbored holes. Plug them with wood or the special plastic plugs intended for veneered particleboard. Screw the back between the ends from outside, in any case. In these joints, a screw spacing of 3 or 4 inches should be satisfactory.

10. Check squareness. Inserting the loose shelves will keep the carcass in shape while you make and fit the doors. The two doors (Figs. 9-2D and 9-3H) can be single pieces of plywood or veneered particleboard without framing. The doors fit under the top, between the sides and in front of the bottom. Allow enough clearance between them. There can be decorative hinges on the surface and spring or magnetic catches where the doors close against the top framing. Fit knobs or handles.

11. Fit the casters.

12. To give extra working area, add a flap (Fig. 9-2E), made in a similar way to the suggested table flap in Fig. 7-2G. There need only be one centered bracket. Put a block thick enough to allow the bracket to fold on the side of the cart and hinge the flap to that.

Materials List for Equipment Cart

2 sides	¾ ×	21	× 32
1 back	¾ ×	25½	× 32
1 top	¾ ×	21	× 26
1 bottom	¾ ×	20¼	× 26
1 shelf	¾ ×	6	× 26
1 shelf	¾ ×	9	× 26
2 doors	¾ ×	12¾	× 32
2 shelf brackets	¾ ×	1½	× 7
2 shelf brackets	¾ ×	1½	× 10
2 framing strips	1 ×	1	× 26
2 framing strips	1 ×	1	× 21
2 framing strips	1 ×	2	× 26
2 framing strips	1 ×	2	× 21

FOOD-PREPARATION ISLAND

If there is space for it, a worktop with storage under it can be positioned away from the walls to let you move all around it. This makes it convenient for a cook engaged in complicated preparations or allows two cooks to work together. Even if there is not space for a permanent island, you can arrange for it to be moved. The island in Fig. 9-4 has two wheels at one end and legs at the other end that lets it stand rigidly in use, but if the leg end is lifted, the island can be wheeled about. A towel rail on the legs doubles as a handle for lifting.

Storage is arranged with a cupboard at the wheel end, with double end doors. There is an open shelf above a compartment that houses two bins. The bins are hinged at their bottom edges and can be tilted outwards, but normally they stay closed under their own weight. The top could be made like a table to suit your needs. It could be solid wood at least 1 inch thick, thick plywood covered with Formica, or veneered particleboard.

The main parts, as described, are veneered particleboard about ¾ inch thick. Nearly all joints can be made with glue and ⅜-inch dowels spaced about 3 inches apart. The wheels are industrial casters 3 inches in diameter. The legs have to be the right length for the island to stand level when resting on the wheels.

The sizes suggested in Fig. 9-5 give reasonable proportions, but check your available space. You might have to adjust some sizes to suit stock widths of veneered particleboard. Cover cut edges that are exposed with strip veneer.

1. The key parts on which most other sizes are based are the division (Figs. 9-5A and 9-6A) and the bottom (Figs. 9-5B and 9-6B). The division fits on the bottom and other parts are related to it (Fig. 9-7A).

2. Make the division and mark on its front the positions of the shelves (Fig. 9-6C). On the other side mark the positions of the shelf and top rails (Fig. 9-6D).

3. Make the bottom and mark on it the positions of the division and the cupboard sides (Fig. 9-6E). Cut around the legs to fit it against the end piece (Fig. 9-6F).

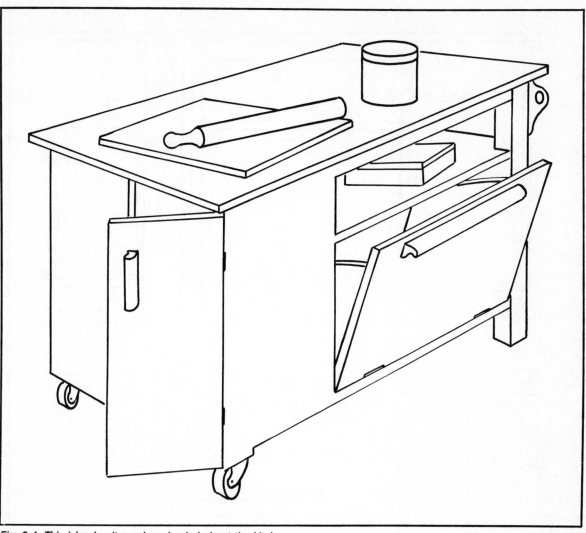

Fig. 9-4. This island unit can be wheeled about the kitchen.

4. Mark and drill for dowels between the division and bottom.

5. Make the pair of cupboard sides (Fig. 9-7B) to fit inside the division and rest on the bottom with the outer edges level. Make and fit cleats to support the shelves (Fig. 9-5C). They could be doweled or screwed from inside.

6. Drill for dowels and assemble the division, bottom, and cupboard sides. Fit a strip (Fig. 9-7C) across the top of the cupboard.

7. Put square blocks under the corners for the casters (Fig. 9-5D). Check the height that the

wheels will raise the bottom to get the length of the legs.

8. Cut the two legs to length, using the division as a guide to the position of parts to be attached to it.

9. Make the end panel (Fig. 9-7D) to fit between the legs, matching their outside width to the bottom. Its lower edge is over the bottom (Fig. 9-6G). There is a strip of 1-×-2-inch wood above the bottom. One comes under the shelf and another is included when the top is fitted. Dowel these parts to the legs.

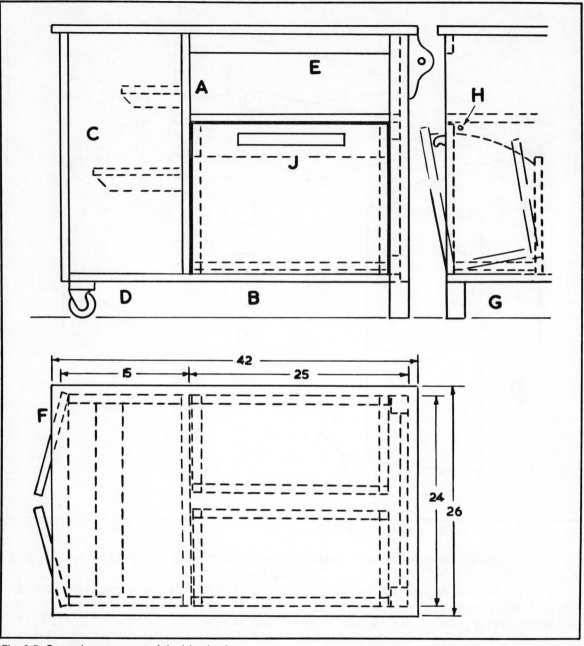

Fig. 9-5. General arrangement of the island unit.

10. Make the main shelf to fit around the legs in the same way as the bottom (Fig. 9-7E). Drill its other end for dowels to the division.

11. Make the two top rails (Fig. 9-5E) to fit between the legs and the division.

12. Assemble all these parts. Check for squareness and freedom from twist.

13. The pair of doors (Figs. 9-5F and 9-7F) fits onto the edges of the other parts, with hinges between and catches at top and bottom. Fit any han-

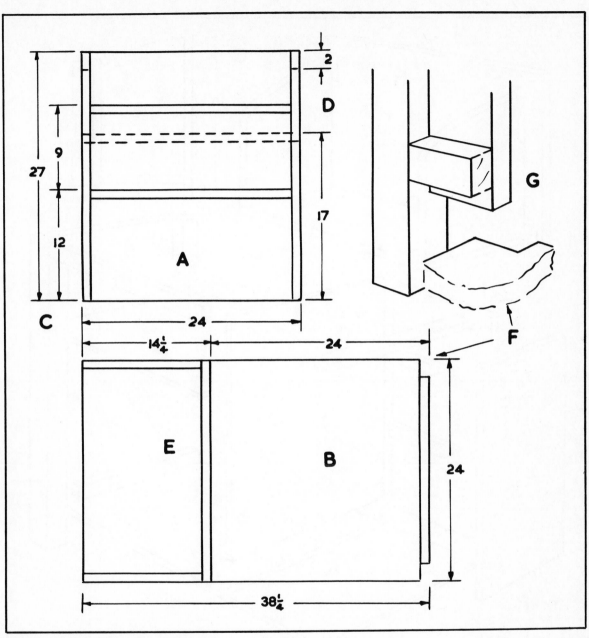

Fig. 9-6. Details of parts of the island unit.

dles or knobs or wait until the bins are made and then use matching handles. Fit secure catches to keep the doors from opening when the island is wheeled.

14. The bins are on opposite sides and are hinged on their edges to the edges of the island bottom (Fig. 9-5G). Draw a side view of a bin (Fig. 9-7G), using the measurements on your island, in case there are any differences.

15. Make the front of each bin (Fig. 9-7H) to make an easy fit in its opening under the shelf. Make the curved ends and bottom. Arrange the

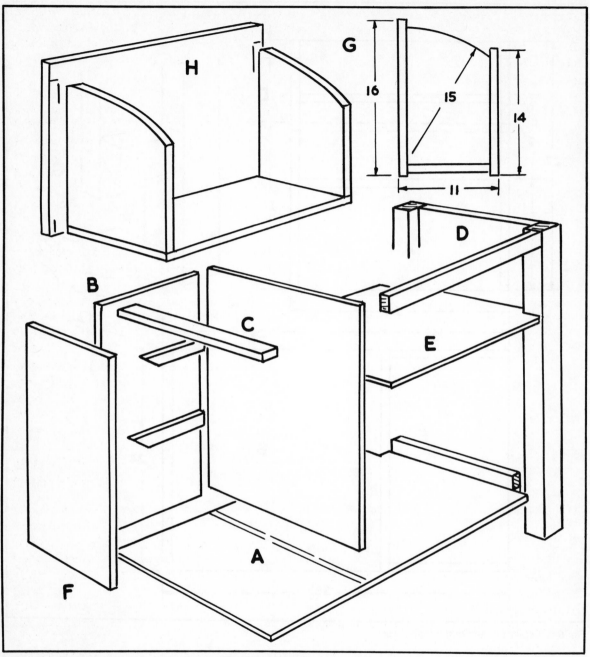

Fig. 9-7. Assembly of the main parts (A-F) and bin details (G, H).

back of a bin to stand above the curve slightly. The bottom should come about ¼ inch above the bottom edges of the front and back. Glue and dowel the parts together. Fit hinges temporarily and try the action.

16. So a bin does not fall open too far acciden-

tally, drill for a ⅜-inch dowel peg through the division (Fig. 9-5H). This will project into the cupboard, where it can be pulled out if you need to release a bin. The back of the bin should stop against this peg in use.

17. If the action is satisfactory, remove the bins and fit handles. Use any type, but long wooden ones, as described earlier for drawers, can be screwed from inside. Assemble the bins in place finally, unless a finish is to be applied first.

18. Make the top according to your needs and attach it in one of the ways described for tabletops. Overhang it 1 inch all around.

19. Fit a towel rail to the legs (Fig. 7-29).

20. Attach the casters.

```
Materials List for Food-Preparation Island

1 division          ¾ ×  24   × 28
1 bottom            ¾ ×  24   × 39
2 cupboard sides    ¾ ×  13½  × 28
2 cupboard doors    ¾ ×  12   × 28
1 shelf             ¾ ×   7   × 24
1 shelf             ¾ ×  10   × 24
1 shelf             ¾ ×  24   × 25
1 end               ¾ ×  21   × 30
2 legs              2 ×   2   × 36
2 top rails         1 ×   2   × 24
3 rails             1 ×   2   × 24
2 shelf cleats      1 ×   2   × 11
2 bin fronts        ¾ ×  16½  × 24
2 bin backs         ¾ ×  14   × 24
1 bin bottom        ¾ ×  10   × 24
2 bin ends          ¾ ×  10   × 14
2 bin handles       1¼ ×  1¼  × 13
2 door handles      1¼ ×  1¼  × 7
```

BREAKFAST BAR

A high counter can serve several purposes in a kitchen. It can be used for eating while standing or sitting on a high stool or as a preparation area at a greater height than most other surfaces. It acts as a room divider, if the one room has to serve more than one purpose. It can also provide useful storage space. The breakfast bar in Fig. 9-8 will suit all these purposes.

It is designed with paneled front and ends. The top is larger than the supports, with a wider overhang towards anyone sitting to eat. Underneath are three broad shelves. One end is flat and projects above the top and is intended to be attached to the wall. The end farthest from it could also be screwed to the floor.

Solid wood is used with plywood panels. If possible, get plywood veneered on one or both sides to match the solid wood. The top is solid with pieces around the edges to give the impression of being thicker. Softwood could be used and finished by painting, but hardwood looks better stained and polished. The paneling will have a Jacobean effect if stained dark brown. Adapt the sizes shown (Fig. 9-9) to suit your needs.

1. Make the wallboard first. Glue pieces to make up the width, if necessary. Mark on it the positions of other parts (Fig. 9-10A) to use it as a guide when marking them.

2. For the further end, make a framed panel of matching height (Figs. 9-10B and 9-11A). The bottom is 6 inches wide. The other parts are 3 inches. Groove them to take the plywood. You could use mortise and tenon joints at the corners, but ½-inch dowels are shown—three at the bottom corners and two at the top. As the finished edges will not show, it does not matter if the grooves run through. Cut the plywood squarely, but not so close as to touch the bottom of the grooves before the joints are tight. Check that the finished end matches the appropriate points on the wall board.

3. The long paneled front (Figs. 9-9A and 9-11B) is made in a similar way to the end. Make the corner joints the same, but groove the intermediate strips on both sides and join them with two dowels (Fig. 9-10D). Space these pieces to size the three panels the same.

4. Arrange cleats for the shelves on the wallboard (Fig. 9-11C) and matching pieces on the end frame. The shelves are simple pieces (Fig. 9-11D), either screwed to the cleats or just resting on them. Drill the paneled frames for dowels to each other and to the wall board. A 5-inch spacing should be satisfactory.

5. Make the top by gluing boards to width

Fig. 9-8. A breakfast bar also provides storage and can be a room divider.

(Figs. 9-10E and 9-11E). Allow a 6-inch overhang on the serving side and end. Curve the end (Fig. 9-9B). At the wall, notch the wood around the wallboard (Fig. 9-9C).

6. Underneath the top, thicken with a 6-inch strip under the curve and 3-inch strips at the sides (Fig. 9-11F). Place the wide piece against the end frame. Lightly round the outer edges. Drill for

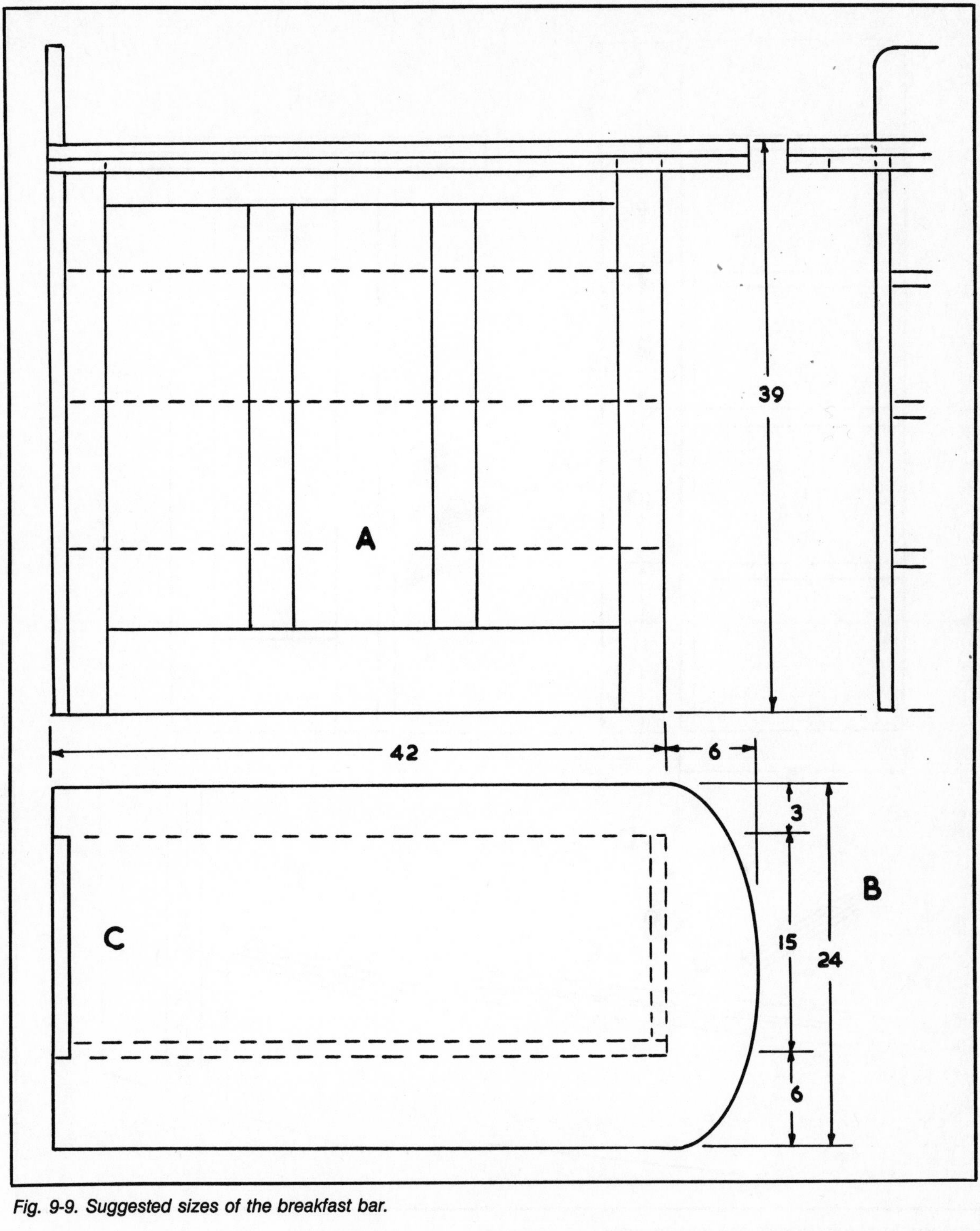

Fig. 9-9. Suggested sizes of the breakfast bar.

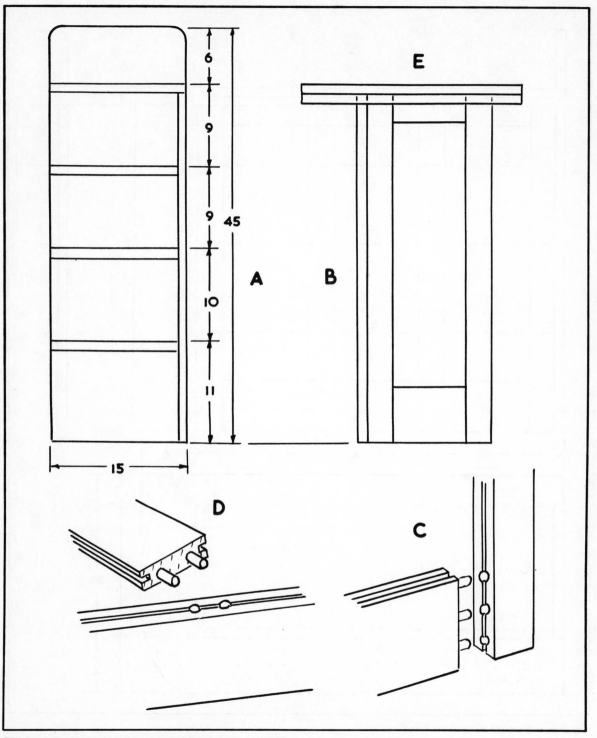

Fig. 9-10. End arrangements and framing joints.

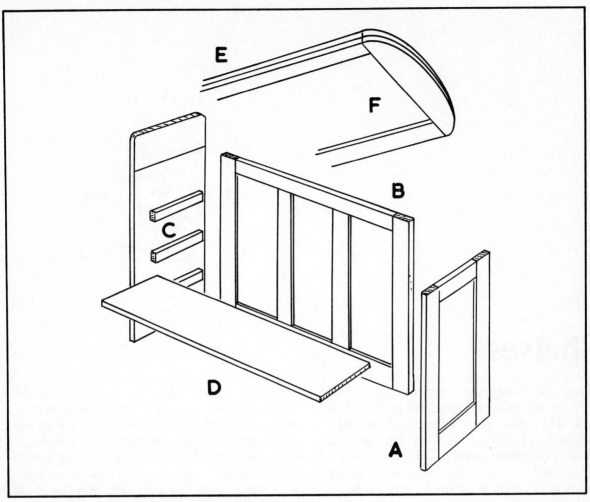

Fig. 9-11. Assembly of the main parts of the breakfast bar.

dowels into the wallboard and the frames.

7. Complete all parts and have the dowels ready. The shelves can be used to hold parts in position during assembly, even if they will not be fixed down.

8. Join the paneled parts together first, then both to the top. Finally bring in the wallboard. See that joints are pulled close and the bar stands level. Drill the wallboard for screws. If the outer end is to be screwed down, put a strip across inside the frame.

9. Finish the wood to your choice. Varnish or lacquer the top so it will resist spilled liquids or leave it untreated so it may be washed.

Materials List for Breakfast Bar

1 wall board	1 × 15 × 46	
2 end frames	1 × 3 × 39	
1 end frame	1 × 3 × 12	
1 end frame	1 × 6 × 12	
1 end panel	10 × 32 × ¼ plywood	
2 front panels	1 × 3 × 39	
2 front frames	1 × 3 × 33	
1 front frame	1 × 3 × 38	
1 front frame	1 × 6 × 38	
3 front panels	11 × 32 × ¼ plywood	
3 shelves	1 × 13 × 41	
1 top	1 × 24 × 50	
2 top sides	1 × 3 × 44	
1 top end	1 × 6 × 25	
6 cleats	1 × 2 × 13	

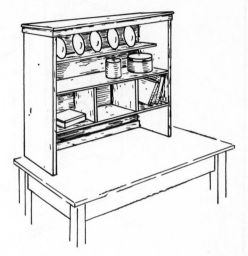

10

Shelves

One of the easiest ways of providing storage is to arrange shelves on any available piece of blank wall. The shelves could be just open-fronted arrangements of boards, or there could be doors made of solid or paneled wood or glass. Open shelves are adequate for things like pans, which can rest inverted on a shelf, but doors are better if the contents are packets of food or cups and plates. Wood doors hide things that otherwise look untidy, but if you want to display the contents, you could make swinging, glass doors or frameless glass pieces that slide.

The simplest shelves are boards on brackets, but an enthusiastic woodworker might want to make something more elaborate. There are many possibilities, but much depends on the available space. Not all shelves have to be independent of other furniture. They could come over a table, countertop, or worktop and be part of it or mounted close to it. In many early homes, the nearest thing to a fitted kitchen was a hutch or combined unit extending upwards and outwards to provide storage and a working area.

When planning shelves, you must consider loads and what effect they might have over a period. A shelf that appears to easily support a load now might develop a sag in six months' time. Solid wood, with its lengthwise grain, is better able to resist bending than plywood or particleboard. Solid wood can be used for longer unsupported shelves than the other materials, although they are suitable for many shelf constructions.

COLONIAL SHELVES

In pioneer homes, one of the first pieces of furniture made was a block of shelves. They might have been crude and simple, but their design can form a starting point for shelf layout in a modern kitchen. If you want a country look, you can make basic shelves, or you might prefer to make something more advanced.

Two or more shelves between ends form a unit that can be moved completely to a new location, if you wish, unlike shelves on brackets that are not so adaptable. The shelves in Fig. 10-1 are shown

Fig. 10-1. A pair of shelves between ends can provide wall or table storage.

as two short shelves between ends, but the length and number of shelves could be altered.

The unit could be made in solid wood or veneered particleboard. The back can be open to the wall or can take a back piece enclosed between the shelves, with a stouter strip above the top shelf.

Alternative methods of construction with different materials are included. Suggested sizes are shown, but they can be adapted to your needs. Solid wood or veneered particleboard ¾ inch thick can be used.

1. For a block of shelves with an open back made from solid wood, prepare a pair of ends (Fig. 10-2A). Mark the positions of the shelves. Shape in any way you wish. If an end is curved, a part of an ellipse (Fig. 10-2B) looks better than part

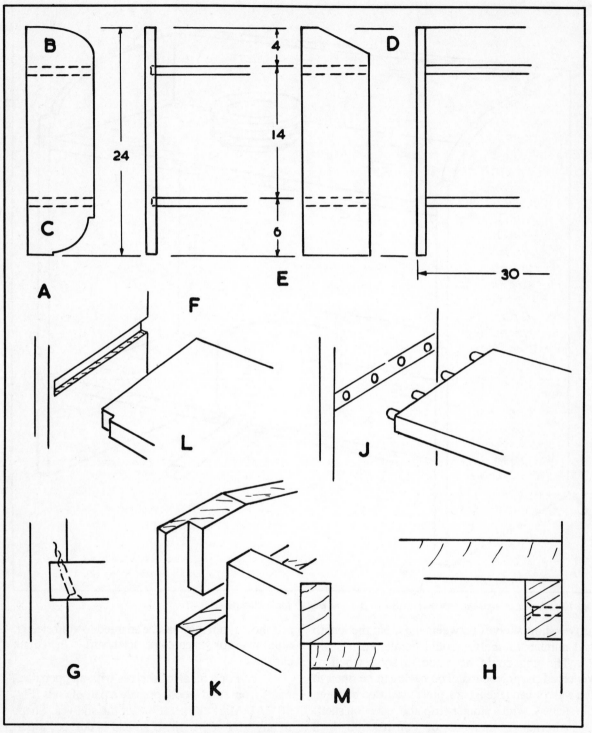

Fig. 10-2. Various shapes are possible for the ends (A-E). Fitted joints (F-M) ensure rigidity.

of a circle. Stop the curve (Fig. 10-2C) to match moldings used nearby. Straight slopes (Fig. 10-2D) might be all you need. If the bottom is to be on or near a tabletop, leave it square (Fig. 10-2E).

2. Make the two shelves and cut stopped dado joints (Fig. 10-2F). If you are making open-backed shelves, strengthen the glued assembly with two screws driven upward near the front and back of each joint (Fig. 10-2G).

3. Hang the assembly from metal screw plates or put a strip under the top shelf (Fig. 10-2H) for screws into the wall.

4. If veneered particleboard is used, cut edges have to be veneered. Because it is difficult to do this on curves, shape the tops and bottoms of the sides with straight cuts (Fig. 10-2D).

5. Join shelves with dowels (Fig. 10-2J) as dado joints are unsatisfactory in particleboard. Fit a strip for screwing under the top shelf, if you wish.

6. The simplest closed back is a piece if plywood or hardboard glued and screwed on, but its edges will show. If that is unacceptable, cut rabbets in the sides if it is solid wood (Fig. 10-2K). With particleboard, the back can fit between the sides on ⅜-inch square strips of wood.

7. For a solid wood unit, it is better to have a thicker piece of wood above the top shelf, with thin plywood or hardboard below. Cut the rabbets (Fig. 10-2K), then widen above for the top piece (Fig. 10-2L). Attach the back parts with glue and screws from behind (Fig. 10-2M). Drill for screws to the wall, either through the top strip or close under the top shelf.

8. Finish to match other furniture.

Materials List for Colonial Shelves	
2 ends	¾ × 7 × 25
2 shelves	¾ × 7 × 30
1 top strip	¾ × 4 × 30
1 back	20 × 30 × ¼ plywood

OVER-TABLE SHELVES

If a table or other working surface is permanently against a wall, a block of shelves will convert it to a hutch or combined unit. The things you need or wish to display can be stored against the wall, leaving lower storage space available for other utensils or equipment.

The block of shelves in Fig. 10-3 is offered as a suggestion; you must adjust sizes and details to suit your needs. The block could go to the ceiling, but at the height shown, the top is about 66 inches with a normal table, and that is as high as a cook is likely to want to reach without a stool.

The assembly is meant to be attached to the wall, but its bottom is on, or very close to, the tabletop. If the table has to be moved occasionally, that would be possible without disturbing the shelves.

The block of shelves will look best if made of solid wood, although plywood with solid wood lips or veneered particleboard could be used. Chosen sections depends on sizes. For the shelves shown (Fig. 10-4), most wood can be ⅞ inch thick. It would be unwise to use wood thinner than ¾ inch whatever you make the overall sizes. The construction described uses dado joints, but many parts could be doweled, if you wish.

1. Prepare the wood for the pair of sides (Fig. 10-5A). Rabbet the rear edges for the plywood back. Mark the length and the positions of the shelves. Two shelves are the full width, but the top one is reduced to 7 inches.

2. At top and bottom, the back is stiffened with strips across (Fig. 10-4B). Their ends should be notched into the sides (Fig. 10-5B) to keep the outside surfaces level with the bottoms of the rabbets.

3. Make the three shelves. Mark and cut stopped dado joints to the sides (Fig. 10-5C). Strengthen the joints later with screws driven from below (Fig. 10-2G).

4. For divisions between the lower shelves (Fig. 10-4C), match their lengths to the spacing on the sides. Cut stopped dado joints (Fig. 10-5D).

5. To display plates on the top or other shelf, make something to stop them from slipping. If you have the equipment to make it, cut a V groove 2 inches from the back of the shelf (Fig. 10-4D). An equally effective stop is a ½-inch square strip (Fig. 10-4E).

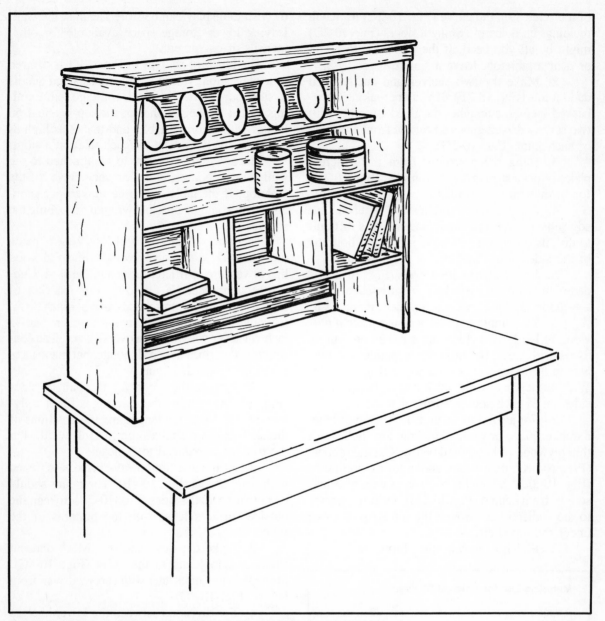

Fig. 10-3. A block of shelves over a table provides a display area and storage.

6. Have the plywood back ready, cut with square corners, to be fitted to hold the assembly in shape. Assemble the divisions to their shelves, then the shelves to the sides with the back strips, then fit the back plywood. Work on a flat surface and be careful that there is no twist in the assembly.

7. Cut top strips (Fig. 10-4F) to fit across the front and across the sides with mitered front corners (Fig. 10-5E). Leave the lower edges square, round or bevel them, or work a bead or other molding (Fig. 10-4G). Fit the strips with a stiffening piece (Fig. 10-4H) behind the long strip.

8. The top could be a solid board, but it is shown as framed plywood (Fig. 10-5F). Prepare

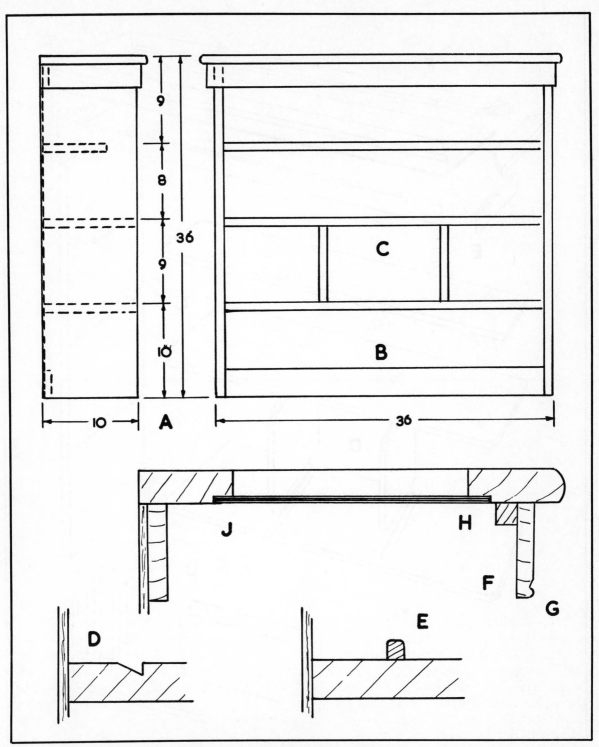

Fig. 10-4. Suggested sizes (A-C), shelf details (D, E), and top section (F-J).

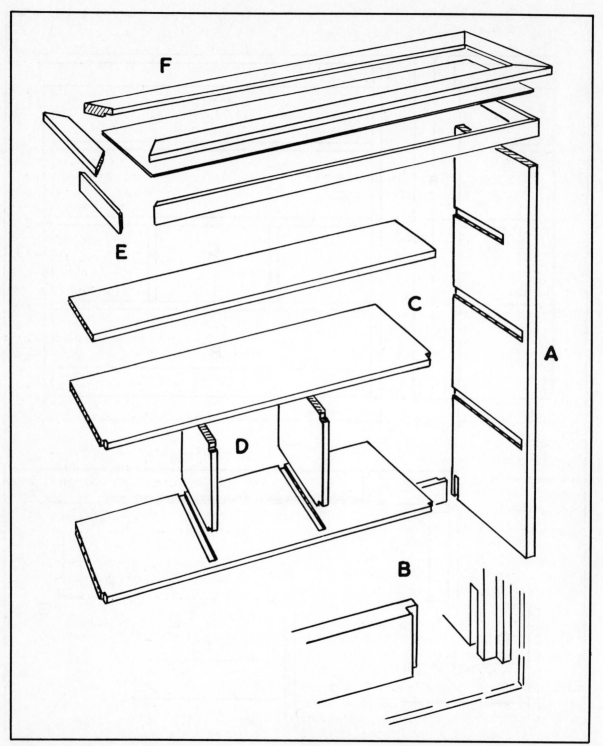

Fig. 10-5. Assembly of the unit parts.

wood for the top framing with rabbets for the plywood (Fig. 10-4J). Leave the rear edge flat but round the exposed edges.

9. Cut the plywood to size. Miter the corners of the frame. Drill for screwing into the parts below. Although the mitered corners are glued, there will not be much strength in these joints alone; but when the wood is screwed down, the strength will be adequate.

10. Match the finish to the table or other furniture. Cloth glued to the bottom edges of the sides will reduce scratching or accidental movement.

Materials List for Over-Table Shelves				
2 sides	7/8	×	10	× 37
2 shelves	7/8	×	10	× 37
1 shelf	7/8	×	7	× 37
2 back strips	5/8	×	2½	× 37
1 top stiffener	7/8	×	7/8	× 37
2 divisions	7/8	×	10	×12
1 top strip	½	×	2½	× 39
2 top strips	½	×	2½	× 12
2 top frames	7/8	×	2½	× 40
2 top frames	7/8	×	2½	× 12
1 back	36	×	36	× ¼ plywood
1 top	8	×	34	× ¼ plywood

GLASS-FRONTED SHELVES

Glass about ¼ inch thick either clear or patterned, can be made into sliding doors without framing if the edges are rounded and finger holes or handles provided. The doors slide in grooved pieces of wood and can be arranged to lift out for cleaning or a clear access to the space behind.

The block of shelves in Fig. 10-6 has an enclosed space between shelves and an open narrow shelf above. The sides are shown with shaped ends, but you could leave them plain or decorate them in another way. If sizes are altered, do not make the doors too narrow in relation to their height, or they may not slide easily. As a guide, the width is better no less than the door height.

The instructions apply to solid wood. Veneered particleboard could be used with dowel joints, but solid wood can have dadoes. The glass slides should be straight-grained hardwood, in any case. The back is plywood, preferably veneered to match the solid wood.

1. Prepare the wood for the pair of ends (Fig. 10-7A) with rabbets for the back.

2. Mark out the ends. The main shelves stop 1 inch from the front, and the top shelf is 5 inches wide.

3. Make the shelves and cut the dadoes in the ends (Fig. 10-8A).

4. Groove the glass guides wide enough for free movement (Fig. 10-7B). They are shown 3/8 inch wide (Fig. 10-7C). Clearance must be at least 1/16 inch. The bottom guide has grooves 3/8 inch deep. The top guide has grooves twice as deep (Fig. 10-7D). Glass has to be made to a depth that will allow it to be lifted into its top groove while its bottom edge clears the bottom guide and lifts out. In use, the glass is held down by its own weight. Make the two guides. Smooth the bottoms of the grooves and lightly round their edges. Glue the guides to their shelves. Put a few nails or screws in the bottom of the grooves.

5. If the sides are to be shaped, use the squared drawing for the outline (Fig. 10-8B). Round all of the forward edges.

6. Assemble the parts. Drive screws diagonally upwards into the main shelf joints. Squareness at the front is important for the proper fit of the glass doors.

7. Have the glass cut so the pieces overlap at the center (Fig. 10-7E) and with holes or handles at the outer edges. If the doors are to slide fully to one side, any handle must not project more than the thickness of the guide between the grooves—in this case, 3/8 inch.

8. Finish the wood to match other furniture. Wax the grooves to let the glass slide smoothly. Screws through the back into the wall will be inconspicuous under the upper wide shelf.

Materials List for Glass-Fronted Shelves				
2 ends	¾	×	11	× 34
2 shelves	¾	×	9¾	× 37
1 shelf	¾	×	5	× 37
1 guide	5/8	×	1 5/8	× 36
1 guide	1	×	1 5/8	× 36
1 back	34	×	36	× ¼ plywood
2 glass doors to suit				

Fig. 10-6. This block of shelves has sliding glass doors between the wide shelves.

SHELF VARIATIONS

With most kitchen shelves you merely put things on them, but when you make your own, you can fit the shelves to hold particular items. Racks can hold special pans, blenders, and other things that need careful storage, yet are still accessible.

One way of providing special storage is to extend a bottom shelf outside its support. This involves loads pulling downward on a joint, so it should be strong. Dowels are not a good choice, as the load is in the direction of pulling them out, and security depends on glue only. You could drive

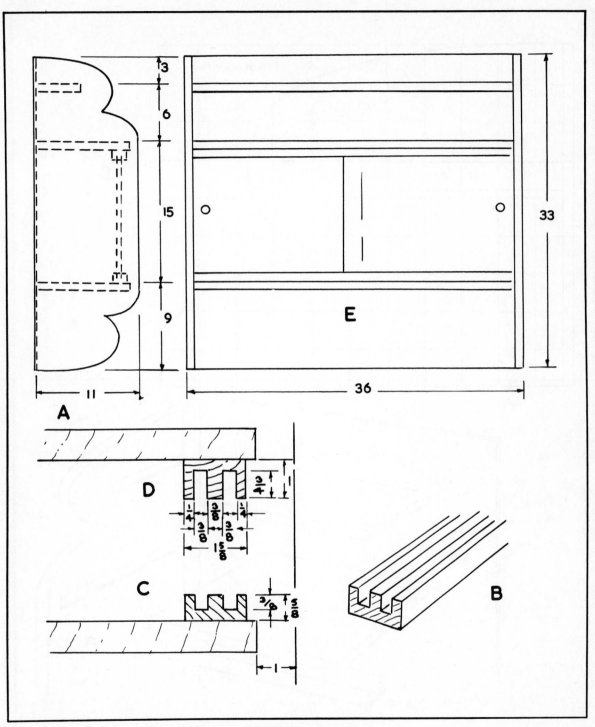

Fig. 10-7. The glass doors slide in grooved pieces attached to the shelves.

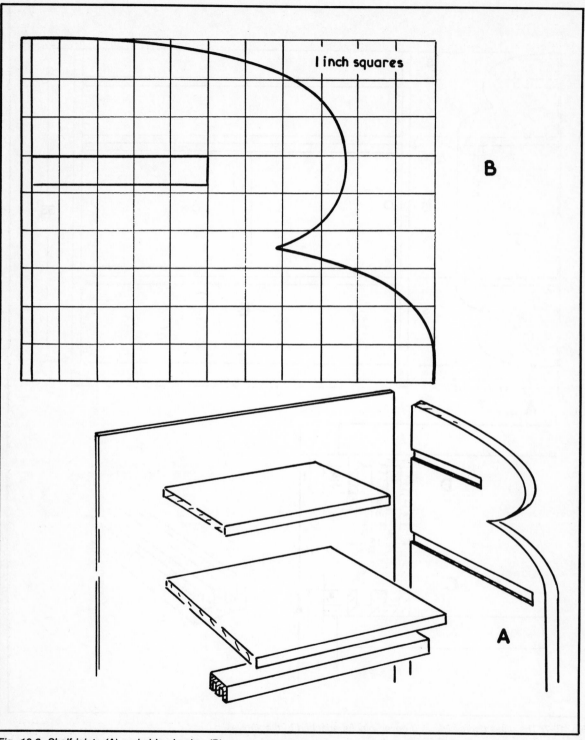

1 inch squares

B

A

Fig. 10-8. Shelf joints (A) and side shaping (B).

upward, and this might be the only satisfactory way for particleboard. With solid wood, use long screws to grip well in the end grain. A good way of increasing strength is to put a dowel across for each screw to go through (Fig. 10-9A). If you do not want dowels to show on the outside, drill holes for

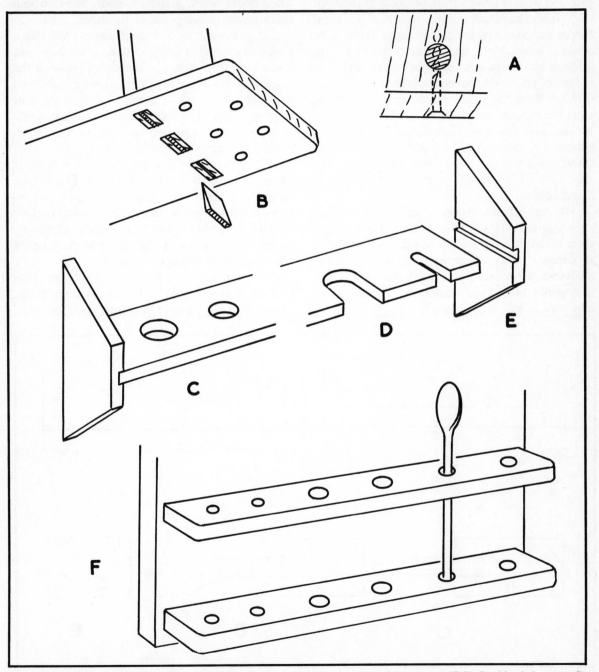

Fig. 10-9. An extending shelf needs secure joints (A, B). A shelf can be pierced for storage (C-E). Double shelves can fit inside a door.

them partly through from inside. A better joint for solid wood is mortise and tenon, with several tenons across the width of the boards. Secure with glue and wedges driven from below (Fig. 10-9B).

There are many things that can be fitted through shelves. Holes can be made from quite small to those able to take mugs or beakers (Fig. 10-9C). For things you might prefer to insert from the front, you could convert the holes to slots (Fig. 10-9D). Round all edges and corners. Do not cut slots too close because of the weakening caused by the short grain between them. The example shown is a narrow shelf between brackets (Fig. 10-9E), but you can make holes and slots in any shelf, even a wide shelf where large things are stood behind.

Some kitchen tools and other items are better supported at two levels (Fig. 10-9F). The arrangement is shown inside a door, and this is convenient if narrow shelves will be adequate. Mark out the shelves together and drill through the top one, but only partly through the bottom one. The hole sizes can vary to suit your needs.

You can fit doors between shelves or make sliding plywood doors, like those described for glass in the previous project. A combination of plywood doors below and glass doors above would make an attractive piece of furniture.

If you want to fit hinged doors, there is a choice of method of fitting. All older furniture, and much new furniture, has the doors between the sides (Fig. 10-10A). If you are making traditional or country furniture, this must be the method of hanging a door. The door is inside at top and sides. At its bottom, it can also be inside or allowed to overlap a narrower bottom shelf.

The alternative is to put the door in front of the sides and shelves (Fig. 10-10B). This choice particularly suits veneered particleboard construction since it simplifies fitting. This method of door hanging does not require quite such precise work as the first method. It also gives slightly better clearance when the door is open.

The simplest door is a piece of veneered particleboard. It will hold its size and will not warp. Plywood of comparable thickness could be used,

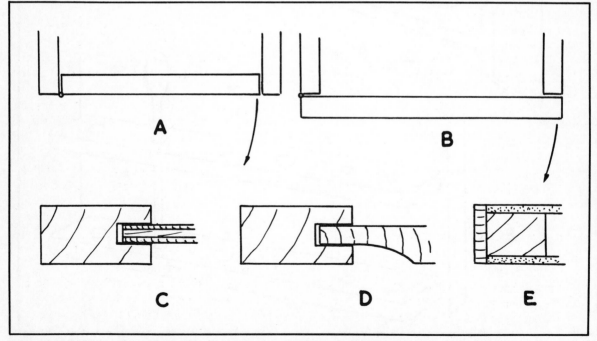

Fig. 10-10. Doors can fit between sides (A) or overlap them (B). Doors can be paneled or built up (C-E).

but edges should be lipped with solid wood to hide the ply edges.

In many situations framed and paneled doors are better. The panel could be plywood (Fig. 10-10C). Make it so it does not touch the bottom of its grooves. Use corner joints for the frames as described for several earlier projects.

An alternative to plywood is a raised solid wood panel (Fig. 10-10D) that can match other furniture in the kitchen. Fit it and frame it in the same way as plywood.

A door can be made with hardboard or thin plywood on each side of solid wood framing (Fig. 10-10E). Include framing across the body of a large door or where a lock or anything else has to be attached. Lip the edges.

HUTCH

A wide shelf at table height, with more shelves above and below, makes a hutch or Welsh dresser. This storage item gives plenty of display or storage space above. If the lower shelves are hidden by doors, a large number of items can be packed away where their appearance will not matter.

The hutch in Fig. 10-11 has a working surface at standing height, shelves within reach above, and a pair of doors in front of more shelves below. The upper shelves are framed at the front, and there is an overhanging top. The doors below are shown as framed plywood, but other types are possible.

Construction is with solid wood, though details could be altered slightly to use veneered particleboard or lipped plywood. The ends are each made of two boards glued together. Shelves are joined to them with dadoes. Gluing all joints and arranging ½-inch dowels at about 3-inch intervals should be satisfactory. Door frames will be stronger with mortise-and-tenon joints.

For softwood, finish it with paint or stain and varnish. If hardwood is chosen, give it a polished finish to match other furniture.

Sizes (Fig. 10-12) can be adapted to suit available space. Most parts are 1 inch thick. This might finish ⅞ inch, but shelves should not be less than

that, unless they are very short, or they might sag after long use.

1. Start by making the pair of sides (Fig. 10-13A and B). Cut rabbets in the long pieces for the plywood back. The shelf dadoes are the same at all positions and taken about halfway through the wood. The bottom could have dadoes, but it is shown doweled (Fig. 10-13C). The front narrow part (Fig. 10-13B) comes up to the bottom edge of the central dado on the long piece. Glue these parts together. Reinforce the joints with dowels if necessary.

2. The shelves (Fig. 10-14A and B) are the same width and length. You could fit wider, lower shelves by continuing the dadoes into the front pieces of wood.

3. Glue pieces of wood to make up the width of the worktop (Fig. 10-12A and 13D). Its rear part is the same length as the shelves, but the front part is cut to overhang the sides by 1 inch. At the front, the worktop overhangs the doors by 1 inch.

4. Make the bottom (Fig. 10-13E) to match the sides, with allowance for the doors, and drill it and the sides for dowels. Make a plinth (Fig. 10-12B and 13F), set back 1 inch under the bottom. Glue it to the bottom with a few dowels and drill its ends for dowels into the sides.

5. Put strips (Fig. 10-13G) on the sides to take screws upwards into the worktop, when that is fitted.

6. Make a piece (Figs. 10-12C and 10-14C) to fit across inside the plywood back. Drill it and the sides for dowels.

7. Have the plywood back ready, cut square, but leave the final planing of the edges until it is fitted. It need not extend below the bottom but should come level with the strip at the top (Fig. 10-14D).

8. Assemble the crosswise pieces to the sides. Drive screws diagonally upward through the dado joints, if you wish, but other framing will probably provide adequate stiffness. Fit the plywood back to hold the assembly square.

9. Make two strips to fit in front of the sides above the worktop (Figs. 10-12D, 10-13H, 10-14E) and a strip across between their tops, with

Fig. 10-11. A hutch with hinged doors, shelves, and a work surface.

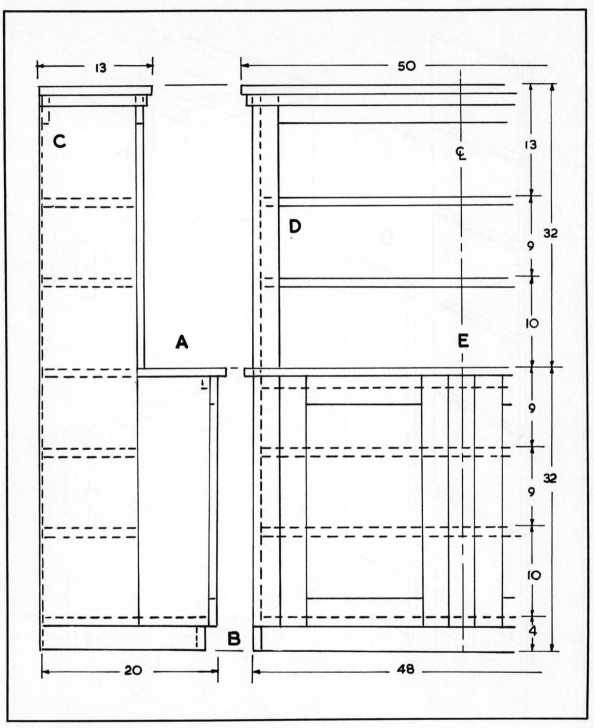

Fig. 10-12. Sizes of the hutch.

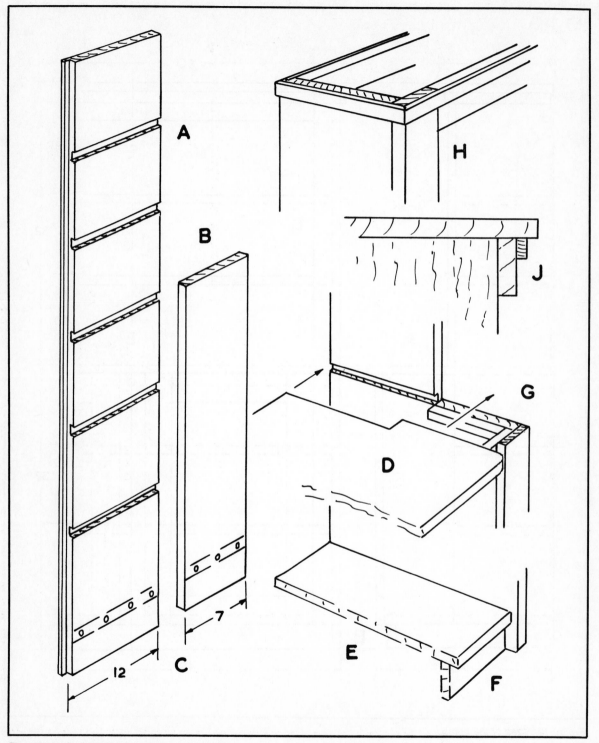

Fig. 10-13. Constructional details of the hutch.

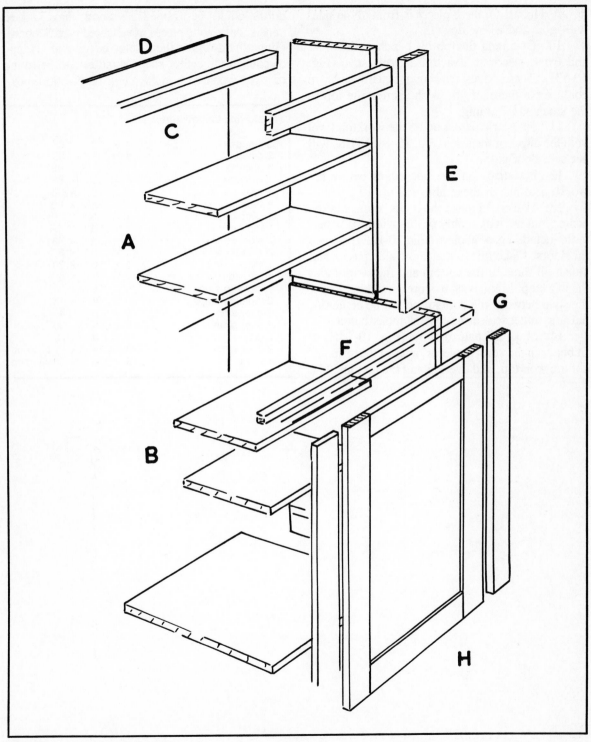

Fig. 10-14. Assembly of the hutch.

doweled joints. Fit these pieces in front of the sides with glue and a few dowels.

10. Overhang the top by 1 inch at the sides and front. Decorate it with a narrow strip (Fig. 10-13J). These edges are shown square, but you could mold them, if you wish. Screw the top to the sides and framing.

11. Put a strip across under the worktop level with the edges of the sides (Fig. 10-14F). This will act as a door stop.

12. Put strips on the side edges below the worktop to match those above (Fig. 10-14G).

13. You could make the doors to meet at the center, but in an assembly of this width, it is better to include a central piece (Fig. 10-12E) between the doors. Make this to match the side pieces and attach all three to the bottom and the strip under the worktop. If you wish to store something large, the strip between the doors need not be centered, but a symmetrical arrangement looks better.

14. Make the pair of doors (Fig. 10-14H) to fit between the vertical pieces, against the strip under the worktop, and overlapping the bottom. The doors could be framed plywood, have raised panels, or be solid pieces of veneered particleboard. Hinge the doors at their outer edges and arrange catches to the center strip. Handles can be round or strip wood or bought metal or plastic types.

Materials List for Hutch				
2 sides	1 ×	12	× 65	
2 sides	1 ×	7	× 32	
4 shelves	1 ×	11¾	× 49	
1 worktop	1 ×	21	× 52	
1 top	1 ×	13	× 52	
1 bottom	1 ×	18¾	× 49	
1 plinth	1 ×	3	× 49	
1 top rail	1 ×	3	× 49	
2 side strips	1 ×	3	× 33	
2 side strips	1 ×	3	× 30	
1 center strip	1 ×	3	× 30	
1 top strip	1 ×	3	× 42	
1 molding strip	½ ×	1	× 50	
2 molding strips	½ ×	1	× 13	
1 door stop	1 ×	1	× 49	
4 door sides	1 ×	3	× 30	
4 door sides	1 ×	3	× 20	
2 door panels	20 ×	24	× ¼	plywood
1 back	48 ×	62	× ¼	plywood

Index

Other Bestsellers From TAB

☐ **THE PORTABLE ROUTER BOOK—**
R. J. DeCristoforo

If you've always thought of your portable router as a pretty unexciting tool, capable of little more than producing decorative edges on certain types of woodworking projects . . . then this book is just what you need to start taking advantage of all the creative possibilities that the router can really offer! Plus, you'll find how-to's for making your own router stands, jigs, fixtures and guides for use in creating such special effects as fluting, reeding, tapering, and peripheral cutting. 368 pp., 466 illus.

Paper $14.95   **Hard $24.95**
Book No. 2869

☐ **SMALL ENGINES: OPERATION, MAINTENANCE AND REPAIR—AAVIM**

This time-, money-, and aggravation-saving sourcebook shows how you can service, operate, maintain, and repair any air-cooled, spark-ignition, one-half to approximately 15 horsepower engine yourself . . . and save hundreds of dollars in repair bills! If you wish to expand your knowledge beyond the service and operation of small engines, part two briefs you on the procedures and techniques you need to know to tackle major maintenance and repair work. 288 pp., 529 illus., 8 1/2″ × 11″.

Paper $14.95   **Hard $24.95**
Book No. 2813

☐ **133 *USEFUL* PROJECTS FOR THE WOODWORKER—***School Shop Magazine*

A wealth of information for beginning and advanced hobbyists . . . tools, techniques, and dozens of exciting projects. Here's a handbook that deserves a permanent spot on every woodworker's tool bench. Packed with show-how illustrations and material lists, this invaluable guide provides you with a wide variety of useful, and fun-to-make woodworking projects: a spice rack, a wall clock, a plant stand, a cutting board, a wooden chest, a magazine rack, a serving cart, a child's playhouse, and more! 160 pp., 280 illus.

Paper $12.95   **Hard $19.95**
Book No. 2783

☐ **DREAM HOMES: 66 PLANS TO MAKE YOUR DREAMS COME TRUE—**Jerold L. Axelrod, architect

If you are planning on—or just dreaming of—building a new home, you will find this book completely fascinating. Compiled by a well-known architect whose home designs have been featured regularly in the syndicated "House of the Week" and *Home* magazine, this beautifully bound volume presents one of the finest collections of luxury home designs ever assembled in a single volume! 88 pp., 201 illus., 8 1/2″ × 11″ Extra Large Format. 20 Full-Color Pages.

Paper $16.95   **Hard $29.95**
Book No. 2829

☐ **HOME PLUMBING MADE EASY: AN ILLUSTRATED MANUAL—**James L. Kittle

Here, in one heavily illustrated, easy-to-follow volume, is all the how-to-do-it information needed to perform almost any home plumbing job, in both water and waste disposal systems. Whether you want to learn something about household plumbing so you can save time and money next time a problem occurs, or you're thinking of making major plumbing or septic additions or repairs to your home, this is the place to start! 272 pp., 250 illus.

Paper $14.95   **Hard $24.95**
Book No. 2797

☐ **77 ONE-WEEKEND WOODWORKING PROJECTS—**
Percy W. Blandford

Let this guide put the fun back into your hobby! Overflowing with step-by-step instructions, easy-to-follow illustrations, dimensioned drawings, and material lists, this indispensable guide includes plans for 77 projects: tables, racks and shelves, a take-down book rack, corner shelves, a vase stand, beds and cabinets, yard and garden projects, toys, games and puzzles, tools, and more. 304 pp., 226 illus.

Paper $14.95   **Hard $23.95**
Book No. 2774

*Prices subject to change without notice.

Look for these and other TAB books at your local bookstore.

TAB BOOKS Inc.
P.O. Box 40
Blue Ridge Summit, PA 17214

Send for FREE TAB catalog describing over 1200 current titles in print.
Or Call For Immediate Service   1-800-233-1128

EAU CLAIRE DISTRICT LIBRARY